Zane Grey's Wild West

Zane Grey's Wild West

A Study of 31 Novels

VICTOR CARL FRIESEN

McFarland & Company, Inc., Publishers
Jefferson, North Carolina, and London

A version of Chapter 1 appeared originally in *Zane Grey Review* 16, no. 4 (June 2001); Chapter 8 appeared in *Zane Grey Review*, 25, no. 1 (May 2010); Chapter 14 appeared in *Zane Grey Review* 25, no. 3 and 4 (December 2010); a version of Chapter 18 appeared in *Zane Grey Review* 16, no. 1 (December 2000); and a version of Chapter 25 appeared in *Zane Grey Review* 24, no. 4 (December 2009). Chapter 15 was originally published in *The Concord Saunterer*, New Series 6 (1998), and appears here courtesy the Thoreau Society Collections at the Thoreau Institute at Walden Woods.

LIBRARY OF CONGRESS CATALOGUING-IN-PUBLICATION DATA

Friesen, Victor Carl.
  Zane Grey's wild west : a study of 31 novels / Victor Carl Friesen.
      p.   cm.
  Includes bibliographical references and index.

  ISBN 978-0-7864-7779-1
  softcover : acid free paper

  1. Grey, Zane, 1872–1939—Criticism and interpretation.
  2. Western stories—History and criticism.
  3. West (U.S.)—In literature. I. Title.
  PS3513.R6545Z626 2014
  813'.52—dc23   2013037337

BRITISH LIBRARY CATALOGUING DATA ARE AVAILABLE

© 2014 Victor Carl Friesen. All rights reserved

No part of this book may be reproduced or transmitted in any form or by any means, electronic or mechanical, including photocopying or recording, or by any information storage and retrieval system, without permission in writing from the publisher.

Cover art: Charles Marion Russell, "A bad hoss," 1905 color lithograph from original 1904 painting (Library of Congress)

Manufactured in the United States of America

McFarland & Company, Inc., Publishers
  Box 611, Jefferson, North Carolina 28640
  www.mcfarlandpub.com

To my fellow members of Zane Grey's West Society

The heavens were clothed in driving clouds, piled in vast masses one above the other, ... far too grand and durable to be disturbed by the fitful efforts of the lower world. —James Fenimore Cooper, *The Prairie*, 1827

I would have every man so much a wild antelope, so much a part and parcel of nature, that every person should ... remind us of ... [that] nature which he most haunts. —Henry David Thoreau, "Walking," 1862

What is become of the horseman, the cowpuncher, the last romantic figure upon our soil? ... His wild kind has been among us always, since the beginning: a young man with his temptations, a hero without wings. —Owen Wister, *The Virginian*, 1902

Contents

Preface	1
The Novels	7
1. *Betty Zane:* The First Western Frontier	11
2. *Riders of the Purple Sage:* Mill-Wheel of Place and Action	18
3. *Desert Gold:* More Than Money	25
4. *Last of the Duanes:* Undying Passion	33
5. *The Light of Western Stars:* Living Western Style	39
6. *The Rainbow Trail:* Love Story	46
7. *The Border Legion:* Titanic Evil Forces	52
8. *Wildfire:* The West Ablaze	59
9. *The U. P. Trail:* Romance of a Railroad	65
10. *The Man of the Forest:* Mind and Instinct	72
11. *The Desert of Wheat:* I.W.W. and WWI	78
12. *Wanderer of the Wasteland:* Learning to Live	85
13. *To the Last Man:* A Feud Mentality	92
14. *The Call of the Canyon:* Going Home	99
15. *The Vanishing American:* A Thoreauvian Native	105
16. *Tappan's Burro*: No Greater Love	113
17. *Code of the West*: Growing Up in the Twenties	119
18. *The Thundering Herd:* A Buffalo Saga	125
19. *Wild Horse Mesa:* One Grand Spectacle	132

20. *Under the Tonto Rim:* A Backwoods Tale   138
21. *Forlorn River:* Prolonged Drought and Money Madness 144
22. *Valley of Wild Horses:* A Cool Reckless Spirit   151
23. *Nevada:* Life of a Gunman   157
24. *The Shepherd of Guadaloupe:* Love and Malice   164
25. *Rogue River Feud:* Low Ebb and Recovery   171
26. *Robbers' Roost:* Road to Regeneration   176
27. *The Trail Driver:* An Arduous Trek   182
28. *Thunder Mountain:* Gold-Rush Cowboy   188
29. *Knights of the Range:* Western Chivalry   194
30. *Woman of the Frontier:* The Best Years   200
31. *Western Union:* A Great Achievement   207

Bibliography   215
Index   219

Preface

There is some difficulty in selecting 31 of Zane Grey's Westerns, half his total output, for inclusion in a book of literary discussion. Of course, a volume with continuing popularity has to be included. I am thinking now of *Riders of the Purple Sage*, the best-selling Western ever written (and its sequel, *The Rainbow Trail*). But once one gets beyond a dozen or so obvious choices, gradations in literary worth become more debatable. Different critics will disagree as to which plots are better written; what seems overdramatized to one may not be distracting to others if the characters are sufficiently gripping. Also, personal taste becomes a factor, where subject or locale and "memories connected with first readings" play a part (see Pfeiffer, *So You Want...*, 2, in the bibliography; page references other than to Grey's novels pertain to this bibliography). My choices stem from wishing to best show the scope of Grey's interests in the West and his powerful descriptions of the land. How does he convey the ideals of this opening territory—his stated aim?

My selection of novels provides as wide a sampling as possible, a range of subjects encompassing frontiersmen, horse wranglers, cowmen, gunmen, prospectors, bandits, Native Americans, backwoodsmen, hunters, fishermen, foresters, farmers, teachers, and construction workers (on railroad and telegraph lines). The work of all these people is predominantly outdoors, with wild nature as setting, a determinant of action and often of character too, particularly effective as desert in *Wanderer of the Wasteland* or deep woods in *The Man of the Forest*. Besides these locales parklands, canyons, mountains, rivers, lakes, and an ocean are the backdrops in some fifteen states—from West Virginia in the East (the first western frontier) to Arizona in the Far West, the setting for nearly half the novels (it is Grey's favorite state), and even beyond to California.

The time of the 31 books dates from events leading to the last battle of the Revolutionary War, at Fort Henry on the Ohio River, 1782 (*Betty Zane*), to the flapper era of the 1920s (*Code of the West*). A cluster of books deals with the cowboy world that developed in the western states or territories following the Civil War, the late 1860s through to the 1880s. It was the cow pony that raised the rider above the rest of us earthbound beings and made him a folk hero. Grey builds up this fact in such books as the spirited *Knights of the Range*. And gunmen-cowboys can be heroic too, as in *Robbers' Roost* and *Nevada*, the latter at the turn of the century. In *Last of the Duanes*, the title character is in fact the ultimate gunslinger. (Heroes with the lesser role of shoot-out artist appear in at least half a dozen other books considered here, Lassiter in *Riders* being an obvious example.)

Another cluster of books pertains to World War I. *The Desert of Wheat* graphically describes battle scenes and a soldier's subsequent convalescence. *The Call of the Canyon*, a fine sociological study, and *The Shepherd of Guadaloupe* show returned veterans trying to adjust to an uncaring Roaring Twenties society (in *Shepherd*, the quick-witted jibes of a secondary female character pretty much steal the show). Grey sees some hope of veterans finding themselves in the elemental West, its simpler, richer lifestyle, rather than in the East ("that man is richest whose pleasures are the cheapest," affirms naturalist Henry David Thoreau [*Journal* 8:205]). Sometimes, as well, we see an Easterner, man or woman, a newcomer to the spacious West, find his or her real home and vocation under *The Light of Western Stars* (in this book a New York woman, a socialite, successfully runs a ranch). While a character's real battle may seem to be for mere survival and/or material success, it is really for inner fulfillment.

Several novels have women as main protagonists, like *The Call of the Canyon* above. In *Woman of the Frontier* Grey's understanding portrayal of the title character makes it one of his best books. *Under the Tonto Rim*, another example, pictures a teacher in a hillbilly setting. The women are drawn from real life, people Grey knew (Wheeler, "Two Roads...," 8; see also Pauly, 114–20). He presents such a variety, in principal or supporting roles, all uniquely characterized, that on the whole they seem more interesting than the men, who are generally involved in physical action. This is the case in *Wild Horse Mesa*, where three women are portrayed, playing off each other to reveal their individualities, while a commenting hero looks on. Grey's sure ear for dialogue between women or men (or between both) is key to his vivid delineation of these people.

I have included most books focusing on horses—*Forlorn River* is one, *Wildfire* a particular favorite. Grey knows and loves these animals, and depicts them well. Also, there is a good proportion of novels of direct historical interest, *The U. P. Trail* being an example, where East meets West through railroad building in the 1860s. Cattle drives, extending through several states/territories from 1867 to 1882 before more railroads ended their necessity, are picturesquely captured in *The Trail Driver*. And the near extermination of buffalo in Texas, 1874, is accurately told in *The Thundering Herd*. Gold-rush fever is described in *The Border Legion* (Montana, 1863) and *Thunder Mountain* (Idaho, 1906). As well, I have included Zane Grey's very first novel, self-published *Betty Zane* (1903); the last published in his lifetime (and written in the first person), *Western Union* (1939); and one recently published in book form, the previously mentioned *Last of the Duanes* (1996).

The inclusion of two other books, generally not considered among Grey's best, needs some explanation. Another war-veteran account, *Rogue River Feud*, is hardly a Western, as the term is commonly defined, for its overall subject is fishing—commercial and sport. However, the setting is certainly as far westerly as one can be in the contiguous United States, down Oregon's most scenic river to the Pacific coast, and there *is* a lengthy horseback journey as well. The second book, *Valley of Wild Horses*, of course, has its horse theme, but more interestingly it starts at ground zero—literally. The book begins with the hero's birth at the edge of a field in the Texas Panhandle, and his boyhood is fully described. With Grey's facility in describing a great river in one book and a young boy's development in another (along with his ear for recording conversation, serious and humorous, of various people), we can only wonder how he might have fared in writing a "Huckleberry Finn" Western. Mark Twain himself seems to ask for such a sequel when he has Huck say at the end of the classic tale that he is going to "light out for the Territory" (that is, the West) (245).

Included here too is *Tappan's Burro*, a long short story or novelette and a variation on Grey's novels about horses. It is another favorite of mine, its shortness a guarantee of no overwriting, a weakness sometimes attributed to Grey. Incidentally, three regular-length novels contain chapters that, when excerpted, make splendid short stories. They are chapter 17, "Wrangle's Race Run," from *Riders of the Purple Sage*; chapter 29, featuring Casey's railcar dash, from *The U. P. Trail*; and the prologue to *Desert Gold*, a many-faceted adventure yarn. These books were serialized, as were most of Grey's novels, so that many readers would have read the three accounts as "short stories." (Years of serialization for all applicable books, the first installment, are given in the text.)

I have used the word "novel" several times with reference to Grey's work. He himself, in a foreword to *To the Last Man* (an exposition of feud mentality), preferred to be called a romance writer. He really is not part of his contemporary literary world, that of Theodore Dreiser and Sherwood Anderson, who pessimistically saw man trapped by world forces over which he had no control. Grey's heroes and heroines are more likely to be masters of their fates and captains of their souls (Henley, "Invictus," 84). Grey fits in better with earlier generations of writers, say, Cooper and Thoreau in the United States, Scott and Dickens in Britain—reference is made to these four writers, and others, in some of the chapters. Note that I cite very few specific commentaries on Grey. An expository treatment such as mine requires that I go directly to Grey's books and see what *he* says; I am not trying to see his work in the light of someone else's criticism. Having said that, I wish, however, to single out two comprehensive studies here whose broad understanding makes them superior works: Joseph Lawrence Wheeler's "Zane Grey's Impact on American Life and Letters: A Study in the Popular Novel," 1975; and Charles G. Pfeiffer's *Zane Grey: A Study in Values—Above and Beyond the West*, 2005.

Grey, again in the foreword, sees himself in the tradition of not only Walter Scott, but also Victor Hugo "and likewise Kipling, Hawthorne, Stevenson" (i–ii). People want to "live for the *dream* in their hearts" (my emphasis). It gives meaning to their lives. He paraphrases a sonnet by the Romantic William Wordsworth ("The World Is Too Much with Us," 182) to claim that the *business* world is too much with them, laying waste their powers—"with never a breath of the free and wonderful life of the open!" (ii)—that of his West, depicted by him in all its vastness, its wilderness, color, and beauty.

Romance, he continues, is "only another name for ideals" (i), and he is trying to inspire ideals in his readers, a *Code of the West*, where values tried and true win out. His work of that title—written, serialized, and published in book form during the Roaring Twenties—looks at some of the decade's fun-crazed antics affecting even the spirit of his cowboy country, presents them with humor and pathos, but speaks for a saner world. His idealism, too, makes Grey a defender of our natural resources, an ecological voice in almost every novel/romance, much ahead of his time. Similarly, he wants better treatment of Native Americans, speaks indirectly for their welfare in many books, and dedicates one whole book, *The Vanishing American*, to their cause. His ideal is a fellowship of humanity, of all races.

My treatment of Grey's books is to devote one chapter to each work considered. That chapter discusses whatever to me seems pertinent to it. There is an outlining of the story itself, with quotations enough—a word or clause, a whole paragraph sometimes—to show the author's apt phrasing and to catch the flavor of the writing. Included are comments on how the book "works," it being on the whole not just another typical Western. Specific criticism of some characteristic writing trait may be examined for one book, if cropping up frequently, then passed over in another. Grey respects his craft and subject, researching each new undertaking meticulously, and my intention is to approach his work, in all its diversity, positively.

My personal assessment could be termed popular scholarship, having in it a more colloquial English, in keeping with Grey's own style, even with some humorous asides. Note my use of the present tense throughout. It is in fact my metaphor to describe an author who maintains a large readership right into our own time. Today Zane Grey's West Society, founded in 1983, holds well-attended annual conventions to celebrate his works.

I should conclude by saying something about how I, a Thoreau specialist, came to write about Zane Grey. Actually, it was because of Thoreau, who has no real connection to Western literature. He, the philosopher-naturalist, spent his short life (he died in 1862 at age 44) in his native town of Concord, Massachusetts, writing about the New England natural world. As for me, a century later I read through his complete works and completed my M.A. thesis (1965) on his approach to nature.

During some intervening teaching years, I looked about for a doctoral dissertation topic. I had grown up on a farm in the prairies of Western Canada, driven a horse-and-cutter to a country school as a youngster, and dreamed then, as did most fellow students my age, of being a cowboy some day. As an adult, things Western still fascinated me. I noted that even Thoreau began his daily walks *westerly*, the West being wildness, representing for him his primal home, a resource to be preserved—and to preserve man. A person literally came to his (five) senses there, like an animal in the wild. When he himself "headed west" (a colloquial expression for dying), he appropriately uttered two last words—"moose" and "Indian" (Harding, 466)—epitomizing wildness, a sacred place and God's realm.

So I thought I would do something on the "idea" of the West in American literature for my doctoral studies, a broad subject to be sure, and I read Frederick Jackson Turner's *The Frontier in American History*, 1920, and Henry Nash Smith's *Virgin Land: The American West as Symbol and Myth*, 1950, as seminal works. A short time later I discovered, in perusing an academic journal, that someone else had just written a book on my chosen topic. Well, it was back to Thoreau for me, to expand my master's thesis for a Ph.D. degree (1975). The latter research was published as a book, *The Spirit of the Huckleberry*, 1984, by the University of Alberta Press.

Then one day, a half dozen years later, while rummaging in a used book store, I came upon Grey's *The Vanishing American*. As a nine-year-old, I had received a Christmas gift of his first book, *Betty Zane*. And while I had read this somewhat fictionalized account of the author's great-grandaunt several times, I had never read another Grey book until I happened upon this one in adult life, 55 years later. The book held especial interest for me. The title itself has become a memorable catch phrase, and the subject matter, the Native American, a lifetime interest. As a boy, I had made a fairly broad collection of arrowheads and stone mauls from blowouts caused by Great Depression dust storms right on our own sandy farm and those of the neighbors. (Thoreau, incidentally, had collected 900 such artifacts at Concord.)

When I started reading the book, I was struck by the many similarities between Grey's title protagonist, Nophaie in Arizona, and the New England Native as Thoreau himself described him. What was even more impressive, it seemed to me, was that these Natives were very much like their respective scribes: Grey, the outdoorsman, like Thoreau, could never have enough of nature and embraced it sensuously, enraptured by kaleidoscopic cloud cover above and the wind-scalloped sandy reaches underfoot. Both writers were readers of Wordsworth, kindred spirits in appreciating nature and sensing man's unity with it.

The parallels were so striking that I soon set to work on a comparative study, a lengthy essay, fully documented, on Thoreau and Grey, as revealed in his 1925 novel. It was published in *The Concord Saunterer*, 1998, an academic journal of The Thoreau Society, of which I am a life member. Then another member, from South Wales, Great Britain (and also of Zane Grey's West Society), felt that the Zane Grey people would be interested. He sent a copy to the editor of the *Zane Grey Review*, who wished to reprint it. Thus I was sent a copy of the publication with my article, in 1999. I became a member of Zane Grey's West Society a short time later, read more Zane Grey novels, and wrote further articles for its journal. Some of them are now chapters in this book.

The order of the chapters is chronological, depending on when the book each features was written (see The Novels, which follows), rather than published. Page references here are to any Grosset & Dunlap edition, unless otherwise stated. (These would be the same as found in the original Harper & Brothers edition or in the later Musson Book Company or Walter J. Black editions.) I hope this preface is also something of a summing-up chapter and that readers of the whole work will be stimulated enough to read more of Zane Grey and consider his remarkable achievement themselves. I would like to express my appreciation to Yvonne Giesbrecht, who patiently and painstakingly typed the manuscript. To my wife, Dorothy, I express my gratitude for her special care in reading it.

The Novels

Main characters (hero and heroine first; "villain[s]," if any, last):

I am indebted to Charles G. Pfeiffer's handy reference, *So You Want to Read Zane Grey and Don't Know Where to Start*, 2006, in listing (or confirming) the year(s) of composition as well as the time and setting of each novel.

1. *Betty Zane:* written—1902; time—1781-82; place—WV (Betty Zane, Alfred Clarke, Lew Wetzel, Ebenezer Zane, Bess Zane, Isaac Zane, Myeerah, Ralfe Miller)

2. *Riders of the Purple Sage*: 1911; 1871; UT, AZ (Jane Withersteen, Lassiter, Fay Larkin, Bern Venters, Bess Erne/Oldring, Wrangle and Black Star and Night (horses), Bishop Dyer, Elder Tull)

3. *Desert Gold*: 1912; 1912-13; AZ (Dick Gale, Nell Burton, George Thorne, Mercedes Castañeda, Tom Belding, Yaqui, Charlie Ladd, Jim Lash, Blanco Sol (horse), Ben Chase, Radford Chase, Rojas)

4. *Last of the Duanes*: 1913; 1870s; TX (Buck Duane, Jennie Lee, Euchre, Bland, Kate Bland, Captain MacNelly, Cheseldine, Poggin)

5. *The Light of Western Stars*: 1913-14; ca. 1913; NM/AZ (Madeline "Majesty" Hammond, Gene Stewart, Bill Stillwell, Florence Kingsley, Monty Price, Don Carlos)

6. *The Rainbow Trail*: 1915; 1886; AZ, UT (John Shefford, Fay Larkin, Nas Ta Bega, Joe Lake, John Withers, Shadd)

7. *The Border Legion*: 1915-16; 1863; ID, MT (Joan Randle, Jim Cleve, Jack Kells, Bate Wood, Red Pearce, Sam Gulden)

8. *Wildfire*: 1916(?); 1860s; AZ (Lin Slone, Lucy Bostil, Wildfire and Sage King (horses), John Bostil, Creech, Joel Creech, Cordts)

9. *The U. P. Trail*: 1916 or 1917; 1866–69; NE, WY, UT (Warren Neale, Allie Lee, General Lodge, Larry King, Casey, Ruby, Beauty Stanton, Durade)

10. *The Man of the Forest*: 1917; 1880s(?); AZ (Milt Dale, Helen Rayner, Bo Rayner, Tom Carmichael, Roy Beeman, Jim Wilson, Beasely)

11. *The Desert of Wheat*: 1918; 1917–18; WA, Europe (Kurt Dorn, Lenore Anderson, Chris Dorn, Anderson, cowboy Jake, Neuman, Glidden)

12. *Wanderer of the Wasteland*: 1919; 1878+; CA (Adam Larey, Ruth Virey, Guerd Larey, Margarita Arallanes, Dismukes, Oella, Genie Lockwood, Magadelene Virey, Elliot Virey)

13. *To the Last Man*: 1921; 1887; AZ (Jean Isbel, Ellen Jorth, Gaston Isbel, Lee Jorth, John Sprague, Jim Colter)

14. *The Call of the Canyon*: 1921; 1919; AZ (Carley Burch, Glenn Kilbourne, Flo Hutter, Virgil Rust, Haze Ruff)

15. *The Vanishing American*: 1922; 1900–1918; AZ (Nophaie, Marian Warner, Gekin Yashi, John Withers, Blucher, Morgan)

16. *Tappan's Burro*: 1922; ca. 1900; AZ, CA (Tappan, Jenet (burro), Madge Beam, Jake Beam, Jess Blade)

17. *Code of the West*: 1922–23; 1920s; AZ (Georgiana Stockwell, Cal Thurman, Mary Stockwell, Enoch Thurman, Tuck Merry, Bid Hatfield)

18. *The Thundering Herd*: 1923; 1874; TX (the buffalo, Tom Doan, Milly Fayre, Jude Pilchuck, Clark Hudnall, Catlee, Hank Follonsbee, Andy Pruitt, Randall Jett)

19. *Wild Horse Mesa*: 1923–24; 1890s(?); UT (Chane Weymer, Sue Melberne, Brutus and Panquitch (horses), Ora Loughbridge, Sosie Nokin, Mel Melberne, Jim Loughbridge, Toddy Nokin, Bent Manerube)

20. *Under the Tonto Rim*: 1925; 1920s; AZ (Lucy Watson, Edd Denmeade, Clara Watson, Joe Denmeade, Lee Denmeade, Mrs. Denmeade, Jim Middleton)

21. *Forlorn River*: 1925; ca. 1900; CA (Ben Ide, Ida Blaine, Nevada, Hettie Ide, California Red (horse), Hart Blaine, Amos Ide, Marvie Blaine, Madoc, Less Setter)

22. *Valley of Wild Horses*: 1925–26; 1890(?); TX, NM (Pan(handle) Smith, Lucy Blake, Blinky Moran, Bill Smith, Jard Hardman, Dick Hardman)

The Novels

23. *Nevada*: 1926; ca. 1903; OR, CA, AZ (Nevada (Jim Lacy), Hettie Ide, Ben Ide, Marvie Blaine, Rose Hatt, Judge Franklidge, Cash Burridge, Cedar Hatt, Clan Dillon)

24. *The Shepherd of Guadaloupe*: 1928; 1919+; NM (Cliff Forrest, Virginia Lundeen, Ethel Wayne, Jed Lundeen, Clay Forrest, August Malpass)

25. *Rogue River Feud*: 1929; 1919+; OR (Keven Bell, Beryl Aard, Garry Lord, Mr. Bell, Gus Atwell)

26. *Robbers' Roost*: 1929–30; 1871; UT (Jim Wall, Helen Herrick, Bernie Herrick, Smoky Slocum, Bill Heeseman, Hank Hayes)

27. *The Trail Driver*: 1930; 1871; TX, OK, KS (Joe (Texas Joe or Tex) Shipman, Reddie Bayne, Adam Brite, Pan Handle Smith, Less Holden, Deuce Ackerman, Rolly Little, San Sabe, Ben Chandler, Roy Hallet, Ross Hite)

28. *Thunder Mountain*: 1931–32; 1906; ID (Kal(ispel) Emerson, Ruth (Nugget), Sydney Blair, Mr. Blair, Jake Emerson, Cliff Borden, Rand Leavitt)

29. *Knights of the Range*: 1931–32; 1870; NM (Holly Ripple, Renn Frayne, Brazos Keene, Cap Britt, Laigs Mason, Ride-'Em Jackson, Sewall McCoy, Russ Slaughter)

30. *Woman of the Frontier*: 1933; 1885–1918; AZ (Lucinda Huett, Logan Huett, children [George, Abe, Grant, and Barbara], Matazel)

31. *Western Union*: 1938–39; 1861; NE, WY (Wayne Cameron, Kit Sunderland, Vance Shaw, Jack Lowden, Tom Darnell, Ruby, Edward Creighton, Red Pierce)

1

Betty Zane:
The First Western Frontier

For Christmas, 1942, my brother gave me an abridged edition of Zane Grey's first book, *Betty Zane*, published by Saalfield in 1940. I was already familiar with the author's name from reading his "King of the Royal Mounted" in the funnies section carried by the farm weekly we received. Drawn by Jim Gary in those days, it featured a police sergeant's adventures on Saskatchewan prairie, in the Far North, and along Canada's coastal waters—a Mountie always getting his man. It was my favorite funny paper, and I was happy to have a whole book by Grey.

Grey had published *Betty Zane* in 1903, himself, to celebrate his own ancestors' arrival in the Ohio River Valley in 1769–70 to found a settlement on the east side of the river near Wheeling Creek. There a few years later, 1774, the Zane family, with other settlers, built Fort Henry as protection against the Native Americans.

The settlers feared an attack from those Natives siding with the British during the Revolutionary War. Indeed, a prefatory note in the full edition I later bought (Grosset & Dunlap) refers to a cairn in Wheeling, West Virginia, which commemorates "the siege of Fort Henry, Sept. 11, 1782, the last battle of the American Revolution" (vii). Grey's book is also a commemoration of this event—and the incidents leading up to this climax where his great-grandaunt proved her heroic mettle.

Grey elucidates further that had it not been for the heroics of Elizabeth (Betty) Zane, the city of Wheeling would "never have existed" (vii). He knew the story of her exploits—and those of her brothers Colonel Ebenezer Zane, the head of the community, and Isaac, eventually married to an Native princess—as oft-repeated family tales. He recalls that his grandmother as a little girl had heard the stories firsthand from Betty herself, then an old woman.

I myself had read the abridged novel more than once, not knowing that its events were mostly about real people, when I came across an account of Fort Henry and Ebenezer Zane in an old set of *The Book of Knowledge*. It even mentioned Betty's famous dash to the fort through a gauntlet of enemy rifle fire. Slung over her shoulder was the bag of gunpowder that saved their stronghold. It was with renewed interest that I read the novel again, and several more times, in my boyhood.

In the first chapter, Grey outlines all the essentials of the story—the Ohio Valley setting, the likelihood of siege or attack, and Betty's acquirements of "fleet foot" and "daring spirit" (20), key to her heroic run in the penultimate chapter. Grey also hints at a love interest with the coming of a new soldier, Alfred Clarke, to help protect the fort, while establishing the real-life character of Lew Wetzel, who might have been a rival for Betty's hand had he not been the silent, restless borderman later called "Deathwind" (106) by the Natives he pursued. Chapter 1, as well, gives some inklings of Isaac's strange case. He was captured by Wyandottes/Hurons because of their princess Myeerah's love for him. The course of this love provides a comment on Betty and Clarke's relationship.

In a foreword to a later novel, *To the Last Man*, 1922, Grey gives his writing credo: "My inspiration to write has always come from nature. Character and action [i.e., plot] are subordinated to setting" (ii). Certainly in *Betty Zane*, there are some splendid descriptions of the setting, some short, some long. The account of a fishing excursion (86–95) is typical with its reference to an old sycamore shading a quiet pool, a doe and her fawn drinking in the shallow water, an eagle circling slowly high above a bluff. Betty's exclamation is, in fact, Grey's too: "It is the association which makes fishing delightful. The canoe gliding down a swift stream, the open air, the blue sky, the birds and trees and flowers—these are what I love" (84).

Elsewhere Grey refers to Isaac's affinity for nature, and we can be sure the author once more is speaking of himself: "like all the Zanes he had born in him an intense love for the solitude of the wilderness" (101). This feeling jibes well with his saying in the previously quoted foreword that the secret of his ambition as a writer is contained in the Wordsworth statement—"The world is too much with us" (ii).

Despite Grey's assessment of his works in this manner, character and action are hardly subordinated to setting in his first novel. The author shows Betty to have the foibles of one who has several older brothers to spoil her and has had a maid to wait on her since she was a baby. Ebenezer, as the oldest brother, has undertaken to look after her, but he "rather indulged her caprices" (217), for he is a "kind-hearted brother" (280). He fondly calls her "Betts" (19), although he is not beyond referring to her as "that young firebrand" (178) or "Her Highness" (279).

Some of Betty's traits are brought out humorously, again supplied by Ebenezer's wry comments, and in the light, bantering conversation she herself has with her girlfriends (the amount of both humor and banter in this book is characteristic of several Grey novels). Betty is "passionate," "quick[-]tempered," but "generous and tenderhearted" too (41), feeling miserable when her impatience has hurt someone. She does "everything well" (138) (but wants "her own way" [34]), and is "mischievous" (19), "quick as a steel trap" (138), and self-centered—"not used to being unnoticed" (199). In short, Grey has created a memorable character for his great-grandaunt.

Grey's great-grandfather, Ebenezer, and his wife, Bess or Bessie (herself half Native), are also well portrayed. He is a genial but commanding figure, age thirty-three to thirty-five in the novel, a nation-builder who in later years, at President Washington's request, built a national road from Wheeling, West Virginia, to Maysfield, Kentucky, called Zane's Trace. It opened southeastern Ohio to pioneer settlement. What is interesting in Grey's description is that Bess in her own way is as competent as her husband. Early on she is depicted as a woman "of remarkable force of character as well as kindness of soul" (15), bravely tending to injuries incurred by her neighbors. And she "knows" Betty better than does Ebenezer, who, "blind as brothers are in regard to their own sisters" (58), wonders how his little sister, "breaking her heart over [Clarke] all these months," can remain so "cool" in greeting him when he comes to propose. Bess "indignantly" asks her "worthy spouse": "Would you expect Betty to fall into his arms?" (281). The by-play between husband and wife throughout the novel is a nice touch, humorous too, and revealing of Grey's keen understanding of marital relationships, even though he himself would not be married for another three years after the writing of this book.

The action is as vivid as one might expect in a frontier setting, with the time span but one-and-a-half years, from spring, 1781, to fall, 1782, when the siege at Fort Henry occurs. In this interval Betty and Clarke fall in love, but their love story could best be described by a line from Shakespeare's *A Midsummer Night's Dream*: "the course of true love never did run smooth" (1.1.132). They are two of a kind, proud and prejudiced—one is reminded of the twists and turns in Jane Austen's novel *Pride and Prejudice*, 1813, and Elizabeth Bennet's statement in that novel could well apply to both of the Grey characters speaking of each other: "I could easily forgive *his* [*her*] pride, if he [she] had not mortified *mine*" (21).

It is Wetzel, in talking to Clarke, who understands the situation: "You fly off 'en the handle too easy. And so does Betty. You both care fer each other and are unhappy about it. Now, you don't know Betty, and she keeps misunderstandin' you" (221). In my mind's "ear," I keep hearing this as if said by John Wayne—it has that certain turn of phrase. (I think Wayne would have made a perfect Wetzel in a movie production of the book.)

Meanwhile, Betty has another suitor in Ralfe Miller, new to the settlement. His outright failure to win her combined with his zealous hatred of Clarke lead to the stabbing of his rival while the man is asleep. Before disappearing into the night to join renegade forces, he pauses beneath Betty's window with these final words, "Now, go to your lover. You'll find him cold" (223). Wetzel later gives chase, and Colonel Zane says, truly, that he "would not give a snap of [his] fingers for Miller's chances" (226). The episode is graphically related. Clarke survives.

Wetzel's words to Betty on leaving explain the triangular relationship of her, Clarke, and, yes, himself: "I knew how it was with him so I told him. I knew how it was with you so I told him, and I knew how it was with me, so I told him that too." Betty realizes she has not really known this man, her best friend, who had always been so protective of her; now she understands why. Wetzel continues in his John Wayne manner: "That kind of gives me a right, don't it, considerin' it's all fer your happiness" (228).

Grey has said, halfway through the book, that "Betty was a Zane and the Zanes came of a fighting race.... It gave her ... the resolve to fight against the longing in her heart" (141). So when in the final scene of the book Clarke tells her not to fight any longer, she, a true Zane, and true to her character, replies, "But I can't help fighting" (286). It is her last resistance, however, and she is, as her loving brother says to end the story, "tamed at last" (288).

Ebenezer's words are fitting comment because of the several references to Betty's "wildness" earlier in the book. Her capacity for understanding has grown through her travails, and the progress of the story might have been called—again, with reference to a Shakespearean play, its title significantly altered—*The Taming of the Wild Heart*.

All this love story is played out against the action leading up to and including the siege of Fort Henry. Grey devotes two chapters to the siege itself, a chapter for each day of the conflict. The writing is exceedingly graphic. Described are heavy casualties on both sides, these being the results of black-powder riflery, cannon blasts, axe wielding, and flaming arrows at night.

We already know the layout of the area on which the drama unfolds. The fort is 365 by 150 feet, a twelve-foot stockade with bastions at each corner marking its boundary. Inside, farm families have taken refuge, and the fighting force is but forty-two, even counting any women and boys able to handle rifles. Luckily, a crew of four men transporting a cannon and cannonballs down the river that morning become part of the group. A blockhouse of two stories and several cabins provide additional protection for them.

Outside the wall, at the distance of a hundred yards, is Ebenezer's house. The owner and three extra marksmen are stationed there—to safeguard the structure and, because it is on higher ground, help to maintain a crossfire and so aid those in the fort.

The enemy, arriving by late morning, is six hundred strong, two-thirds of that number Natives, with their red-coated, British-soldier allies in the rear. They have just crossed the Ohio from the west and are demanding unconditional surrender. Simon Girty, an American pioneer who has taken to leading Indian raiding parties against the colonists and who now sides with the British, is one of the spokesmen.

There will be no surrender, only warfare, and a cloud of black-powder smoke quickly lies over the site. It is in the little details of battle, Grey's attention to individuals' well-being, that the siege is described. We see a bucket of water at each porthole where a woman dips a hot rifle barrel and wipes it dry before handing the weapon back to the man shooting. Thus we know something of the rapidity of gunfire. "Hearing" the tearing up of bandages, we learn of the wounded and dying. Fifteen of the forty-two defenders are killed the first day.

The second day brings a new concern—the gunpowder is gone! What to do? Grey skillfully builds up the suspense: the silence of shock, the wild searching for the explosive, the repeated cries of "Gone!"—all this in contrast to the "calm, resolute, self-contained" figure of Betty ladling hot lead into a bullet-mould (269), a task she has been at for almost forty hours. It is she who will volunteer to run to Ebenezer's house for more gunpowder.

Fleet of foot and a woman, she has the best chance of success. That she is not shot on her easy run to the house is but quiet prelude to the dangerous flight back. At the house a keg of powder is hastily dumped onto a tablecloth, the ends caught up to form a bag, and Betty is off, the enemy no longer in doubt about her mission. It is a sense of speed and danger that Grey wishes to convey here, and he does so admirably: "The reports of rifles blended in a roar.... The bullets were raining about her. They sang over her head; hissed close to her ears, and cut the grass in front of her..., but still untouched, unharmed, the slender brown figure sped" (274).

The fort is saved, and the next morning a relief party appears. Carlton Jackson—in his critical study, *Zane Grey*, 1973, in Twayne's United States Authors Series—says that Grey, despite employing some dramatic license in telling his tale, "showed how one incident of the Revolution helped produce a nationalistic experience" (23).

Grey's treatment of the Native Americans in his first book, with regard to their relation to settlements in the whole Ohio Valley and elsewhere, is interesting. The author seems to glory in the heroics of Wetzel, who is, after all, a professional "Indian hunter," but he sides with the Natives. The beginning of chapter 6, a half dozen pages, talks directly of their situation, how they were treated since the time of their earliest contact with the white man. Inroads were made onto their lands, says Grey, and this "invasion" made them a "fierce and relentless foe" (117). They suffered "long years of deceit and treachery" (119) at the hands of the whites and were "cruelly wronged" (120).

In fact, Grey's one-and-a-half page discussion of how white man's rum degraded them touches on the Noble Savage theme: "the steadily increasing tide of land-stealing settlers rolling westward, and the insidious, debasing, soul-destroying liquor were the noble redman's doom" (122). Later in the book, Grey has Colonel Zane, whose opinions we have come to respect, say this: "The Indians consider that they have been robbed and driven from their homes. What we think hideously inhuman [in their fighting] is war to them" (159).

And the final paragraph of the book is reserved for the Native Americans, recalling those who had originally roamed the area (yes, and those descendants who had besieged Fort Henry): "Sad ... is the thought that the poor Indian is unmourned. He is almost forgotten" (291). Grey, however, would not forget. One of his greatest books would deal exclusively with the Natives' changing circumstances, as the author saw them, vis-a-vis the rest of society—*The Vanishing American*, 1925. (He was proud of his aboriginal ancestry.)

My introduction to Zane Grey, by merest chance back in 1942, was a very good one. Not only did I read Grey's *first* book—a fair place to start—but it was, in a sense, his first "Western." He thought of the area settled by his ancestors, as he makes clear in the opening note and prologue, as "our western border" (vii), "the frontier" (xii), and part of "that unknown west" (ix).

In ending the story, Grey already includes a scene that would become a staple in so much Western literature—the loser in love's triangle disappearing, as it were, into the sunset. Here Betty and Clarke, finally together, watch Wetzel's departure up a hill: "They looked and presently saw the tall figure of the hunter emerge from the bushes. He stopped and leaned on his rifle. For a minute he remained motionless. Then he waved his hand and plunged into the thicket. Betty sighed and Alfred said: 'Poor Wetzel! ever restless, ever roaming'" (287).

Betty Zane paved the way for Grey's writing of his some sixty Westerns set in the *Far* West. Jackson tells us (28) that when Grey suggested to Charles Jesse "Buffalo" Jones in New York that he, Grey, accompany Jones back to Arizona in order to write about their experiences on that frontier, Jones wanted assurance that Grey could write. Grey gave Jones a copy of *Betty Zane* to read, Jones was convinced, and the rest, as they say, is history.

A literature professor of mine once remarked that a novel still widely read after one hundred years may indeed be a lasting work of fiction. *Betty Zane* is now more than that age. I am happy to say that I was able to first read it some seventy years ago.

2
Riders of the Purple Sage:
Mill-Wheel of Place and Action

Riders of the Purple Sage, 1912 (serialized in *Field and Stream* the same year) is a complex book, a weave of intertangled relationships that come to light only as the novel progresses. Eventually, we see that the life and death of Milly Erne before the story begins propels all the action—of two plots, each with its own hero and heroine. She is Lassiter's lost sister—Lassiter, a gunman (Grey's first), mysterious, somber, dressed in black leather, who rides into the Mormon community of Cottonwoods. There, he meets Jane Withersteen, whose father had founded it and left her a huge ranch. Beautiful and self-assured, she has angered her fellow Mormons by giving from her wealth to needy non-Mormons just as freely as she does to members of her own religion.

Bern Venters heads the riders of the purple sage, the cowboys tending Jane's herd of seven thousand cattle. As one of the non-Mormons (referred to as Gentiles in this book), he admires his employer for her kindness to him and is seen by church-elder Tull as a rival for Jane's hand. When one herd of cattle is stolen, he sets out for Deception Pass after rustler Oldring and his Masked Rider to retrieve them.

Venters shoots the rider, finds that he has wounded a young woman—Bess, Oldring's girl, or so she says. She in fact is Milly's stolen child (and thus Lassiter's niece—her true identity is not revealed till much later in the book). He nurses her back to health in a secret valley away from all the hubbub, and says that he is sure that helping her will help him—a comment from the author on the meaning of life.

Meanwhile, Jane hires Lassiter as a rider to protect her cattle—from the Mormons, who have begun harassing her to keep her in line. She has mixed feelings. She may not fully understand her own thoughts about the man, but she senses "a sadness, a hungering, a secret" (8) in his make-up, and is attracted. Still, she knows that he is a gunman and has heard him say about her church people—"To hell with Mormon law!" (10).

She resolves to keep him nearby so that she can change his attitude and prevent him from killing them. He, however, believes that it was an overly zealous, proselytizing Mormon who had run off with his sister and that his actions had somehow led to her death. He is out to kill Milly's oppressor, and he has traced her last whereabouts to Cottonwoods. Jane now reveals that Milly had been her "best-loved friend" (17) and is buried on her property.

"Oh, what a tangled web" has been woven (Scott, *Marmion*, 6.17.27). The course of events could make the story but a soap opera, or rather, a horse opera, with no end of coincidences, mistaken identities, misconceived actions, and miscarriages of justice, always with much accompanying melodramatic sentiment. But Grey manages to avoid most such pitfalls in this the bestselling Western of all time (its sales well over a million copies in hardcover alone). He does so by creating a strong female lead in Jane Withersteen, who "asked only the divine right of all women—freedom ... to love and live as her heart willed" (26). (Grey's chief criticism of the Mormons of the time, 1871, is what he considers its mistreatment of women and the apparent fanaticism of some of its leaders—men, of course. Jane, herself, is a forerunner of a changing Mormonism.)

She, at age twenty-eight, is powerful enough to stand up to the domineering men of her church, while still having the grace to live "for happiness and the day at hand" (15). She can excuse the men, who, she says, "have been driven, hated, scourged till their hearts have hardened," but adds, "we women hope and pray for the time [they] will soften" (13–14). She maintains a home with bright-colored rugs, a "cozy corner with hammock and books" (15). No austerity there! "There's no one," she feels, "with a right to question [her] actions" (14).

It is about Jane that what is happening ever whirls. Even Venters, off with Bess in his Surprise Valley, survives by "stealing" a few of Jane's stolen cattle—he sees the irony of his act—from Oldring! (And Oldring's rustling of them, we learn, was made possible when the Mormons, to thwart Jane, called in her Mormon riders.)

The author has firm control over the stampeding events: seems to "mill" the two plots around, in and out of Surprise Valley, ultimately bringing everything to a standstill, and secures Jane's (and Lassiter's) safety and wellbeing within the Valley, having had Venters and Bess flee elsewhere. This occurs with Lassiter's tumbling down of Balancing Rock to seal off their retreat: "The crag thundered into atoms. A wave of air—a splitting shock! Dust shrouded the sunset rim of shaking rims.... The outlet ... closed forever" (335).

Presaging this book-enveloping mill-wheel effect is Lassiter's actual milling of a stampede of Jane's cattle early on in the story when he first begins working for her. Mormons had purposely frightened the steers by flapping a white sheet at them, and Lassiter rides out to control the melee, to end it—all magnificently described over two pages. He crowds the herd leaders, sheers them to one side, so that they gradually turn around *into* the last of the run, making for a ground-quaking great upheaval; then the "inner strife ceased, and the hideous roar and crash.... [A]nd the pall of yellow dust began to drift away in the wind" (81).

Really, the plots of Grey's Western are Elizabethan, the bare bones of a Shakespearean drama, if you will, fleshed out not in royal court and historic battlefield but in the court*yard* of a ranch house and the nearby sagebrush desert and canyon country of southeastern Utah. Venters's well-watered Eden of Surprise Valley could be another Arden, as in *As You Like It*, a refuge from the troublous outside world, a sometime retreat for Venters and Bess, as Arden was for Orlando and Rosalind in Shakespeare's play (also with both women appearing there as other than whom they really are). For Jane and Lassiter the retreat appears permanent.

There is an element of mystery about things, apart from the identity of Bess. "What might not be possible in this stone-walled maze of mystery?" (62) asks Venters (and Grey) about the red-rock environs, the hub of open space and outlying spokelike canyons (another mill-wheel image, this time of setting). Which spoke, followed up, will provide some answers? Venters wonders if Oldring's rustling of cattle, now hidden in one of the canyons, is a cover for some other devious activity (he is mining for gold). What part did Bess have in all this? is another question he ponders, concluding: "It may have served Oldring to create mystery" (57). Certainly, the reader's interest is sparked.

What Grey is doing is to lead the reader into a book of great potential, where the conflicts are great, along with the evils and loves. Jane has the greatest conflict, trying to be true to her Mormon faith while some of its adherents are ravaging her holdings. The ignominy of men such as Elder Tull is exposed in their heinous acts behind religious motives, equivalent to the early New Englanders' burning of witches in order to get them to confess and so save their souls.

One such act in *Riders of the Purple Sage* is these men's oiling and setting afire the tail of a live coyote, then having the animal stampede Jane's cattle yet again—to bring her to her knees. And when Jane, entrusted with caring for a Gentile's little girl, Fay, will not give her a Mormon upbringing, Bishop Dyer "thunder[s]" that she must do otherwise, or she faces "the damning of [her] soul to perdition" (150). (It was Dyer who, in effect, had killed Milly

Erne.) More conflict for Jane, more self-righteous evil from a church mentor. Grey's message is—Don't be fooled by outward religious appearances; look for, and emulate, a genuine Christ-like behavior (166, 174).

The great loves are not without conflicts, and evil too. The most obvious emotion is the young love slowly developing between Venters and Bess, living like Adam and Eve in Surprise Valley. Its beginnings are told with fine subtlety: "she turned her head and saw him. A swift start, a change rather than rush of blood under her white cheeks, a flashing of big eyes that fixed their glance upon him, transformed her face in that single instant of turning; and he knew she had been watching for him, that his return was the one thing in her mind.... [S]ome unfamiliar, deep-seated emotion, mixed with pity and glad assurance of his power to succor her, held him dumb" (128–29).

Unfortunately, though their love has been declared, the "eternal feminine" (296) (as Goethe defines it, 413) rears up when she detects that one of the bales Venters brings back from Cottonwoods has been packed by a woman (Jane)—so there *was* a woman in his life, something he previously denied. This is only a slight tiff, but what is found in many of Grey's books, what could be called the "eternal masculine," a flaw with usually much more serious ramifications, appears here as well. This is a man's obsessive concern with his sweetheart's previous love life. Venters knows she is Oldring's "girl," thinking this means his mistress rather than his daughter, and vows to shoot the man on first sight.

The depiction of Venters stalking Oldring at a bar and killing him is exceptionally graphic (258–60): Venters can only speak in a whisper. He feels "frozen, mechanical, incapable of free thought," and everything around him seems "coldly distant." He is robotic, as though not in control of his own actions when he calls Oldring to step outside, then has a hot, "unutterable fiendish joy" in killing him, ending his "magnificent manhood."

The description following, of Venters's reaction while returning to Bess and the ensuing conversation with her, may be some of the best writing in the book (one needs to read all of pages 262–68 to get the full impact): "He caught glimpses into himself, into unlit darkness of soul. The fire that had blistered him and the cold which had frozen him now united in one torturing possession of his mind and heart, and like a fiery steed with ice-shod feet, ranged his being, ran rioting through his blood, trampling the resurging good, dragging ever at the evil" (262).

He does not tell Bess what he has done, but the "perverse jealous devil" (266) within him will not let him be. He must know what she was to Oldring, and when she says, "his daughter," he flounders like a drowning man, his "queer fancies" contrasting abysmally with her pure innocence, the unknowing "innocence of lonely girlhood" (267). He can only cry out: "My God! ... My God! ... Oh, Bess! ... Forgive me! Never mind what I've done—what I've thought. But forgive me. I'll give you my life. I'll live for you. I'll love you. Oh, I do love you.... Oh, Bess, I was driven! And I might have known! ... God! How things work out" (268). Lassiter had said that "gun-packin' in the West ... has growed into a kind of moral law" (157), but youthful Venters's "gun-packin'" here, Grey would say, is a corruption of that law.

The love between Lassiter and Jane is much different. At thirty-eight, he is ten years older than she, and though this is a first love for them both, they talk about it calmly and rationally because such are their personalities. To start with, Jane had used all her feminine wiles to win him over in order literally to dis*arm* him, to have him give up his guns: "I wanted you to care for me so that I could influence you." And he had responded, equally casually, "What you meant is one thing—what you *did* was to make me love you" (155). (This is still in the first half of the book.) It is left for one of Jane's riders to state their case more emotionally: "Jane turned his head. He's mad in love over her—follers her like a dog. He ain't no more Lassiter! ... He hasn't thrown a gun, an' he won't!" (256).

Later, nonetheless, the two "lovers" continue their same rational analysis. Jane says, "I *think* I care a great deal. How much, how little, I couldn't say" (my italics). He replies with an observation that could apply to them both, and to everybody else, "Habit of years is as strong as life itself" (271). That is, they are older and cannot change their lifestyles easily (as Venters and Bess can, for instance, to accommodate a growing love). Grey's portrayal of the two couples is a study in contrasts, and also, here, some very fine writing.

Lassiter concludes, "I reckon, Jane, that marriage between us is out of all *human reason*?" (again, added emphasis) (271). She agrees—because she is still a Mormon woman, and he is still Lassiter, a gunman. For answer he unbuckles his gunbelt and lays it on her lap—and she, realizing that she has been given the power of Samson's Delilah, buckles it back around his waist "where it belong[s]" (272). She had wanted to disarm him, yes, but now, she knows, not to *unman* him.

But can she marry him? Lassiter suggests they ride out of Utah, on her fine black racers, Black Star and Night, where he can be a man without guns. She, however, cannot leave her gray sage country with its purple distances, the land she loves so well. Her habit of years appears incorrigible, while he is trying to show her that he, through love, can be regenerated.

Then little Fay is stolen by Dyer, and all Jane's life seems "to fall about her in wreck and ruin" (283). Her response is irrational—she wants to just give up, accept Dyer's yoke, and marry Tull. She becomes another woman—

weak, pleading, melodramatic. But Lassiter is again Lassiter, and enough is enough. He remembers that his sister's child was stolen too, and he is ready to gun down Dyer. He tries to stop Jane's tirade with "Woman—don't trifle at words!" (285), but is unsuccessful. She will do anything to spare her bishop—even ride away with Lassiter, leaving the purple sage behind forever. His answer is a cold, ringing "No!" (286).

Jane's continued frantic pleas do not ring quite true. "Lassiter, would you kill me? I'm fighting my last fight for the principles of my youth—love of religion, love of father..." sounds somewhat stilted. Also, "Lassiter, *I do love you*! It's leaped out of my agony. It comes suddenly with a terrible blow of truth. You are a man!..." (286) is a bit much. (One could argue, I suppose, that Grey, who otherwise records conversation with such a sure hand, is deliberately writing as he does to reflect Jane's distraught frame of mind.)

Good old Lassiter!—he sees things clearly and says, "Jane, ... you're ... blackenin' your soul with lies" (287). But she cannot stop: her final plea is in behalf of her father, who, she admits, sent out Dyer to proselytize Milly. Lassiter in turn tries to bring her to the reality of the present moment: "This thing I'm about to do ain't for myself or Milly or Fay. It's not because of anythin' that ever happened in the past, but for what is happenin' right *now*. *It's for you*!" (287–88). Jane faints.

When she comes to, she is again a rational woman—and a lot has happened in the interval: Lassiter has shot Dyer, secured a gunman's justice, not a negotiated peace. Grey, through his hero, speaks later of how "hard an' cruel this border life is.... But it can't last always. An' remember this—some day the border'll be better, cleaner, for the ways of men like Lassiter!" (326). She is now ready to go with him, anywhere, and quotes the Biblical response of Ruth to Naomi (Ruth 1:16): "Your people shall be my people, and your God my God!" (294).

They leave on the two racers—for Deception Pass and the temporary safety of Surprise Valley. Lassiter had earlier tracked Venters there, showing that the Valley is not completely safe from attackers. (Unless, of course, the huge Balancing Rock is rolled off its pedestal. For defense, it had been chipped by early-day cliff-dwellers to balance perfectly, ready to be dislodged and start an avalanche, thus blocking the entrance, coming in *or* going out.) For this reason Venters and Bess are leaving the Valley, hoping to get away on their burros, when they meet Lassiter and Jane, escaping from Tull and his men.

Jane is still the center of the action. She offers an exchange of mounts, knowing that the young couple need fast horses to get through to the nearest railway without being stopped. Venters had previously been given Jane's fastest horse, Wrangle, and he had ridden out on this great sorrel to get another fast horse for Bess, only to be waylaid by Tull's associates, who were running off with Jane's racers. He had retrieved the stolen horses and returned them to her then, but in so doing Wrangle was killed. Now the burros will do for Jane and Lassiter.

They get to Deception Pass, where Lassiter discovers some "fellers [he's] been lookin' for" (325). He approaches them secretly, Jane hears a fusillade of shots, and he returns with little Fay and two horses. It is rush, rush again to gain Balancing Rock and behind it, Surprise Valley. The pursuers are in sight, and Lassiter, with Jane crying out, *"Roll the stone! ... Lassiter, I love you!"* sends the huge rock bounding down upon Tull and company, closing the outlet in a "long-drawn rumbling roar" (335). The milling wheel of events in this book has come to a full stop.

Venters had once mused that he and Bess would have had enough in edenic Surprise Valley to live there all their lives; besides its rich bounty of wild animals and edible growing things, he had brought into it eight live beef calves—from, of course, Jane's rustled herd. All this will now provide for the newcomers. Jane and Lassiter and Fay, however, do not always remain in the Valley. A sequel, *The Rainbow Trail*, 1915, with a story of its own, tells how their departure comes about years later.

3
Desert Gold: More Than Money

The prologue to *Desert Gold*, 1913 (serialized in *Popular Magazine* the same year), is a complete short story in itself. Its somewhat ponderous, intense prose is unlike that in the rest of the book but anticipates much of the writing in *Wanderer of the Wasteland*, published ten years later. In each instance the style is appropriate to the subject matter—lonely prospectors in a "drear ... infinitude" of desert, a "vast silent world" (1, 3).

Of the two miners in the prologue, the one called Cameron (really Robert Burton) has sought the desert to better remember a woman whom he had wronged and lost, to dwell on his guilt in the "limited abode of ... desolation" (5). He chooses the Sonora Desert along the southern border of Arizona during the late 1800s. There he meets another lone wanderer, an older man whose name he learns only weeks later. This miner has come to the desert to forget a woman, his disgraced daughter, who went West to work and live for her baby girl. Both men pace the sandy wastes at night, separately, suggesting to us in their plodding manner the helplessness of man. The surrounding desert, meanwhile, is "austere, ancient, always waiting" (9).

It is when the second prospector reveals his name, Jonas Warren, that Cameron knows, as we suspected, that the person haunting both men is the same woman, Nell. Cameron had always felt that he was somehow part of an "inscrutable purpose" (10), and now feels that his meeting with Warren here is a kind of providence, an enactment of the desert's "simplicity, its truth" (13). He reveals all to his companion, that he was Nell's lover. Therewith, the old man rises in terrible anger, grapples with him and tries to kill him in a primeval struggle. Though he weakens, the two are left half-stunned, facing each other, and panting for speech.

It is as if the encounter is between two great natural forces, even geological ones colliding, in which there can be no winner, only an adjustment, a realignment of the same spent energies, now next to each other—"the distant rumble of a slipping edge," "the silken seep of sifting sand" (15). The affray is no longer one of good versus evil but of two opposing destinies meeting. Cameron reaffirms to Warren his attempt at making amends by marrying Nell later, but they could not live together. The two men become reconciled and face an oncoming sandstorm, each thinking of the other's welfare. But Warren dies, just after Cameron finds that all the scattered rocks about them show gold, desert gold!

He keeps vigil, thinking of the mother and girl, who are close to him then. "Time and distance were annihilated.... The fateful threads of the past, so inextricably woven with his error, wound out their tragic length here in this forlorn desert" (21). Before long, he dies, too, but before doing so, he scribbles a message on his marriage certificate, something he always kept with him to prove to himself that he had done right, and places it in a little tin box for another person, following in the steps of her destiny, to find. Then he gives up his soul to the desert's "passionless serenity" (22).

Chapter 1 introduces us, a decade or so later, to Dick Gale, a spoiled Easterner, age twenty-five, who has come West to show his father that he has some gumption. A star athlete in college, particularly in football, he just could not fit in the business empire his father was building in Chicago. He wanted adventure, not office work, so the year 1911 finds him in the Southwest border town of Casita, with a Mexican revolution and guerilla warfare occurring immediately south. He hopes to see some "stirring life" (23).

Dick is not disappointed. He meets a former college friend, George Thorne, who is now in the United States cavalry, patrolling Arizona's international line. Thorne has assisted refugees fleeing into the States from Mexico, including a Mercedes Castañeda from an old wealthy Spanish family. She had been captured by a rebel bandit named Rojas and escaped to Casita, but Rojas knows of her whereabouts and is here to recapture her. She and Thorne are in love, and he wants to get her safely farther into his country to marry her. Will Dick help him?

Dick likes the adventurous challenge. He meets the beautiful Mercedes, who is "all fire and soul and passion" (37). He also catches a glimpse of the "evil visage" of Rojas in a saloon, he with his "dandified dress" and diamonds on his fingers (39). They both appear here like stock-in-trade heroine and villain, but their characters are more fully delineated as the story proceeds. Mercedes, of course, is not the primary heroine, and Rojas may be more than someone calling himself a revolutionist "just for an excuse to steal, burn, kill, an' ride off with women" (50).

Dick uses his football training to start a row in the saloon, rushing at Rojas with "his old line-breaking plunge" (40), thus creating enough disturbance to allow Thorne and Mercedes to get away. Rojas suffers "a smashed finger, a dislocated collarbone, three broken ribs, and a fearful gash on his face" (89) (is hospitalized for a month). Two cowboys in attendance help by shooting out the lights. Thorne has to hurry back to his cavalry unit, so Dick is left alone to shepherd Mercedes to a refuge in the desert. Fortunately the two cowboys, Charlie Ladd and Jim Lash, happen along and become major players in the action. They all find safety at the Tom Belding ranch, where the wife is the former Nell Warren, and her daughter (and Belding's stepdaughter) is Nell Burton, almost twenty.

Young Nell is described by Belding as "wilder than any antelope" and "full of the devil" (65). But she matures instantly when she meets Dick, not the first time a girl has done so when she first sees the love of her life. She not only wants Dick as her husband but wants to deserve him. She now is somewhat constrained. As for Dick, Thorne's Spanish lady had awakened something in him, and he is ready now for a love of his own in Nell. Belding always seems to be getting the two together, for he thinks they would make a good match. His wife is more hesitant; she, *we* know, is thinking of her own earlier marital problem.

As Inspector of Immigration for the federal government, Belding needs riders to patrol the border for smugglers and raiders. He hires Ladd, Lash, and Dick, too, to be border rangers. Dick is particularly delighted to have an outdoor job with a possibly dangerous duty to perform. Thus he is drawn into the desert crucible, experiencing its power to work a spiritual change in him. He feels

> the white sun, with its glazed, coalescing, lurid fire; the caked split lips and rasping dry-puffed tongue; the sickening ache in the pit of his stomach; the insupportable silence, the empty space, the utter desolation, the contempt of life; the weary ride, the long climb, the plod in sand, the search, search, search for water; the sleepless night alone, the watch and wait, the dread of ambush, the swift flight; the fierce pursuit of men wild as Bedouins and as fleet, the willingness to deal sudden death, the pain of poison thorn, the stinging tear of lead through flesh; and that strange paradox of the burning desert, the cold at night, the piercing icy wind, the dew that penetrated to the marrow, the numbing desert cold of the dawn [97].

Externally he is miserable, but internally he is exulting with a "strange, wild glory" (103). He had never been of any use before, to himself or others, but now he uses his hands, senses, and wits to survive, and the superficialities of life, like dead scales, drop from him. He has a faithful horse, Blanco Sol, one of the original stock of big, strong, white horses that Belding had brought up from Durango, Mexico, and from which the rancher had bred a hundred more to sell to equine fanciers in Texas. And Dick has love in his heart; he sees Nell's face in every cloud by day and in the flames of every campfire by night.

Sitting before a fire, he also thinks of other wanderers of the desert, of drifters leaving ruined lives behind or memories of lost sweethearts, and he compares their fate to his that promises such joy. Here Grey is purposely harking back to the prologue, and pointing ahead to the book's conclusion. This chapter, entitled "The Yaqui," is well-wrought, depicting not only the hardships of desert life for Dick but its blessings too: "The dark mantle [of night] turned gray, and then daylight came quickly. The morning was clear and nipping cold. He threw off [his dew-wet] blanket and got up cramped and half frozen. A little brisk action was all that was necessary to warm his blood and loosen his muscles, and then he was fresh, tingling, eager. The sun rose in a golden blaze, and the descending valley took on wondrous changing hues" (106).

When Dick tries to get a drink for his horse (and himself) at a much used well, three Mexicans are already there with stolen horses. As he watches, two Natives, one a Yaqui, ride up on burros and are shot. The Yaqui, only injured, is nearly trampled to death, purposely, by one of the mounted Mexicans. Dick, firing, goes to his rescue—the horses stampeding, the Mexicans skedaddling—and takes him home to the ranch on his horse, a day's journey away. As Dick walks beside Blanco Sol, keeping a firm hand on the helpless Yaqui, he earns the Native's undying gratitude. We are never told his actual name; he is simply—"Yaqui."

In the days that follow, back at the ranch, we learn something of Dick's engineering expertise, acquired at college. He discovers an ideally located arroyo that could be dammed by simply dynamiting the cliffs above it and so creating an inexhaustible storage of water from the Forlorn River flowing into it. Crops could be irrigated, and there would be water for mining purposes as well, for there is gold in the hills. The whole area would prosper. Dick, Ladd, Lash (and Thorne, too) will all stake out claims in nearby quarter-sections of land.

Mexican raiders now steal several of the ranch's prize white horses, but not Dick's mount. Belding, his three riders, and Yaqui track the thieves; and what transpires is a race, described over eight pages, between Ladd on Blanco Sol and one of the Mexicans on his newly stolen horse, Belding's favorite. It is an account to rival that of the great run of Bern Venters's fine sorrel, Wrangle, in *Riders of the Purple Sage*, published just the year before. Dick watches spellbound as the dust from both horses rolls "in a funnel-shaped cloud from the flying hoofs" (143). But Blanco Sol's running is "that of a sure, remorseless driving power—steadier—stronger—swifter with every long and wonderful stride" (144). Belding gets his horses back.

Blanco Sol is featured in one more spectacular dash. Nell Burton secretly rides off on him to Casita to get word about Thorne, still stationed with the cavalry there. Mercedes, her good friend now at the ranch, is terribly worried. The ride takes five hours. We learn what happens through Charlie Ladd's colorful speech—he had followed her, later, to be of assistance. At the camp Nell finds that Thorne is actually being held prisoner by Rojas, across the border. The cavalry has been hesitant about rescuing him, but when Nell takes off to get him, someone catches hold of her horse ("an' that feller invite[s] himself to the hospital"); then the whole troop follows ("Looks like there'd been a cattle stampede on the desert"). Rojas and his men temporarily flee ("vamoosed without a shot"); Thorne ("black and blue all over, thin as a rail") is saved and brought to the ranch (162). Recovered, he and Mercedes marry.

Belding knows that Rojas captured Thorne only to make him tell where Mercedes is hidden. He sums up Rojas's mindset and activities: "The bandit's crazy over her. That's the Spanish of it." He loves her as a woman, hates her as a Spanish lady, and later swears he will give up robbing and killing when he marries her. His is a peon's "insane passion." And with Thorne, a rival, and Mercedes both at the ranch, "Our troubles have just begun" (163). Rojas has no knowledge of the marriage.

It is only a matter of days before Rojas and his band appear. He wants Mercedes delivered within twenty-four hours or he will fire the buildings and "hang the children on cactus thorns" (175). Belding's advice to his household members is that Mercedes and Thorne, with Dick, Ladd, and Lash for support, and Yaqui as leader of them all (a real "godsend" here [179]), leave in the dark of the night and circle around the enemy camp to seek safety at Yuma, three hundred miles away. It is February, and the heat should not be too oppressive. The six of them will each ride one of the white horses, taking two extras along. (Belding wants his best horses to escape too.) On leaving, Dick proposes to Nell, and she accepts.

The riders always have to watch the back trail—Rojas is sure to follow—and the forward one as well—for sign of other rebels. This gives Grey the opportunity to scatter his narrative with short descriptions of scenery, not only describing the surrounding country the six are escaping through, but also how it contributes to the atmosphere of their flight. When they see needle points of light, they know these are rebel campfires, and they need to head south into the Mexican Sonora Desert as a roundabout route.

This is Yaqui's home territory. There, they come upon fluted saguaros, fifty feet high, whose branching arms add "a grace to the desert," or basin mirages, where "inverted mountains h[a]ng suspended in the lilac air" (188). Elsewhere, dome-shaped hills, "sunset-colored above, blue-black below" (189), lead to great lava beds, where a choking dust rising up makes the riders cough, the horses snort. It is still thirty miles to the next waterhole.

Dick and the others look no more at the scenery: The "magnified[-]clinker" landscape (193) makes them lead their horses, to save them and to watch their own footholds. Rojas, with some dozen men, they now discern, is coming up the difficult jagged lava field too, a full day's travel behind. This is a "lonely, fierce, and repellant world" (197), fit stage for a showdown battle between the two forces. Grey is like a movie director, staging the most appropriate vistas as backdrops to the action.

As a break for the reader from all this desolation, and as a way of emphasizing its repulsiveness, Grey presents one contrasting vista. Yaqui has gone ahead into a crater zone, and the others, looking up, see him on a rim silhouetted against the sky—"and his great horse, dazzling white in the sunlight, with head wildly and proudly erect, mane and tail flying in the wind, ma[kes] a magnificent picture" (197–98).

The battle itself is staged along the brink of a crater several miles in circumference and a thousand feet deep. Grey calls it "The Crater of Hell" (199), also title of the chapter delineating the warfare. Fortunately, a fissure opens into an arroyo with grass and water, where the horses are left. There is a lot of long-distance sniping and casualties on both sides. Thorne suffers a serious head blow from a glancing bullet, knocking him unconscious; Yaqui, a bullet through the shoulder. Lash and Ladd are also wounded, Ladd badly shot up.

A wounded Rojas desperately tries to get to a screaming Mercedes and does so. While they are fiercely struggling, Dick shoots wildly at them. All this becomes a little melodramatic. Then Yaqui leaps down to the rescue and pursues Rojas along a precarious cliffside ledge in a deliberate stalking that can have only one ending in this story. The trail peters out, to leave Rojas clinging to an unscalable wall of lava. When Yaqui slowly cuts him free, we watch him fall back and downward into the crater's depths.

It takes weeks for Lash and Thorne to recover, Ladd much longer. Spring passes, when they might have returned, but by midsummer the heat is just too oppressive for traveling, and waterholes en route will be dry. Mercedes bears up well when a problem for them all is simply the passing of time; she begins teaching the others Spanish. Dick comes to spend more time with Yaqui, who had bound up his own shoulder; he feels a brotherly bond with him and wonders if he himself is capable of the Native's "tenaciousness of life," let alone his "strange honor, loyalty, love" (278). Thus, Grey speaks for a fellowship of humanity of all races.

Dick knows that the desert has been his principal teacher, that he is now a different man, climbing the lava slopes and sitting stock-still for hours trying to grasp "a little of the meaning of infinitude" (277). (Note that Grey says "stone-still," a particularly apt word, suggesting that Dick has become more a part of his environment, no longer only an observer of it.) He seems to be fighting against an "unfeeling self," to be losing his human powers "to stand up under this ponderous, merciless weight of desert space and silence" (279).

And then the spirit of that infinitude cries out to him, alone on a promontory at night—"Lost! Lost! Lost! What are you waiting for?" (279). These words echo Henry David Thoreau's famous account of confronting wild nature on climbing Mount Katahdin in *The Maine Woods*, 1864. It describes a vast, titanic earth-force, "made out of Chaos and Old Night," pitted against his lone being, so that Thoreau himself cries out: "Man [is] not to be associated with it.... Talk of mysteries! ... our life in nature,—... to come in contact with it[!] ... *Who* are we? *where* are we?" (70–71).

Both Thoreau and Dick free themselves from this sense of alienation, remembering well-loved familiar worlds—the naturalist, his Walden woods and pond; Dick, his sweetheart Nell on the Belding ranch. He must return at once, and an oncoming desert rainstorm makes travel possible.

Much has happened at the ranch. A Ben Chase and son Radford, rich financiers new to the area, have legally jumped the claims of the land staked by Belding's rangers because no improvements, of course, had been made. As a further insult, the father and son team has built the dam and reservoir that had originally been Dick's idea. Then, with influential friends in Washington, the two have engineered Belding's loss of his government job. To top it off, they are harassing the two Nells, mother and daughter, over the seeming illegitimacy in their Burton relationship.

When the fugitives return home, Dick solves what he can of the problems in Western fashion (approved by Grey)—no appeasement for bad actors. He soundly thrashes Radford for insulting Nell Burton, also threatens the father to keep out of his way, thus stripping Ben Chase "of all authority and confidence and courage" (313). And Yaqui, in a final compensation to Dick Gale for saving his life, leads him into the nearby mountains, up to the source of the Forlorn River he had hoped to dam. He could stake a claim there for water enough to meet all the needs of his friends below. Then Yaqui shows him the gold Robert Burton had stumbled upon shortly before his death, as well as the little tin box with a twenty-one-year-old marriage certificate. No more problems remain; Yaqui has paid his debt in full.

In pondering this mountain journey in which Dick needs to go to the top in order to achieve ultimate success, I cannot help wondering whether Grey had in mind at all his own situation a year earlier when his *Riders of the Purple Sage* had been rejected by the editor and staff of Harper & Brothers, even though the company had already published his *The Heritage of the Desert*, 1910. He had then gone over their heads to the vice-president and executive officer for a second appraisal, and the manuscript had been accepted—to become the best-selling Western of all time.

Desert Gold ends with Dick and Nell married—she is his real desert gold—and Yaqui riding west into the sunset—home.

4

Last of the Duanes: Undying Passion

The story starts with a drunken cowboy out gunning for Buck Duane, age twenty-three, in the town of Wellston, Texas. Duane has the driving "blood lust" of his gunman father, killed years ago in a street fight, and the "unquenchable spirit" of his surviving pioneer mother (304–5). He fears no one, only himself, a strange, untested force within him, something over which he seems to have no say at all. He will not be called a coward—"a man simply can't stand that in this country" (15). So there will be a showdown. In *Last of the Duanes* (serialized in *Argosy* in 1914 but not published as a book until 1996), Zane Grey analyses this gunfighter mentality, a kind of basic immaturity to instantly settle disputes in a young Wild West. (Page references are to the 1996 Leisure Books edition by Dorchester Publishing.)

The author refers to these gunfighters as "more variable than children, as unstable as water, as dangerous as dynamite" (90). Here, Duane draws (or throws) his gun "*as a boy* throws a ball underhand" (my emphasis), as if the act is a kind of game, ritually enacted. But death is the abrupt consequence. The description following is fittingly terse, one of short sentences and no wasted words—just a life, where life is cheap: "He pulled twice, his shots almost as one. [The cowboy's] big Colt boomed while it was pointed downward and he was falling. His bullet scattered dust and gravel at Duane's feet. He fell loosely without contortion" (20).

Then back to real life: "in a flash all was reality for Duane." He sees a face now without devilment, just eyes expressing "something pitifully human" (20–21). Such eyes will bother him after each shooting in his gunman life, a "haunting visitation" (27) making him break into a cold sweat days and months after the killing, an "insidious phantom" (30) that does not wear off in time. He finds he can no longer enjoy nature as all Grey's central characters do. He becomes aloof to the world about him so that the author's descriptions of it in this book become terse too—just brief, scattered mentionings such as "the ebony canyons of shadow under the mountains, the melancholy serenity of the perfect night" (99).

Thus begins Duane's "unsought and hated career" (164). He is not really a criminal, as defined then by "any reasonable Texan" (189). He never holds up a man, robs a store for food, nor steals a horse in critical circumstances. As for himself, he feels no remorse about his killings: he has rid the community of an obnoxious character. An objective bystander would say that Duane, a young, inexperienced man, is making himself a judge of things, not knowing how apt we all are at resorting to self-justification and rationalization to explain away our actions. Actions have reactions; sequences of behavior have con-sequences. These slip Duane's mind until he sees his uncle with a getaway horse and gear ready for him. He will have to live as a fugitive, a lone wolf, or in a pack of men repugnant to him.

He rides hard southerly for several days, securing his safety, then approaches the border country along the Rio Grande, much frequented by outlaw gangs. Along the way he becomes acquainted with another rider, also on the dodge, who explains the various gangs' operations. Unfortunately, this new friend dies of gunshot wounds, and Duane has another look at death, a moment elemental and sad, "with a burden of mystery he [can]not understand" (43). He rides south again.

Two days later Duane stumbles into the largest outlaw camp, run by a big-time rustler—Bland by name, but not by temperament. He is a vicious killer, often without cause, but can be cowed by his brazen wife, Kate, who has lovers among the gang members. His response/revenge is to fetch over a girl to be her companion but really someone to possibly replace her and, meanwhile, make her jealous. An older outlaw, Euchre, feels sorry for this poor girl, Jennie, and enlists Duane's aid to help her escape the trying situation.

Kate herself is the chief difficulty in rescuing Jennie. It is hard to pull the wool over her eyes. Grey, over several pages, presents a well-drawn portrait of this woman of discontent. In one instance, we are told, she likely is a liar, one who believes her own lies. Yet when she tells *her* "story," Duane, like us, feels she is telling the truth: "I never see a decent woman or man.... I'm buried here ... buried alive with a lot of thieves and murderers. Can you blame me for being glad to see a young fellow ... a gentleman ... like the boys I used to go with? ... I'm sick for somebody to talk to.... I'm sick of this hole. I'm lonely..." (76). At one moment her eyes glow with fire; another, she is crying. She is both violent and overemotional, but what intrigues Duane is her longing for respectability. He can play on this trait to win her confidence and gain freer access to Jennie with an escape plan.

From Kate's view, Duane is "playing on the game of love" (83), while he, missing nothing, is really playing with death, for he knows the danger of the undertaking. But he glories in the opportunity, it giving some meaning to his life while providing hope to Jennie's desperate plight. Further, he cannot help but think it keeps him "from sinking to the level of her captors" (92–93), whose chief action is ever killing a new man in order to forget the last one. Duane still has other lives to live.

Bland is on to his wife's new fling, although she denies it and says it is Jennie that Duane loves. He then chokes her till she is black in the face and calls Jennie from her room. The girl confirms that she herself is the object of Duane's attention, and that she loves him. Chess Alloway, Bland's lieutenant, on overhearing this, cries out in dismay. We can see what a tangled mess of relationships exists.

Bland "loves" his wife in his own jealous way, even to the point of almost choking her to death; she hates her husband and is beginning to "love" Duane; Alloway, a real ruffian, secretly "loves" sweet, determined little Jennie; Jennie apparently loves Duane (perhaps only saying so to protect shameless Kate); and Duane loves nobody at this point. Such plot encapsulation usually sounds rather silly or comical (try it with a Shakespearean play!), but it speaks to Grey's competence as a storyteller that the whole account, of several chapters, has a strong dramatic validity.

Duane and Jennie make their escape early the next morning from Bland's cabin, the husband and wife still arguing when Duane arrives. He has to gun down Bland, and Alloway, who comes running down the lane when he hears the gunfire. And, yes, it is Kate who almost stops the getaway. When she hears that it is Jennie for whom Duane's attentions are really meant, then hell hath no fury.... She is a tigress fighting him, managing to shoot him through the chest before he throws her against a wall to be rid of her. Thus he and Jennie ride to safety, some forty miles away, before he falls off his horse. He has given her freedom, and she now, in the wilds, saves his life, nursing him back to health. He is in a coma for nine days.

Further aid comes from a friendly rancher and his wife, with whom they stay until Duane is completely recovered. Duane has gained a reputation, here a favorable one, for shooting the gang leaders, and the rancher is most hospitable. He warns Duane, however: every saloon loafer and punk cowboy will now want to shoot *him* "for the glory of it" (122). Duane has time to reflect on his position; how little stands between his better self and another self within him utterably terrible. He is glad he has saved the girl. Doing so distinguishes him as someone with "a human feeling to succor" (125). He feels he is not an outlaw.

Still, he sees his life before him as one of riding, hiding, killing until he meets his own death. It is now Jennie who tells him not to give up hope for better things, just as he encouraged her before *her* escape. "Be a lone wolf," she says. "Fight for your life ... and maybe ... some day..." (127). They will part, but not quite as they had intended. Some riders make off with her.

Duane trails the man he thinks responsible, shoots him, and is wounded himself. (He discovers, much later, that he killed the wrong man—so much for being judge, jury, and executioner. Such "justice" is swift but not always sure.) Another long hiding and recovery period ensue, then a seeking out of the little hut where Jennie first nursed him. He finds some comfort there, for it seems to hold her presence. But for months he mopes, "a prey to remorse, a dreamer, a victim of phantoms" (137). At night especially, he must live with the hellish thoughts thronging his mind, always the unseeing eyes of the men he has killed looking up at him.

All these morbid sensations Grey describes powerfully in a short tenth chapter, a psychological study of a thinking and feeling gunman such as Duane. A page of italicized writing is Duane's own attempt at self-analysis, with voiceless cries like the following: "*Poor fool! No, I shall never see mother again ... never go home ... never have a home.... Better be a callous brute or better dead! I shall go mad thinking! ... What is left? Only that damned unquenchable spirit of a gunfighter to live ... to hang onto a miserable life.* [And to his victims:] *Lie quiet in your graves and give me peace!*" (133). I am reminded here of Robinson Crusoe, alone on his island, calling out in his worst moments of despair. Yet Crusoe survives; so does Duane. Grey points out that his very gunman's spirit made the West livable for those coming later.

After six months of brooding, Duane once more ventures abroad, anything rather than hiding alone. He cannot escape his reputation and must outdraw one Hardin, an ally of Bland, harassing stockmen. Another time he is hounded by bad cowpunchers, not just as a lone wolf fleeing but "enacting the tragedy of all crippled, starved, hunted wolves at bay in their dens" (164). We are seeing in him the same pain and suffering that cornered animals endure when they are about to meet their deaths from man—only Duane has a human mind and feels all the more his plight. He escapes.

Later he finds posted a thousand-dollar reward for himself, dead or alive, wanted for the killing of a rancher's wife. His reputation has become such that he is gaining "fame" even for crimes he has *not* committed. He goes at once to clear his name, is confronted by a lynch mob, and saved only through the efforts of one strong man who insists on first securing all evidence available. Grey uses a whole chapter for this thorough depiction of mob mentality here.

Meanwhile, on several occasions, Duane has received word that a Captain MacNelly of the Texas Rangers wants to see him at their camp after dark. Is this a ruse to capture him? Whatever, he now feels compelled to go. And MacNelly offers to give him a full pardon, makes him a Ranger, and sends him alone, as an undercover agent, into another outlaw gang on the Rio Grande, this one run by the smooth operator, Cheseldine (an outlaw sent to catch an outlaw!).

Duane is to learn its movements and lay a trap so that his fellow Rangers can capture all the leaders, thus breaking up the gang completely. There is only one chance in a thousand that he will get back alive, but he jumps at the opportunity, leaving behind his old miserable existence and again doing something worthwhile with his life, however short it may be. Apparently, a young woman, a Miss Lee, sweet and passionate, prompted MacNelly to recruit Duane as a Ranger.

Duane meets the woman, and she is Miss *Jennie* Lee, the girl he rescued from the Blands, still intent and grateful, but now, he realizes, in talking with her, "his soul—his strength on earth—his hope of heaven" (207). They declare their love for each other, but a problem arises. She had not known of his special Ranger mission and is dead set against it—*he* will be dead, with their love just now discovered and affirmed.

Chapter 16 gives their back-and-forth views about his situation, their understandings and feelings, reasonings and pleas. Grey again, as in other books, is excellent at writing out this kind of dialogue and accompanying descriptive passages. A few lines of quotation here hardly capture the nuances:

> She rose and stood before him, still white, though calm now, with steady hands. Underneath the shadows of love and troubles in her dark eyes smoldered a fire. She looked stronger, older then....
> ...["]Listen, you don't know me. You think you're with the old Jennie. But I'm different. I've suffered, and I've learned in these years. I believe I'm right in asking you to give up this ranger service. Will you?"
> "Jennie, I can't. How could you ask it?"
> "How can you go if you love me?"
> "If you were a man, you'd understand."
> "But I'm a woman. *You* don't understand that!" [220, 222–23].

It is the cumulative effect of speech and action that is telling. He has a promise to keep, pulls her hands loose from his (note it is not his from hers), and backs away—then disappears from her life until the last few pages of the book.

If Duane had mastered the "old, terrible, ... killing instinct" (236) within him, as he "had won a hard-earned victory over longing and passion" (235), he would have survived his "mission impossible" without a scratch. Everything, for once, no matter how difficult, works smoothly. None of his (and

MacNelly's) best laid schemes go awry. He inveigles himself into the Cheseldine gang and wins over its leader by his "monumental nerve" (265), recognizing him when Cheseldine poses as someone else. Befriending another member, he gains a lot of useful information for laying his trap.

It is only the two lieutenants, Poggin and Knell, who can be troublesome. Because of their slick gunmanship—Poggin is reputed to be a greater gunman than even he—Duane wants "to stand over them, to make them see him with their last fading sight" (256). It is conquering this bent to outdo these two rivals personally that presents the difficulty. He has to discipline himself and not forget that he is here to help his fellow Rangers break up the entire gang. His motives can no longer be lone-wolfish.

How Duane succeeds is graphically detailed by Grey in the last quarter of the book. Events center on an attempted major bank robbery by top gang members. Duane has already alerted the Rangers to be there in hiding. He, himself, has separately arrested Cheseldine (a neat bit of policing), escorted him by train to the bank town, and delivered him to MacNelly. Meanwhile, the robbers are riding into town.

All that remains to be done is capturing the men in their criminal act. MacNelly, much pleased, excuses Duane from any further assistance and reminds him he has Jennie to live for. But Duane cannot be so dismissed. Poggin has never left his mind, and he must face him, man to man: "He had no thought of freeing the community of a dangerous outlaw.... He wanted to kill Poggin.... [H]e shuddered under the driving, ruthless inhuman blood lust of the gunman.... He stood stripped bare, his soul naked—the soul of Cain" (304–5). Duane refuses to hide at the bank door, like the other Rangers. Poggin outdraws him. Both go down in a hail of gunfire.

In the tremendous shoot-out, only one of the gang escapes. The Rangers suffer three dead, but Duane is not among them. He recovers, now carrying nine bullets in his body. Jennie, happy, plans for their future married life, away from this gory world of the past. But he cannot help feeling that haunted faces with upward staring eyes will be with him always, though she "need never know" (313).

5
The Light of Western Stars: Living Western Style

> Coyotes stealing away into the brush; buzzards flapping over the carcass of a cow that had been mired in a wash; queer little lizards running swiftly across the road; cattle grazing in the hollows; adobe huts of Mexican herders; wild, shaggy horses, with heads high, watching from the gray ridges—all these things Madeline looked at, indifferently at first, because indifference had become habitual with her, and then with an interest that flourished.... And she divined ... that henceforth there was to be something new in her life, ... something good for her soul in the homely, the commonplace, the natural, and the wild [47].

Madeline Hammond, age twenty-four and a brilliant New York debutante, has just come West to visit her brother, a local cowboy. She has had an outdoor "society" life of tennis, golf, and yachting, but it seems she has never really noticed the great out-of-doors, her only recollections of the "blue-arched vault of starry sky" (3) being from the stage scenery of an opera. She is now "tired" (Zane Grey repeats the word six times) of fashion, polished men, people generally; of showy homes, noise, all ostentation; of even herself (4). What she needs is to be alone, to gaze over a lonely land, to look up at real stars, and to discover her real self.

She arrives at El Cajon in southern New Mexico—when a revolution is going on just across the border in Mexico. No year is stated; however, it must be 1910 or 1911 because Francisco Madero is engaged in ousting dictator Porfirio Diaz (and Madero in turn will soon be ousted by Victoriano Huerta). These events are peripheral to Grey's plot and were still headline news when *The Light of Western Stars* was published in 1914 (it had already been serialized in *Munsey's Magazine* in 1913, the year when Huerta seized power).

Bill Stillwell, who calls himself the last of the old cattlemen, says that Madeline has come at a most interesting time—the cowboys are packing their guns again, just as in the olden days, because of the trouble south of the border. There have been guerrilla groups wandering up—raiding cattle and holding up trains—to get supplies for their revolutionary activities. It's the Wild West once more.

Such is Madeline's first impression upon her arrival one late evening. She is met at the railway station by a drunken cowboy who has just made a bet that he will marry the first girl to step off the train. The cowboy, Gene Stewart, even drags a padre along to perform the ceremony (in Spanish). Then, he is aghast to learn that the girl, nicknamed "Majesty," is the sister of his friend—Stewart, in fact, had admiringly named his prize horse after her.

Meanwhile, a shot is fired outside—someone actually murdered by a Don Carlos vaquero (Don Carlos is a Mexican rebel smuggling arms and ammunition across the border). To think that Madeline "Majesty" Hammond, so far, had never experienced excitement, trouble, or unpleasantness in her life! She is taken to safe quarters for the night, to stay with Florence Kingsley, her brother's fiancée. On the way she sees the light of Western stars for the first time—"she fancie[s] it w[ill] always haunt her" (14). Welcome to cowboy country!

Rancher Stillwell advises her to take things as they come, and not mind them overly much. Stewart, he points out, apart from his drunkenness, is really the pick of his cowboys, chivalrous, and picturesque too, the last of the hard-riding kind. It is to Stillwell's ranch, fifty miles away, that she and Florence ride out the next day—her brother is foreman there. She is determined "to learn a little about this incomprehensible West" (34).

The first activity she sees is a roundup, the driving together of cattle for branding and cutting of calves. It is a time of whirling lassos, seared hides, and bawling critters. Madeline feels sick, stifled by the odors, and choked by all the rising dust; yet she persists in staying and admires the hard-working cowboys: "they went about this stern toil as if it were a game to be played in good humor" (67).

Stillwell explains the cowboy life: "long hours on hossback, poor grub, sleepin' on the ground, lonesome watches, dust an' sun an' wind an' thirst, day in an' day out." They age quickly; beneath their courteous manner there is a hardness caused by their everyday hardships. The rancher sums up their character as "stone an' fire an' silence an' cactus an' force" and yet with a vein of "pure gold" (68–69). They will stand up for the right or for a friend in trouble even at the cost of their own lives. We see such action later when Monty Price challenges the loud-mouthed, swaggering, crooked sheriff and his deputy to draw when they try to arrest Stewart on a phony charge. All three men die in the shoot-out.

Florence adds, elsewhere, that cowmen are "great big simple boys" when it comes to amusement. They play just as they work, giving "their whole souls to it" (182). This trait is best revealed in the book when they play what they call "gol-lof." The juvenility of their antics in showing off before some city women guests at the ranch is almost embarrassing to read about but humorous too, particularly when one says of the others: "All you can do is waggle with a club an' fozzle the ball." "Cow-headed gents," indeed! (184).

One of the guests observes that, yes, they are like children or simply "natural men" or even "nature's noblemen" (248)—a fitting concept, she feels (as does Grey). Madeline concurs after she shows one of them how to use a patented breadmixer. He lords it over his fellow cowboys about his new expertise, and they all line up to learn about it. She holds clinics on the machine for a week, knowing that they need to be humored along.

The cowboys have their own sense of humor too, ably displayed in the tall story. Monty Price again, before he is killed, tells a real dandy to his fellow cowmen and Madeline and her guests around an evening campfire. He is meticulous about having appropriate circumstances to begin it and asks Madeline beforehand to start him off. He wants to appear reticent about telling it. In fact, he protests that "it's too harrowin' fer tenderhearted gurls to listen to" (254). Of course, they want to hear it all the more—this most terrible time he ever had. And so he gives in, then changes his position so that the firelight shines more directly on his face.

Meanwhile, he tells them he will have a hard time deciding exactly which incident was the most terrible. Finally, he gives them a choice of two tales, knowing full well which one they will choose. "All right," he says, but adds that that one is really the hardest for him to tell, "rak[ing] over tender affections long slumberin' in [his] breast" (254–55).

So the tale begins, with his shooting three cowpunchers with his back turned—he doesn't want his identity revealed—and the saloonkeeper there has to go to a sawmill in order to get enough sawdust to cover what is left of them. Then hearing that a gang of cutthroats has holed up in a cabin with a girl as captive, he and a few others go immediately to the rescue. The battle lasts all night; and before it grows light, he slips into the cabin and begins shooting, and dodging bullets. "When mornin' come..., [the gang] was all piled up on the floor, all shot to pieces" (256).

Thus he finds the girl—"Purty! Say, she was boo-tiful." They fall in love and ride off together, but another gang comes along. Monty now admits that he is "some scairt" ("fust time in my life") when the two of them are chased into a herd of stampeding buffalo, but he, holding the girl, jumps "like a shooting star" from buffalo to buffalo right to the edge of the herd—and freedom. But the girl then ups and marries another "feller," and poor Monty is "rankled" in his breast. "Gurls is strange," he moralizes dryly (256–57).

Of course, Grey, via Monty, spins out the tale for a full four pages, increasing the hilarity with every added word. The audience roars, some women laugh till they cry, and Madeline is beside herself with laughter. And we see the versatility of Grey as a writer, this anecdote well worth excerpting for inclusion in an anthology of humorous tall tales.

Now for the plot of the novel. It is this: Madeline (as her brother already has done) needs to shed her aristocratic mindset, adopt plain Western ways and feel at home with them; Gene Stewart has to end his bouts of drinking, find something to live for, and develop his broad capabilities. The two processes are intertwined.

Madeline begins to change when she realizes she has missed something in life, something besides the "pleasure, culture, travel, society, wealth, position, fame" that is already hers (73). She has not really been fully engaged in life, at work in it, and finding happiness from that work. A sentence from prairie writer Willa Cather speaks to Madeline's situation: "I tell you, people are happiest where they've ... struggled along and been real folks and not tourists" (135–36).

So far, Madeline has been a tourist. But when Stewart goes off to fight for the rebels under Madero in the Mexican civil war, he gives his horse, Majesty, to her; and in riding it across the desert wastes, she finds herself alive, what with the "wind in her face, the whip of [the] horse's mane, the buoyant, level spring of a running gait." She is ablaze with nerves and muscles tingling (80–81). Her hat and her hair combs fly away — her hair streams in the wind: all symbolic of her new freedom to find herself and an object for her life.

She is awed by the great distances of the visible landscape, its almost terrifying sublimity, and a thought comes to her. She will start ranching herself, on a large scale, with modern methods. She asks Stillwell for advice, what he would do with unlimited funds. He mentions piping in water, building dams, planting trees, buying the best stock, fencing grazing land, hiring every good cowboy in the country. Ranchers thereabouts, including himself and even Don Carlos, would willingly sell out at the right price.

Her mind is made up. She buys fifty thousand acres of rangeland, with Stillwell as superintendent of it, and begins work for the sheer joy of it, making improvements and developing some ideas of her own, such as bettering the living conditions of Mexicans working her large holding. After half a year, things are progressing well.

Meanwhile, Stewart has won a name for himself, El Capitan, in fighting for the Mexican rebels. But he begins his return as hero by getting drunk and causing a ruckus in every town he comes to. We find him in Chiricahua, Arizona, recuperating from his latest binge before likely being locked up. It seems as if he is trying to get himself shot. Actually, he is in love with Madeline and sees the situation as hopeless. What he needs is to be rescued, by Madeline, from his self-abasement, for Stillwell maintains that he would make a good ranch foreman. Now, these are modern times on an up-to-date ranch, and the new means of locomotion for going long distances is a big white touring car that can exceed speeds of an express train, a mile a minute. It has an enormous engine, and although the make is not mentioned, one has the impression the vehicle is comparable to a Stutz Bearcat. The cowboys think it a species of demon, and the chauffeur, wearing helmet and goggles, a demon driver. It is in this vehicle that Madeline makes her hair-raising ride to Arizona. Her entreaty to Stewart is a few simple words: "I have come to help you, to show my faith in you" (114).

Stewart recovers, becomes foreman, and when not otherwise busy stands in the distance watching Madeline and watching out for her. His is a Lew Wetzel figure guarding Betty Zane. A talk with the padre from El Cajon, ministering to the Mexican workers on the ranch, has given him a fresh sense of responsibility. We will find out why later in the story.

The new foreman does his job well, discovering that Don Carlos's vaqueros are stealing Madeline's cattle—Don Carlos is still living on his old ranch although it has become part of the huge Hammond spread. Madeline's advice to Stewart is to avoid violence, except in self-defense, while taking care that no harm comes to her and her cowboys. This may be difficult. Don Carlos is now working for the Huerta rebels, thus fighting against revolutionaries that Stewart had supported, while trying at the same time to abduct Madeline and have her be "his" woman. One such attempt is thwarted by "intrepid" (146) Florence when she—exchanging horses, hat, and jacket with Madeline—leads the would-be captors astray.

Madeline, however, is later seized by an independent band of destitute guerrillas. Stewart arranges for her ransom, and they ride home together on Majesty. The night wind's loosening her tumbling hair says again that she is free. And the sky is "a dark, velvety blue blazing with white stars" (163). The light of the western stars, we note, is more than the book's title. It has become a motif for Grey, a recurring natural feature that he uses to comment on the heroine's developing adjustment to living western style.

It is after this incident that Madeline's guests arrive from New York (brought the last several dozen miles by the demon car and driver). Grey has Madeline reflect on these women—"longing to break down the bars of their cage but ha[ving] not the spirit" to do so (179). However, they will have some adventures, besides the fast car ride. There are still bandits in the area, and Stewart believes it best that they seek refuge in the mountains—"among the crags and clouds," according to Madeline (208).

Here we get a sense of her love of nature, typical of all Grey's central characters. She likes to be out in the open "in the teeth of the wind and rain and storm." She is humble and reverent while glorying in the "stupendous strife of sound, the wonderful driving lances of white fire" (228–29). When the storm clears, she elects to sleep under the stars. They comfort her.

And Stewart stands motionless on a nearby rim (Wetzel again), "a dark, powerful figure" (237). Earlier, Madeline had not wanted him to fight the bandits because, as she told him, he might get hurt—her first admission of caring. Now she sees him as compelling and vital, a "promise of things to be" (251). Later, however, she sees him alone with another woman, an innocent encounter, but she believes the worst and will not listen to his explanation.

Their "quarrel" remains unresolved because they must immediately flee from Don Carlos. He and his men have tracked them up the mountains. Part of the escape involves hauling some of the women (by lasso) up a ledge, where they can secretly hide. They do get back safely to the ranch eventually.

Stewart can act only like all Western men of "simple, lonely, elemental lives" (157) when he is shunned. He must leave, crossing the border to rejoin Madero's forces, but will not go until he knows for sure where he stands with Madeline. The meeting is one of emotions "unbridled" (323); Grey's overwriting, however, tends to make it too melodramatic. Stewart will not be denied in knowing the "why" of her behavior; she in her "egoistic belief in her fairness" (325) remains imperiously mute, or so it seems to him. The passionate misunderstanding ends with his curt, three-word farewell, with an emphasis on the double meaning of the first word: "*Majesty Hammond, adios!*" (327). That evening the train of stars mock Madeline with "their unattainable painless serenity" (328).

Madeline feels she should leave too, for the East. But she has two visitors. The first is a prospector friend of Stewart who explains away the woman Stewart had met—she is the prospector's wife. The other visitor is the padre that she first met on her arrival in the West. He tells her that she and Stewart, unknowingly, were actually married that night. It was Stewart's learning of this when he became foreman of her ranch that cured him of his alcoholism— he had something to live for, was responsible for her. And now he has gone to get himself shot and so leave her free. In the padre's words "that is beautiful, it is sublime, it is terrible" (339). She realizes she must now be responsible for *him*. She is his wife. She has been blind to his nobility that her initial faith had created.

Then comes the fateful message: he has been captured by Huerta's men and will be executed the next day at sunset. She has time that day to use her "wealth, position, fame" to wire messages herself, to Washington, that will arrange for an exchange of prisoners. Though she has official telegrams back the next morning, can she be sure that the government messages will also reach rebel quarters unimpeded?

There is only one thing to do: get into that demon car with its demon driver—a cowboy along for extra help—and head out to those rebel quarters. A half hour is required to get things ready. Taken also are two heavy planks, for gullies or patches of heavy sand; extra ropes, for pulling or even lifting or lowering the car; several spare tires, for the many inevitable cactus and sharp-stone punctures; and dynamite, for rock-blocked shortcuts.

Grey uses some thirty pages to describe the trip, and a remarkable trip it is, to Agua Prieta across the Mexican border and on to Mezquital, over old wagon trails, across desert wastes with no roads at all, and through almost impassable deep washes. In one instance a lengthy wash seems a total barrier, and the "racers" skirt along it for miles until they find a place where the farther rim is sufficiently lower to jump the car across. The day wears on. Always they are "rushing, rushing, rushing under the wrathful red eye of a setting sun" (372). And they arrive in time, needfully—the messages had not come through.

6
The Rainbow Trail:
Love Story

The Rainbow Trail, 1915 (serialized in *Argosy* the same year), is a sequel to *Riders of the Purple Sage*, published three years earlier. Zane Grey has to give some details of the first novel to lead into the present one, and does so skillfully, a bit at a time, without interrupting the narrative flow. Thus the hero, John Shefford, age twenty-four, journeys from Illinois, where he had been nominally a minister for two years, but really an ungrounded seeker, then dismissed by his narrow-minded congregation. With the wound to his soul not healing and hoping to forget the incident, he is led West by a friend's "strange story" (2).

At Flagstaff, Arizona, he pursues a northeasterly course by horseback toward the Utah border. En route he strikes a man who is threatening a Native girl. The man turns out to be a missionary to the Navajo, and so we have two ministers at odds about the treatment of Native Americans. Halfway through the book Grey provides his view on what should be their proper treatment, by means of a dialogue between Shefford and a Morman rancher. The letter argues: "a good man, strong with his body, and learned in ways with his hands, with some knowledge of medicine, can better the condition of these Natives. But just as soon as he begins to preach his religion, then his influence wanes. That's natural. These heathens have their [own] ideals, their gods" (144). And Shefford immediately exclaims, feelingly, "Which the white man should leave them!" (144). Up to this midpoint, incidentally, Shefford's one blow has been the only violence in the story—something unique in Grey's writing.

It is only at the very end of the first chapter that we learn a little more of the hero's quest. His friend's account told of a girl taken to some hidden canyon called "Surprise Valley," twelve years earlier. Her fate "haunted" him (17). Perhaps, he thinks, the rescue of this imprisoned person, now a young woman, will be his salvation. He, in fact, has unconsciously created a romance between himself and what he considers this "wild ... and lonely girl" (60). A dreamer, he is ever faring forth for some treasure at the end of a rainbow. He is reluctant to face perils head-on.

At the Kayenta trading post he gets a job delivering supplies by burro-train every few weeks to a village of about fifty Mormon women. The early practice of polygamy is being outlawed by the government, and to counteract the new law, the Mormons have established communities of what are called "sealed" wives in hidden locations. Before he heads out, Shefford reveals to trader John Withers further details prompting his search, also pertaining to the Mormons, and described originally in *Riders*.

Jane Withersteen, a Mormon, had adopted the girl he is seeking. Her name is Fay Larkin. Jane's doing so had angered her fellow churchmen because Fay was a Gentile. A gunman, Lassiter, and Venters, a rider for Jane (and Shefford's friend from whom he learned the story) took her side. Venters eventually left the area, after ranching in the hidden valley, and Jane, Lassiter, and Fay sought refuge there, in safety, after rolling a huge rock across the one entrance to block pursuit. The Mormons could not enter, but then neither could the three ever leave.

Shefford's new work will allow him to familiarize himself with the Mormons and maybe gain some knowledge of what happened to Fay. Besides giving him this opportunity, Withers also has some good advice for his employee regarding the young man's doubts about religion and God: "go to the Navajo for a faith" (55). It so happens that Shefford has gained the friendship of Nas Ta Bega, "a noble red man, if there ever was one" (57), who had been stolen and educated in California but now has reverted to his old Indian ways (he is a precursor of Grey's title hero in *The Vanishing American*, 1925, for he believes the Native race is "dying" [65]). He calls Shefford "brother" (62) and will be a big help to him as the novel progresses.

As for this Navajo's faith, it is that the desert is his mother—he is attuned to nature, akin to it. He will travel with Shefford, and the young man can learn from him. Shefford has already learned that the "illimitable expanse of blue sky" and the "dreaming silence ... over the land" are a calming influence (58) (as nature is to Wordsworth, ever an influence on Grey's writing). Divining that his help comes from the desert too, he is ready to embrace "all that wild and speaking nature" about him and surrender himself to it. Even coming to this resolution makes him "wonderfully alive" to the surrounding world (59). He learns about the Rainbow Bridge (Nonnezoshe), which Navajos "worship." It is in accord with his own revered "rainbow."

Going along on Shefford's first trip with the pack-train, besides Nas ta Bega, is Joe Lake, a young Mormon and giant of a man, who, it turns out, is a rival for Fay's hand, but who, later on, will also help Shefford attain his goal. Soon after the men reach the sealed-wife village, a two-day trip, Lake departs for Stonebridge, a regular Mormon village across the border in Utah. With Nas Ta Bega visiting some Navajos nearby, Shefford is left alone to become acquainted with some of the Mormon women. One, called "Mary," age eighteen, draws his particular attention.

The seven pages of conversation between them (101–8) demonstrate Grey's great skill in writing dialogue. Shefford wants to tell her gently why he has come West, to tell her about Fay (and so possibly gain some information). But not knowing "Mary's" background, her understanding of things, her depth of soul, he proceeds slowly, hesitatingly, with pauses so that she can adjust to the drift of his words, so that she will not be unduly amazed by his revelation. We see that his experience as a former minister will help him to select words of kind, impartial tone and win her confidence, at first to listen, then to respond. We see Grey's psychological subtlety here.

He starts by saying that everyone in the village has been good to him, implying that she should be too. Then he says that there is one thing he has not spoken of to the other women that he will to her, thus singling out her receptive nature and making her feel at ease. He says he needs to tell someone who can keep a secret, his way of gaining her confidence (meant in a kindly but not ingratiating fashion). Next he says that the goodness of Mormon women makes liberty of speech difficult for him. So he proceeds by telling some of his own troubles as a former minister and gains her sympathy—she says, "I'm sorry"—and he thanks her for that, and adds, "Perhaps you'll be my friend."

She is certainly willing to try. Then he asks if she can help *him*, for she's "a girl—almost a woman." He hesitates once more, saying that perhaps what he wants to say should be left unsaid. She now is ready to reply, "Tell me what you want." But he waits, and hopes not to wrong her, then says he'll be "perfectly frank." He is now talking as though she is fully adult, a *mature* woman.

He continues by noting that she does not mingle with the other women, that she must be lonely. Then again hesitation—"now I'd like to—to—what shall I say?" He finally suggests that they might help each other, only to ask: "Have I made a mistake?" "No," she replies ("almost wildly," says Grey). Before she can retreat into her shell, he trusts her with his secret, his wish to save Fay Larkin, that doing so would save him, that he would love Fay, his "dream girl," that a curve of a rainbow would lead him down into Surprise Valley. Then he asks her directly, "Mary, do you think *this* dream will come true?"

She is silent a long time before responding—"I think it noble." She admits she has heard of Fay, but about her whereabouts remarks, "She is—dead."

The conversation ends with Shefford striding away in bitter pain. There is one little giveaway phrase for the reader, however, and Shefford himself will pause over it in recollection later. It is "Mary's" exclamation, "Thank God I've met a man like you!" (If she were a Mormon, as he believes, why should she so exclaim?)

Later, "Mary" offers to show him sago-lilies growing wild. This entails much mountain clambering, at which she is an expert. Shefford can ask only how she ever learned to run over rocks so easily. She replies that she has climbed all her life—another hint about her childhood, but he does not realize that it could have been in Surprise Valley, that she in fact *is* Fay Larkin.

He is too caught up in his mountain experience, standing speechless on a promontory with peace pervading his soul (like Wordsworth in the sonnet "Composed upon Westminster Bridge" [170]). He has fallen in love with *this* girl, whatever her real name, and tells her, "This has been the happiest, the best, the most revealing day of my life" (131). The relationship goes no further, for that evening, back at the village, the Mormon night riders arrive to visit their sealed wives, and Shefford leaves, bewildered.

He goes to the Navajos' camp to bring back these herders' wool and goatskins. It is now that Grey gives us a sympathetic four-page description of the Navajo life. Nas Ta Bega's people are "still free, still wild, still untainted" (141). They see with the eyes of their forebears, whose voices they hear in the wind. But Shefford's stay is short; he is kidnapped the next day at dawn by a gang of outlaws, likely led by Shadd, an educated Native (and evil counterpart to the book's "noble red man"). The prisoner is taken into strange territory, robbed, stripped, and, tied up, tossed onto an anthill. With the morning warmth, the activated ants start biting—"a time that was hell—worse than fire" (154): the first extended violence in the story. He is rescued by the exemplary Nas Ta Bega.

Later, in transporting the wool and goatskins by pack-train, the men are attacked by the outlaws and lose the entire train. Shefford ends up in Kayenta, and his work takes him to other posts through summer and fall. Enduring a sandstorm in the desert and standing off a band of desperadoes give him a mental toughness. And half a year passes before he again sees "Mary."

In the meantime the federal authorities have proceeded to prosecute the Mormon polygamists. Government men have discovered the hidden village and arrested the women. Shefford returns just in time to attend the trial in Stonebridge. There, "Mary" testifies under oath that she is not a Mormon, not a sealed wife, and, in fact, not married at all. Nas Ta Bega, who has been doing some investigation of his own, finds out definitely that she *is* Fay Larkin. As it turns out, the court can make no convictions, and Shefford, with Joe Lake, escorts the women back to the village, where he is offered a job as their teacher. He now has ample time to tell "Mary" that he knows who she is and achieve some resolution to his lifetime search for his "dream-girl."

But how to tell her? Again, as in his previous conversation with her, he wants to proceed slowly, gently. He now knows she has been insulated, living in Surprise Valley—hence, her wan, shy, inhibited character. Days and weeks slip by before he dares broach the subject (220–24). He begins by referring to something they discussed six months earlier: their "friendship." She admits he is her "only friend." Because of her trust, he points out that their friendship is "strange"—he being a young man, she a promised "wife." He realizes that she is unknowing of ordinary society's decorum in these matters. She has only "vague perceptions of love and passion"; she does not understand the potential of her relationship to Shefford.

He senses also her feeling of obligation to her Mormon "captors," her sacrificing herself to them, but when he talks of this, her comment is "I must not tell." There is a kind of Henry Jamesian progression here, as in *The Wings of the Dove*, 1902, of truth gradually revealed. "Wait—a—little," Shefford says, "unsteadily," while he tries a new tack, the question of freedom. Hers is an "imprisonment" in a sealed-wife village; she is used to being a "prisoner" and afraid of being free, free from "the living death she believed she lived."

Shefford's careful reticence in speaking of her identity leads to this question that he knows she will answer: "What did I come to this country for?" Of course, it is to find a girl, as she whispers. He can now say that he has found her, she herself, *Fay Larkin*. She falls to her knees in a swoon. So ends the chapter.

With the truth out at last, she tells her own story—how she got into Surprise Valley and how she got out. Grey has ingeniously hit upon the one way possible for her to have left, and readers can find out the details from the book.

But the story cannot end here. Despite the fact that now a "witching, radiant beauty" lurks in Fay's smile, there is something "strange" in it too (236). There is something ethereal about her. Shefford cannot declare his romantic feelings about her because, it seems, she needs time to become accustomed to a world not Mormon. Her awakening to Shefford's world is gradual. And physical complications arise. They have to get away from the middle-aged man, Waggoner, she has been promised to.

A kind of "Wild Justice" ensues in the lawless West—it is the title of chapter 15. Waggoner is found killed outside Fay's cabin, and suspicions fall on the young woman, who is held under guard in the schoolhouse. Joe Lake thinks the Mormon elders will hang her, but Nas Ta Bega has a plan of escape. It involves the complicity of one of the Mormon women and Joe's heroic venture of ferrying a boat down a section of the treacherous Colorado River through the Grand Canyon (he has already conceded Fay to his rival). The Navajo, Shefford, and Fay, when she is freed, first get Lassiter and Jane out of Surprise Valley, then meet Joe, appropriately, at Nonnezoshe, the Rainbow Bridge.

There are adventures along the way—riding mustangs through a maze of perilous cliffs and canyons while escaping from Shadd and company, who are tracking them, all described in vivid detail. Arrival at "the foot of the rainbow" deserves special mention, for the rainbow symbolizes Shefford's dream that for him has now come true. This "rainbow," the bridge, is not transient as one in the sky but "solidified, a thing of ages, sweeping up majestically ... *against* the blue sky" (335; added emphasis). And it is here that he and Fay learn that neither of them killed Waggoner—they too had had their suspicions. Now there is no shadow between them: they are free, young, and in love.

The most dangerous episode of the flight is the boat trip for all of them through the Grand Canyon rapids. Grey devotes seven pages to the actual ride, and just a few lines of it will give you an idea of the hazard:

> Swiftly it came into sight—... a swelling mound, a huge back-curling wave, another and another, a sea of frothy, uplifting crests, leaping and tumbling.... Then as the rumble became a strange, deep reverberating roll, as if the monstrous river were rolling huge stones down a subterranean cañon, Shefford saw with dilating eyes that the Mormon's hair was rising stiff upon his head.
> "Hear that!" said Joe, turning an ashen face to Shefford. "We'll drop off the earth now. Hang on to the girl, so if you go you can go together.... And, pard, if you've a God—*pray!*" [356–57, 360].

The escape down the Colorado is successful. They camp peacefully that night. Next morning Nas Ta Bega and Joe Lake are gone, one to his "vanishing" race of Navajo, the other to his "assimilating" Mormon people. Joe had had a last word with Shefford about any remaining religious doubts: "*Some one* besides an Indian and a Mormon guided you out!" (368). An Epilogue shows Shefford and Fay (and Lassiter and Jane) living happily in Illinois.

Shefford has come to know that "Life [is] eternal.... Love of a woman [is] hope—happiness. Brotherhood—that mystic and grand 'Bi Nai!' of a Navajo—that [is] religion" (344).

7

The Border Legion: Titanic Evil Forces

There are women who fall in love with their teacher, minister, doctor, lawyer, someone of "superior" standing in the community. They may be following nature's way of securing high quality children, a kind of survival of the fittest. A related situation, more primitive, is that of a woman falling in love with her captor. Joan Randle, age twenty, is somewhat that woman in *The Border Legion*, 1916 (serialized in *All-Story Weekly* the same year). The novel is a complex one, however, of primal competing forces, a tide of events carrying a raft of characters along to some expected or unexpected end, preordained by author Zane Grey.

The story is based on the actual life of one Henry Plummer, whom Charles Pfeiffer calls "the West's most infamous sheriff-outlaw" (*So You Want...*, 7). An educated drifter, he tried to make his fortune in the California gold rush of 1849, but was a failure where less capable men were lucky. Falling in with the lawless element there, he became leader of a band of road agents numbering more than a hundred. His outfit later drifted into Oregon, where it established a camp, then headed into Montana with the gold strike at Alder Creek of 1863. Sociable and a man of affairs, he was elected sheriff, a good cover for his life of crime. But he was found out and hanged, with thirty-four of his gang, one of whom seemed more beast than human.

In Grey, "Plummer" becomes Jack Kells (but not a sheriff), while the "beast" is Sam Gulden, memorable villains of different stripe, really forces of evil with which Joan must contend. She, the only woman of consequence in the story, is the author's own creation. Grey draws a "love" triangle of sorts, though the winner proves to be an earlier rejected, easy-going suitor, Jim Cleve. These four make up the story.

It starts with Joan taunting Jim about his never amounting to much, not having even the gumption to be bad. He vows to show her—by joining ruffians Kells and Gulden and their gang on the southern Idaho border. Her retort, "You haven't the nerve!" (6), is silly, adolescent stuff, a turn-off for a serious reader, but if we read further, we see this is but contrasting prelude to the primordial man-woman conflict between Joan and Kells at the end of chapter 3.

The next day Joan finds that Jim has indeed ridden off through the mountains for the outlaw camp, and, remorseful, rides after him. Fortuitously, she comes across a neighbor, and they proceed together, only to be met by Kells himself and two gang members. We have this paragraph then, for Grey still wishes to present the accompanying natural scene of the action, a simple description, with every word just right: "Night settled down black.... The wind moaned in the cedars and roared in the replenished camp-fire. Sparks flew away into the shadows.... Coyotes barked off under the brush, and from away on the ridge drifted the dismal defiance of a wolf" (16).

Joan, someone who as a girl had always looked for something to happen, now gets it in spades. Kells, soft-spoken, amiable, a smile on his intelligent face, bit by bit reveals his true character. Grey is skillful in slowly showing the depths of Kells's evil, letting it seep into Joan (and the reader). We get only hints of his deadly behavior after the fact—shooting the neighbor, then his two companions, after she has gone ahead. "We parted company" (33) is his explanation to her of cold-blooded murder, hiding the truth behind his gentlemanly conduct. Appearance and reality are so much at odds that the evil appears all the more hideous.

Kells is a hypocrite, his education making it easy for him to appear kind, thoughtful, and well-mannered. But we know, as La Rochefoucauld has said in his *Maxims*, 1665, that "hypocrisy is the compliment that vice pays to virtue" (86). That is, there is still a recognition of worthy, higher values that Joan can appeal to (something lacking in Gulden, whom she will meet later, someone possibly worse than a hypocrite, having no values at all). Yet she notes that Kells's eyes hardly seem like eyes, just "gray spaces, opaque openings" (30), "naked abyss[es]," "windows of a gray hell" (41).

She will have to meet him with all the strength at her command—to win him over (with her abundance of missionary zeal) or foil him (with never suspected feminine wiles) or kill him (with his own gun, which she almost does). No more a "thoughtless girl" (37), as she was in taunting Jim, she has to grow up quickly. A black night has indeed settled over her, and the "wolf" is no longer on a distant ridge but here, at hand, "watching stealthily" (38). It is not for a ransom that he is keeping her, as he had first declared.

Her first ruse is to claim she is much younger than she really is, and at another campfire—a good atmosphere for talking about one's better self, about longings, dreams, and hopes for the future—she deliberately emphasizes things of her present *girl*hood. She plays her part well, making herself more at ease than he in his periodic pacing behind her, even though for her it is a "horrible endless night," in which she "age[s] from girl to woman" (53).

What follows at dawn, unfortunately, is *terribly* melodramatic (badly so of the writing, distressingly so for the reader) as she sees him "unmasked[,] the ruthless power, the leaping devil, the ungovernable passion." "*You've* got to pay that ransom!" he cries; "Girl! ... I'm hungry—for you!" (55).

He half drags her to a deserted cabin, bends her backward, kissing her, and she lets herself go with no resistance, the better to seize his gun from its holster and shoot him in the side. The overwritten prose continues in sentences like these: "The black, turgid, convulsed face grew white and ghastly, with beads of clammy sweat and lines of torture. His strange eyes showed swiftly passing thought—wonder, fear, scorn—even admiration." She, in turn, wants to say she is sorry, but cannot: "her tongue cl[eaves] to the roof of her mouth and she seem[s] strangling" (57). In short, he collapses; she faints.

The upshot is that she can now escape but chooses not to. Her woman's choice is to nurse him back to health. He advises her to go because once he recovers he will be his old evil self. But in tending him, she is attracted to him and cannot desert him. A mark of her strength of will, and stubbornness, is that the more he insists, the firmer is her *no*. What happens, however, is not a growing love for Kells—she could never *marry* him—but, during his month-long convalescence, a remembering of her former suitor Jim Cleve, his becoming sweet to her in the solitudinous hours that pass, and she "dream[s] herself into love" (68) with *him*. Grey's depiction of her situation is astute.

It is at this time that some of Kells's men discover them. Gulden is there, utterly huge, and broad, resembling a gorilla, Joan thinks, a monster in whose presence she is absolutely in terror. Grey describes him as an "engine of destruction that needs no rest" (77), a "criminal for the sake of crime" (84). Compared to him the others seem but insignificantly evil. Kells introduces her as his wife—his way of protecting her from them—so she carries on the deception. Willy-nilly, she has become part of the gang, which she names the Border Legion. She is in a worse position than ever, and nature provides this comment: "the coyotes were out in force and from all around came their wild, sharp barks" (75).

The new men with Kells and Joan head out to the home camp, Cabin Gulch. Joan knows that Jim will be there, for the men had spoken of his riding in, completely reckless, a hard fighter quick with a gun, and a "great youngster goin' bad quick" (82). Joan can think only how silly and vain had been her coquetry with him. She loves him all the more and vows to stay with the Legion, even if she could escape the clutches of Kells, in order to save Jim. "Only the future, that contained Jim Cleve, mattered to her" (85). The other Legion members she more or less dismisses. They are hardly individualized, seeming but spokesmen for different aspects of evil. Only Bate Wood, a "hardened old ruffian" (91), and possibly Red Pearce show any real concern about her welfare, although at times all "remembered in her a mother or a sister" (181) (However depraved, they are still human.)

In camp Joan has a backroom all to herself off the main quarters, where she is a virtual prisoner but can spy on happenings. (As readers, we seem to be spying with her, and so Grey cleverly involves us in the story.) She finally spots Jim, no longer an overgrown boy (he has aged too), but a powerful and lithe, sad-faced man, actually handsome from the tragedy of having to live his new, desperate life. If Joan needs any reinforcement of her love, she has it now. For Kells has been continually dropping by to win her over, saying he will change his ways, marry her, and, together, they can live among decent people. Her answer is ever that she does not love him, but she believes also, "missionary" that she is, that her presence and his desire for her can uplift him.

In their one actual physical tussle here, when he tries to kiss her, she overpowers him (because he is still weak from having been shot). This is real enough, but their following drawn-out discussion is another bit of melodrama, particularly when he throws her his loaded gun and tells her to kill him, for he does not want to live if he cannot have her. "*My* life or *your* soul!" is his ultimatum (emphasis added) (126).

The conflict/argument takes on real-life tones as she is inspired by woman's "incalculable power to allure, to change, to hold" (127). She first tries to convince him that by giving in she would not be the woman he says he loves, but only a husk of her. He would embrace only what he himself had degraded. Then she draws closer with "the wondrous subtlety of a woman in a supreme moment" (127) and shows him the difference, slipping eagerly into his arms and warmly giving him that wanted kiss. Immediately, she falls away, astounded by her boldness, while he says, "My God!" (128) and leaves her.

Joan then throws herself on her bed, seeking "the relief of blinding tears" (128). She has bested Kells and is overcome by her victory. She need not fear him—ever. Should he threaten to abandon her to Gulden, since he himself cannot have her, to the giant's brutal caveman ways, she can counter that he would never do so, that he cannot be that kind of man anymore. She, we are told later, is "always mindful of her influence" (234). A reader cannot help thinking that Joan's action, too, is something of a last fling—the elemental attraction of captive for captor not to be experienced again.

News of a big gold strike east, across the border at Alder Creek, Montana, now energizes everyone. Kells has been waiting for it all along, and to reap maximum benefit from this bonanza, will reorganize his Border Legion, himself in absolute control. He knows that miners in a great strike "become like coyotes at a carcass" (231) (those coyotes again!)—each out for himself. Grey devotes a page-long paragraph to describing the gold-rush mentality, which he describes as a "régime of wildness":

> Men frenzied by the possession of gold or greed for it responded to the wildness.... The gold-lust created its own blood-lust.... With distrust came suspicion and with suspicion came fear, and with fear came hate—and these, in already distorted minds, inflamed a hell.... Men fought for no other reason than that the incentive was in the charged air.... [T]he worst of men's natures stalked forth, ... roaring for gold, spitting fire, and shedding blood.... [M]otives and ambitions and faiths and traits merged into one mad instinct for gain.... It was a time, for all it enriched the world with yellow treasure, when might was right, ... when death stalked rampant. The sun rose gold and it set red [241–42].

Kells is sure the Legion's operations will be lost in the deeds ordinarily committed. His plan, once at the site, is to have his gang spread out, make a pretence at digging, and mix with the real miners. All thefts will be done masked so that his men may "work" through the summer without anyone suspecting. Meanwhile, he will pose as a business magnate buying claims, establishing a reputation as an honest man of affairs—"we shall have them helpless" (164). He dreams of building an empire of crime.

There are two forces of evil in this budding empire that Grey wishes to posit here. One is a scheming, mind-dominated evil; the other, one of brutal physical ferocity. Kells and Gulden, the respective spokesman for each, appear at times not so much as men living out their individual lives but as representatives of forces of mythic proportion contending with each other. Such conflict plays out in Kells's demand that all present ritually sign their names in his book, pledging themselves to the Alder Creek undertaking. (We are mindful of Captain Ahab, in "The Quarter-Deck" chapter of Herman Melville's *Moby-Dick*, 1851, engaging his crew to pursue the white whale above all else, the mates eerily crossing their lances, the harpooners drinking a commendation from their harpoon-chalices, the others quaffing their grog in assent.)

With the Border Legion, there is now a huddle—a resolution between Kells and Gulden, Kells confirming his authority, Gulden the freedom to kill at any time. Kells, with "infinite depth and craftiness" and dismissing his "hate and loathing" of Gulden, allows the giant alone, after considerable harangue, this special privilege (165–68). Jim Cleve remains indifferent to joining, but in a misunderstanding about Joan's true relation to Kells, on seeing her with the gang, he also signs up. (The intense atmosphere surrounding the whole proceeding makes it comparable to that in Melville.)

Joan has a chance to see Jim alone, explain how she came to be with the outlaw gang, and professes her love for him. He realizes he has "run off like a coward" and "brought her to this calamity," and she, "white-hot with passionate purpose," a "missionary" again, convinces him that if he had nerve enough to be bad, he can find nerve enough to save her (189). He now matures quickly, as she had done earlier. "I begin over from this hour," he says (192). They talk of escaping but realize any such effort then would be fruitless and must wait till all of them reach the gold camp.

On the way Joan hears Legion men discussing among themselves whether they will abide by Kells's plan despite the signing. Already we are given a hint that the chief problem about their venture may be in themselves. At Alder Creek, a thousand men live along a two mile stretch of the gulch, easy prey for the outlaws, whose early ventures are hugely successful. And Kells creates "an impression of character and importance" (232)—by placing Joan in a situation where she will be insulted and he can appear her protecting hero. Grey adds little touches like this throughout the novel to show the complexity of Kells's character. Here Joan thinks Kells a villain, but another time his genuine protection makes her feel "grateful to him" (248).

Joan lives in quarters similar to her previous ones, again a virtual prisoner. But she does have a small window, through which she can have a nightly rendezvous with Jim, and where, because of his impatience, they are secretly married by the gold-camp's minister. Meanwhile, some of Kells's men have grown suspicious of Jim, who has worked hard at his mining activities. They think he is an honest person and not a bandit. So they give him a nefarious job to do alone in order to "clear" his name—that of killing Gulden, who with his backers has split from the Border Legion.

Before Jim can act, news comes that the Legion has been double-crossed by one of Kells's own men and that the miners have formed a vigilante group to oust them, everyone. Some are already caught and being hanged. The gang, including Gulden and his faction, are as one again. They plan to escape back to Cabin Gulch, but in leaving they meet the vigilantes and "instant pandemonium" (309) breaks out. The bandits are temporarily dispersed. Joan and Jim get free of the melee and make their own private escape, by stage. What they do not know is that the gang members get free too and organize one grand heist before leaving for good—of the same stage, which is carrying a huge shipment of gold. The couple has to pretend it is part of this plot, faithful to the now gleeful Legion, returning home.

At Cabin Gulch, the bandits are like "boys, half surly, half playful, at a game" (338). They have the gold to divide, and when some disagreement arises, Kells, confidently, says he will win the disputed amount back in cards. The men start gambling immediately, and drinking—both are their chief amusements at any time—and Joan in her back room fears a "dread climax" (343). The bandits are no different from the miners Kells had so easily exploited in *their* fateful desire for gold: "The evil, the terrible greed, the brutal lust, were in the hearts of the men. And hate, liberated, rampant, stalked out unconcealed, ready for blood" (344).

Finally, only Kells and Gulden are left to gamble, and they start a new game, a quick cutting of cards. Silence and suspense grip the audience, the giant showing no emotion, Kells a whirligig of hope and rage. And Kells is cleaned out. Gulden rises over his mound of gold and challenges the loser to one more bet, one cut of the cards, winner take all—for Joan! "No!" Kells cries out (348), and then he cannot resist—and loses. Joan will have to live her worst nightmare.

Kells and Jim hurry to the distraught girl. Kells now learns that Joan and Jim are married—Jim who had saved his life in a dispute at Alder Creek, Joan who had fanned the spark of goodness in him. He borrows Jim's gun so that he now has two, conceals a knife up his sleeve and re-enters the gambling den.

There he stabs Gulden in the neck, and blazes away at the others. Firing becomes general, mixed with yells and clouds of smoke. Gulden, not dead, remains "a terrible engine of destruction," firing at random. It seems that everyone is shooting at everyone else. All shots fired, the "groping giant" tears a leg off an upturned table as an instrument of attack. He approaches Kells, falls; and Kells, tottering, drops too—the last to succumb in one horrendous blood-bath (354–56). Joan and Jim alone are left, to pursue a normal life together.

Frank Gruber, the official biographer of Zane Grey, credits the author with depicting the "most vicious and savage fight ever portrayed by any writer," yet writing it in a way that is entirely plausible (124). Grey should also be given credit for trying to cast it as more than just a bloody gunfight but something of a titanic struggle, Western style, between two great forces of evil ever present in our world.

8
Wildfire: The West Ablaze

Readers of Zane Grey's most popular novel, *Riders of the Purple Sage*, 1912, will recall the author's superb portrayal of heroine Jane Withersteen's prize horses, Night and Black Star. They were modeled after two of Grey's own horses, and in his lifetime of exploring the West, he came to know many others. Having an author's necessary qualification of being someone "on whom nothing is lost" (Henry James, "The Art of Fiction," 390), he studied these animals in detail, then described them in his fiction, where they were significant to the action.

Only in one full-length novel, however, was a horse, as noted by Carlton Jackson, the "prime mover of the plot" (91). That book was *Wildfire*, 1917 (already serialized in *The Country Gentleman* the previous year), surely one of the most powerful of all Grey's writings. How Grey accomplished this feat is the subject under discussion. Wildfire, the horse, literally runs away with the story.

Wildfire is first mentioned in chapter 4, and is first seen in the following one. Grey uses the opening three chapters to lay the groundwork for his book and give the appropriate setting of people and places for his wild stallion, "red as fire," "gigantic," "every line of him ... instinct with wildness" (69).

From the start we learn of the heroine, Lucy Bostil, who has ridden off on a horse, forbidden her, to celebrate her eighteenth birthday, a time to become her own mistress. She loves horses, and "free, proud, untamed," imagines herself "like a wild horse" (2). She wants something to happen to her, something wonderful, even though it may be terrible too.

Riding up to a vantage point in the canyon and desert country that is her home, she is sensuously alert to all the world below her: the drear barren heights and the bright peaks caught in sunlight, the roaring of river and the silken swish of a swallow's flight over the water, the fragrance of pungent cedar and the perfume of mescal flowers, the mushrooming "cloud pageants" against the "deep velvet azure" of sky (3, 2).

This world is "hers always" (Grey repeats the phrase three times), a country of superlative grandeur—"leagues and leagues" of desert, canyons "great," cliffs "giant," monuments "noble," and horizons "endless" (3). And the dominant color is red: "the red, sullen, thundering river" and the "frowning mass of red rock, upreared, riven and cañoned" (2). What a setting for that giant of a horse, whose "red coat seemed to blaze" (98)—Wildfire!

The locale is along the south shore of the Colorado River in northern Arizona, the stupendous terrain of the Grand Canyon, with Monument Valley and the Painted Desert nearby. The plot centers on Bostil's Ford, a small trading community, named for Lucy's father. Bostil is described as half horse himself, a man owning many fine horses (including his prize, Sage King), coveting any other fine horse, and not above going to any lengths to get it. His main ambition is acquiring some great wild stallion.

In the meantime, his onetime friend, Creech, will not part with his roan racer, a rival to Sage King as the fastest horse in the area, and Bostil, in a petty act of spite, makes sure that Creech's horses are marooned across the flooding Colorado, to be starved and finally put down. (Grey skillfully uses the river's rising current, as a parallel natural force, to describe the hatred welling up in Bostil's soul, a hatred fierce enough to give impetus to such a heinous deed.) Joel Creech, the son, vows his own revenge—on Bostil and on Lucy, for she, after being insulted by him, carried off his clothes when he was swimming. He says he will tie her to a horse and drive her through Bostil's Ford, making a spectacle of her. But everybody knows he is not quite right in his mind—he has been kicked in the head by a mustang. Another threat to Lucy comes from Cordts, a horse thief, who vows to kidnap her as a means to obtain Sage King. It seems that one horse or another is involved somehow in the story's plot.

We are ready now to be introduced to the standout horse and title "character," Wildfire, and to the horse wrangler determined to catch him, Lin Slone. Grey likely had a reason for choosing this spelling for the man's name, rather than the more common "Sloan." The word "lone" is characteristic of this man (one could read the whole name as *Lin's lone*, that is, *Lin is lone*), for his parents were killed in a wagon-train massacre when he was ten. Now he has "no past to think about, and the future [holds] nothing except a horse" (54). His is a "lone camper's heart" (58), and he prefers to trail the horse by himself, being glad when his companion wranglers give up and leave.

The chase begins north of the Arizona border, in Utah, where Slone has already named the stallion for his appearance at a distance—like a "running streak of fire" (68) (twice the name will relate, dramatically, to the animal's involvement in a real fire). The wrangler's plan is to track the wild horse as a cougar would trail a deer.

The chase leads eventually into real "lion country" (56), the Grand Canyon. Grey well knew this area from his trip West with Charles Jesse "Buffalo" Jones in 1907, when he helped Jones capture cougars for zoos and later wrote about the experience in *Roping Lions in the Grand Canyon*, 1924. In *Wildfire*, the author shows the horse making his way *through* the canyon, seemingly trying to put this exhausting course between himself and his pursuer. The pursuit not only allows Grey to describe a familiar locale again but, more importantly, makes it possible to link its beauty, wildness, and splendor with the quarry.

Herman Melville, too, writing of the mighty whale, Moby Dick, catches something of its greatness when his narrator, Ishmael, depicts the ocean in which it lives as representative of all time and space: the other oceans are but its arms; its waves wash the recency of America and the antiquity of Asia. Similarly, Grey gives us Slone's reaction on first seeing the grand abyss, wondering whether he has come to the end of the world. He is "staggered" comprehending it, "intoxicated" by the varied mix of yellow slopes and smoky clefts, so that his eyes fill with tears, and he is "confounded" by its ultimate immensity (62). "This place fits you, Wildfire," he mutters in conclusion (63).

By describing Slone's tough going inside the canyon, Grey is really showing the mighty qualities of the horse that can traverse it—and the dogged perseverance of Slone in continuing to trail him. Thus, "it was hard, rough work, and risky because it could not be accomplished slowly" (66). Again, "the trail was like a twisted mile of thread," always "crags and towers and peaks and domes, and the lofty walls of that vast, broken chaos" (76, 75).

Then the chase leads us through the Painted Desert and into Monument Valley, where the experience takes on an epic quality. Slone begins to lose track of days, weeks, and even months, as the venture has no apparent end. In what Grey calls the "strange, solemn, lonely days and silent, lonely nights" (81), Slone becomes an unthinking being, reverting almost to the primitive, nearly starved in a quest that holds him in its spell.

His mind becomes clear when a hot, west wind sweeps through a large basin, a depression several miles across filled with dry, dead grass. Wildfire has made a mistake entering it, for there is no other outlet. Slone, determined and grim, vows to fire the grass and make the horse "run with [his] namesake" (83) in his attempt to escape back through the entrance, where the wrangler will be waiting.

What follows are several pages of superb description, building into a fury of excitement, as the conflagration sweeps through the valley at night. The effect seems to be planetary, even the moon and starlight paling as the wildfire races on. And somewhere within the melee of rolling smoke (and the great, silhouetted monuments "retreat[ing]" in it) is a "fleeting phantom" and the sound of hoofbeats growing louder, creating an altogether "unearthly spectacle" (88, 89).

Wildfire approaches Slone, but is driven back from the entrance, and, in trying to escape up a slope, is trapped, up to his flanks, in a sandy avalanche of his own making. The wild horse is captured, with Grey magnificently detailing the intense passion of the moment—in both exhausted man and beast. Slone gazes at the creature "in admiration and pity and exultation" (92).

Lucy, on one of her customary rides, discovers them, badly in need of care, and tends to Slone and Wildfire over many visits. And she and Slone fall in love. The ten or so pages of chapter 10 in which Grey delineates their growing affection is done through their conversations. The author here is not merely *telling* things but *showing* us the developing relationship dramatically, and that is good writing. What is not said (the half statements, for example, where Lucy holds back her feelings—indeed, she does not always understand them) is just as revealing as what is said. We see Slone's stolid simplicity and Lucy's joyous vitality, carrying the couple "irresistibly to [their] fate" (139).

A further outcome of their meeting is that Lucy decides she will ride Wildfire in the annual race sponsored by her father and so challenge Sage King's supremacy. We already know from earlier in the book that she can ride "like a burr sticking in the horse's mane" (9). For his part, Wildfire, "that wonderful flame of a horse!" (116), can run "like fire before the wind" (142). This last comparison hints back to the horse's capture but also prefigures yet another and even more sensational ride—in fact, a ride for life—that ends the book.

The various elements of plot are now coming together. Lucy wins the race, although not in a clear-cut victory because Wildfire bumps Sage King. Wildfire simply runs away from all his competition (like another big, red horse in real life—Secretariat winning the Belmont in 1973!). Then it is Creech and Joel, not the horse-thief Cordts, who kidnap Lucy and take her away amid canyon lands to hold for a ransom, which will be Bostil's racing horses. These will make up for Bostil's having, in effect, killed Creech's racers. Thus Creech obtains Sage King. But Cordts is on their trail, seeking his own horse-thieving ends. And Slone, on Wildfire, is not far behind, trying to rescue the woman he loves.

There are several hints along the way of a terrifying, fiery ending. As Lucy and the Creeches travel through pine forest, she smells the "dry" fragrance of the trees and cannot help but think of the possibility of fire, for the trunks, although standing far apart, hold up "intermingled" foliage (262). And deranged Joel, "crazy on fires" (201), is with her. A half-dozen pages later, Creech has to build a rock barrier around his campfire to prevent the flames from firing the grass, and in another half-dozen pages the dry wind increases to a blast. All this foreshadowing shows how carefully Grey works toward the climax.

Then events come tumbling in upon one another. Joel kills his father in an argument, ties Lucy to Sage King for a wild ride (fulfilling, in a way, his earlier threat), and sets the grass ablaze. Slone is close enough that Wildfire smells the smoke, and he rides in. "Joy, agony, terror in lightning-swift turns" (303) grip the wrangler, while his mount lunges out and runs Joel down (and kills him). The horse's whistle, his challenge to King, another stallion, sends that horse rearing in fright and leaping over the line of fire. Wildfire, too, leaps in pursuit, and the great race is on, a desperate rematch of their previous run.

Wildfire carries the heavier rider but gains on Sage King and Lucy. However, the race is not just between the two horses. The flames have run up the pine trees, and the wind creates a fiery gale roaring through the tops. Horses and riders will have, as well, a fierce race with fire.

Again, the effect seems planetary, for "the tumult was the roar of avalanches, of maelstroms, of rushing seas, of the wreck of uplands and the ruin of the earth" (306). The race continues for miles, graphically described, as the steeds sweep along "under a canopy of fire" (309), no longer as competing stallions but in sheer abject terror.

And then the horses burst free of the woods, to safety, Sage King stumbling to his knees in utter exhaustion, Wildfire collapsing nearby, run to his actual death in saving Slone and, indirectly, Lucy. Slone has no sooner rescued her in undoing her ropes, when a shot rings out from a nearby cliff. He crumples too, though merely wounded—by Cordts, in ambush with an accomplice. As the horse thief starts to scramble over, Lucy, protecting Slone, fires back, and hits him (it's shoot or be shot). Cordts catches at his partner, and both plunge downward, "vanishing in the depths" (312). Lucy and Slone return to Bostil's Ford on Sage King, to be greeted by Bostil, who is pleased that his horse has "won" this last race, glad to have his daughter again, and willing, at last, to give his blessing to her and Slone's marriage.

Peace has returned to the valley. Every morning, the sun rises to a clear sky, and every afternoon, clouds line the horizon, bringing needed rain: "the dim blackness of the storm-clouds [are] split to the blinding zigzag of lightning, and the thunder roll[s] and boom[s], like the Colorado in flood" (319–20). The forces of nature still are powerful, mighty in scope, dwarfing the activities of mere man below.

Yet these forces seem now to have a kinder aspect, too, and Grey uses them to comment on the gentler times ahead, just as fire and flood commented on, and were parallel to, the extreme violence before. The storm clouds yield rainbows "beautiful and ethereal" (319). And Lucy and Slone ride off—not into the sunset, for they have just begun their life together—but into "this rainbow day, with storms all around them, and blue sky above" (320).

As with naturalist-philosopher Henry David Thoreau, who said, "In Wildness is the preservation of the world" ("Walking," 202), so Lucy and Slone have had their lives enriched by knowing and experiencing Wildfire, the horse, and the wildness in nature he represented. Such wildness is at the heart of their own very being and gives them strength of character. They will never want to be far from it in the natural landscape at any time, however manifested. Wildness is a resource to be often recalled, re-sensed, relived.

9

The U. P. Trail:
Romance of a Railroad

In the front pages of *The U. P. Trail*, 1918 (serialized in *Blue Book*, 1917), Zane Grey refers to Robert Louis Stevenson's saying that the building of the first railway across the West would be fit subject for "an enduring literary work," what with border ruffians of all nationalities "gambling, drinking, quarreling, and murdering" during the construction. It would have "epical" significance. It was left to Grey to see the "romance" of the subject, as he says, the wonder and dignity, the heat and labor, the heroism and sacrifice.

The first chapter, one page in length, gives the setting, in 1865, from Nebraska's plains through Wyoming's Rocky Mountains and into the Wasatch Range of northern Utah; from buffalo grazing grounds through rocky gorges and snowy peaks to lush valleys and hazy uplands—all "solemn and silent under the endless sky" (1). Chapter 2, a half page longer, reveals a lone Sioux warrior in the Wyoming Hills looking down from "a wide and wonderful prospect" (2) on a small caravan moving east on the Laramie Trail, eventually to halt in a circle for an overnight camp. The Sioux rides off wildly.

The following chapter introduces the members of the caravan, one of whom, a fifteen-year-old girl, Allie, will be the heroine of the story. They are interrupted at their evening meal by a hard-riding trapper, Slingerland by name, who warns them of an oncoming Sioux attack. He rides off for help from the soldiers with a party of surveyors ahead, laying a line for a railroad. The others break camp immediately and hurry on as best they can.

The girl's mother, fearing imminent massacre, realizes it is time to tell her daughter the truth about their past. Allie's father is not Durade, the pathological gambler they have lived with and just escaped from—he had used the woman as a lure to attract customers to his gambling dens and has the same intentions to so use the daughter. Years before, the mother had been forced to marry an Allison Lee, the real father, but had run off with the adventurer Durade before Allie was born. It is well that she reveals this: the Sioux attack at dawn, killing everybody but the girl.

In chapter 4 we meet the hero, Warren Neale, age twenty-three, self-educated, and "wild for adventure, keen for achievement" (16). His daring and intuitive grasp of how to survey the railroad line through difficult terrain has already made him a favorite of General Lodge, chief engineer of the corps. Neale had got on staff by blurting out that there *was* going to be a railroad when naysayers were claiming otherwise. Lodge overheard the remark and said he could use more young fellows like him.

Neale puts up with the bedlam that is a construction camp. In time he comes to see "the bewildering turmoil of plans, tasks, schemes, land-grants, politics, charters, inducements, liens and loans, Government and army and State and national interests, grafts and deals and bosses—all that mass of selfish and unselfish motives, all that wealth of cunning and noble aims, all that congested assemblage of humanity which went to make up the building of the Union Pacific" (106). To him all aspects seem part of a "beautiful romance," his outlook being one of "golden ambition and illimitable dreams." He is an incurable romantic, idealizing the future, but this same idealization will later make him critical of the all-too-human present, the here and now, with its corruption and greed. He wonders, rather naively, "Why could not all men be right-minded about a noble cause and work unselfishly for the development of the West and future generations?" (106).

General Lodge anticipates a *wild* West. He points out there will be thousands of soldiers in camp (for protection against the rampaging Sioux, who are fighting for *their* way of life—and Grey is sympathetic), also thousands of others, the camp followers—merchants honest and dishonest, "whisky men, gamblers, desperadoes, bandits, and bad women." Neale exclaims, "It will be great!"; his superior replies gravely, "It will be terrible" (26).

The first of many "terrible" events for Neale is accompanying the soldiers summoned by Slingerland. They find the mutilated bodies from the massacre, all but Allie's. Neale is the last to leave, then goes back on a hunch and finds the girl, hidden but physically unharmed. However, she is wild, out of her mind from shock. He carries her all the way, on horseback, to the trapper's cabin, which is closer than the surveyor's camp, and tends to her there for a few days until she becomes quiet and rational, then returns to his post.

There, Lodge teasingly sums up what will happen: the girl will grow up into a beautiful woman, Neale will become an important person in the U. P. and they will marry each other—a fine romance! Indeed, this is what happens, eventually, but winding is the trail each follows, the course of their lives. Associations along the way, with the "whisky men, gamblers, desperadoes, bandits, and bad women," affect what they do in successive construction camps as the railroad forges on. Even Larry Red King, a "droll, lazy Southerner" (25) from Texas, has an important role to play. He is Neale's sidekick, true as steel, with a bent for "gun-throwing" (53).

Neale's visits at the trapper's cabin give Allie something to live for so that she watches for him to come—and then hides. Such behavior shows that she is getting better. He rouses her from her horrific memories when he begins fishing at a stream, where she has sequestered herself, and almost loses a huge trout at the shore (of course, Grey was always a keen fisherman—see *Zane Grey on Fishing*, 2003). She leaps up to secure it, and Grey admirably shows (not tells of) her gradual recovery through the conversation that follows. Neale proposes to her before he goes, and leaves a ring from his little finger as a pledge. He knows he cannot come back until fall, three months later.

Then, she is a joyous, gleaming young woman, who runs out to meet *him*. She has been "doing everything under the sun" (76), cooking, sewing, and fishing to regain her health (Grey is a great believer in work, activity, as a curative). In fact, Neale is caught quite off guard, not ready for her display of so much emotion. "Love of him ha[s] saved the girl's mind and ... made her beautiful and wonderful" (81). He vows to be worthy of her. In that winter's work, while staying with Slingerland and Allie, patrolling the nearby mountain pass to check what snows will do to it, he finds that toil is good for him too, making him hardened and tough.

Neale reports back to his regular work in spring, 1866. Rails are now being laid across Nebraska, and when fall comes, he is ordered farther east to Omaha. There he sees firsthand the business dealings behind the building of the railroad. The government sends out "expert" commissioners to examine the track, but many of them are incompetent, expert only at swindling that same government, for example, by reporting that a length of track is substandard and has to be rebuilt. Five miles of reconstruction costs an extra forty-six thousand dollars a mile, from which corrupt commissioners receive a kickback. And Allison Lee, Allie's father, is one such commissioner!

Finally, in the spring of 1867, Neale and Larry King ride out to see Allie, but find only a burned-down trapper's cabin. She had been kidnapped by four ruffians while Slingerland was away. Although she manages to escape, she is soon captured by a Sioux war party, apparently to be a chief's second wife. The jealous first wife helps her to flee, but then she is "rescued" by a wagon train led by Durade. She is now his prisoner, part of his nefarious life.

Neale is not aware of this whirl of events, just completely dejected at the loss of his sweetheart. Now *he* has nothing to live for, loses his romantic enthusiasm for his work, and begins to drink and gamble. It is Larry's presence that tempers his actions. Unfortunately, he is again confronted with Lee's barefaced corruption, also an accusation of his surveying figures being false. Neale is outraged and quits his job with these words: "To hell with your rotten railroad!" (118).

Durade's destination is the latest construction site of the ever advancing railroad, the camp-*city* of Benton, where he will set up his biggest gambling hall. Grey prefers to call it a "gambling-hell" (168), and he is right—Benton, is the worst of all the construction camps: "three men for every man's work. That lays off two men each day. Drunk or dead. The place is wild" (166). A girl who works at a dancing-hall/brothel says, "We're all going to hell here, and the gamest will get there soonest" (176).

Neale—ever restless, haunted by the memory of Allie Lee, and unable, it seems, to leave the railroad hives of activity he once waxed romantically about—has drifted from Kearney and North Platte in Nebraska to Cheyenne and finally Benton in Wyoming Territory. There he meets some of his former fellow-railroad workers, including Casey, a colorful Irishman. (Grey has some fun capturing the man's lingo and sense of humor when Casey boasts of attackers he has shot: "Jist thirty wus moine" [194].) What Neale notices about these laborers is that, unlike him, they are no longer the ordinary men they had been. They have grown—because of the great endeavor, building a national railway, that has caught hold of them. They have imbibed its spirit and shine out (Grey's restatement of the work ethic). Neale, in contrast, has stopped growing; he feels "an inexplicable littleness in their presence" (185).

It is at this time that Neale is asked to rejoin the railroad crew to tackle another troublesome survey. He refuses; he feels he cannot put his mind to it—a black spell is "enfolding" him (197). General Lodge then summons Neale to a work camp outside Benton and speaks to him personally, in a fatherly fashion, both flaying him for drinking and gambling his life away and appealing to his sense of duty to aid a short-staffed corps. Lodge really wants someone to stand by him till the last spike is hammered home.

Neale's romantic soul is roused, and he accepts the challenge. Then Allie bursts into the room, and it is her strong arms that enfold him, no longer his black spell. She has escaped Durade's clutches, and that is reason enough to bring him back to his job, Neale says. But Allie explains Lodge's approach: he "cared enough for you to want you to come back to your job for your sake—for his sake—for sake of the railroad. And not for me" (209).

Allie's safety, unfortunately, is not long lasting. The Sioux attack the camp, and Durade and his men, unrecognized, have sought its shelter for the night. In the turmoil of the ensuing battle, Durade makes off with Allie once more. Neale, again, frequents gambling dens and dance halls, when he is not working, but now only to find some clue about Allie's whereabouts.

What happens is that Neale becomes philosophic about the hell-hole that is Benton, the "product of this great advance in progress," the railroad. The U. P. R. goes on, but the workers in the halls and dens are simply "poor creatures sucked into the vortex" (243–44). He offers one, Ruby by name (fitting for a "scarlet woman"), a chance to escape. It is never too late, is his assurance. He will find a real home for her, with good people, but she cannot accept.

Next day, she is found dead in her room, by her own hand—had he "awakened conscience in her?" He visits her unmarked grave, beside yet another, that of a railway worker killed on the job. He thinks: "As the workman had given his life to the road, so had the woman" (243–45). Her life was precious: "She had been a child once, with dancing eyes and smiles, loved by some one, surely, and perhaps mourned by some one living." Nature, however, makes no comment: "The low hum of Benton's awakening night life was born faintly on the wind. The sand seeped; the coyotes wailed; and yet there was silence. Twilight lingered. Out on the desert the shadows deepened" (245).

Then there is Ruby's employer, thirty-year-old Beauty Stanton, who holds "the haunting ghost of beauty still" (171). Grey refers to her as "a cog in the wheel, a grain of dust in a whirlwind, a morsel of flesh and blood for the hungry maw of a wild and passing monster of progress" (321). She has an opportunity to be something else through Neale, with whom she has become infatuated. His manner is always courteous and deferential to all women, that being the code of the West, even though he wishes to have nothing to do with her. One might say she is wanting something she cannot have—his loyalty to Allie is constant. But I also think there is something here, too, of her following the fellow who follows a dream, and Neale certainly is a romantic dreamer. Such a tack has its downside for the woman when the romantic's dreams do not include her.

Now a situation arises where Beauty can win his gratitude, and glory in it. Allie Lee has been captured from Durade and delivered to her for safekeeping—in one of her brothel cubicles. She will find Neale and tell him the news: "He was going to hear the blessed tidings from a woman whom he scorned" (322); "now as a good woman, with pure motive, she would win his friendship" (323–24). But in her excitement to tell her message, she says only that he should come, and he thinks she is importuning *him*, professionally. When she finally blurts out Allie's name, he thinks this is only an added inducement to her come-on. He calls her a vicious name and strikes her.

She runs out blindly into the street, and what follows is some of Grey's most powerful writing in the book. "There is no flame of hate so sudden and terrible and intense" as hers. His "vile interpretation [of] her appeal" changes a mind "lately fixed in happy consciousness of her power of good" to one in which flashes "a thousand scintillating, coruscating gleams of evil thought," an "inspiration straight from hell." In her "immutable passion to destroy," she will give the next customer entering her establishment the key to Allie's room. It is the cumulative effect of Grey's description that is so telling (326–27).

Beauty Stanton's scheme goes terribly awry, for who comes sauntering in but Larry Red King, half-drunk. She knows what a malicious gunman he is, not that he is a friend of both Neale and Allie. When his dazed mind grows clear enough to understand the real situation, he leads Allie outside, literally shooting his way past five of Durade's henchmen, who have come to reclaim her, and Beauty herself, who tries to stop him. He kills them all, although she lives long enough to write a farewell letter to Neale, explaining things. Grey's description of her death is superb: "she did not cry out, or complain, or repent, or pray.... Memory called up only the last moments of her life.... She would have been glad—if only Neale had understood her! ... Then came a moment, the last, ... when [her] soul lingered on the threshold of its lonely and eternal pilgrimage, and then drifted across into the gray shadows" (340–41).

Larry King is shot himself, and dies on the street, standing up, lodged against a building. Allie, alone, her strength failing, reels, and is grasped by—Durade. For some readers, his johnny-on-the-spot appearance occurs once too often in this busy novel.

We now have another graveyard scene, where Grey gives us an entirely different picture than we had for Ruby's burial. We see Casey and his Irish buddy as gravediggers for the last seven killings and their comments hark back to Shakespeare's yokels at the same trade in *Hamlet* (341–44). Casey's comments on life and death are matter-of-fact: "shure yez hev a cleaner grave than yez hed a bed.... Nice white desert sand." Grey's are more philosophical: "in the eternal workshop of nature, the tenants of these unnamed and forgotten graves [will] mingle dust of good with dust of evil, and by the divinity of death resolve equally into the elements again."

The following chapter, 29, features Casey solely. He sacrifices his own life, riding a gravel car on a downhill twenty-mile run to warn an oncoming train carrying Lodge and his staff of a Sioux ambush at an in-between pass. He knows the Natives will not really bother with his lone car. The problem is that the car's brake is broken, and he must stop somehow and not ram into the train. The account is complete in itself.

Casey had recovered Beauty's farewell letter at the grave, and it is found clenched in his teeth. The first part is read aloud by Lodge's crew before they realize it is a personal note intended for Neale. But that first part seems to implicate Neale as Beauty's lover. Neale is in trouble. Later, he comes across Durade, who is arguing with Allie and Allison Lee, and kills the gambler—by grasping his knife-wielding hand and forcing him to stab himself. More trouble! Allie goes sorrowfully to live with her father, leaving Neale alone.

Neale, having recently been promoted to chief engineer, must commit himself to the hardest of manual labor—carrying and laying rails, spiking them tight with sledges—must persist in "sustained physical action" (383) to maintain his spiritual well-being (Grey's work ethic yet again). Of course, this is all delineated vividly over several chapters, giving Neale (and the author) still another opportunity to speak of the grand achievement of building the railroad: he feels "the majesty of common free men, sweating and bleeding and groaning over toil comparable to the building of the Pyramids[,] ... these simple elemental toilers.... He s[ees] the thousands of plodding, swearing, fighting, blaspheming, joking laborers..., red and bronzed and black, dust-begrimed; and how here with the ties and the rails and the roadbed was the heart of that epical turmoil" (388–89).

Misunderstandings are finally resolved. Neale stands at Promontory in Utah Territory, 1869, hears a man of God offer a prayer at the official ceremony marking the joining of the railroad from the West coast with the Union Pacific, then sees the last spike driven home. And Allie, newly arrived, slips her hand in his. They are married by the minister who gave the prayer.

All's well that ends well, but in the last two short chapters Grey concludes the book with two other observations. One is from the viewpoint of Slingerland, the trapper, whose means of living will change. He hates the great, shining steel band before him. Progress is great, "but nature undespoiled [is] greater" (406). The second comment applies to the Sioux, who fought so valiantly to forestall this "progress," and to other Natives as well. Their hunting grounds are doomed, and an old chief watches a train moving along swiftly, disappearing in the distance, "a symbol of destiny of the Indian—vanishing—vanishing—vanishing" (209).

10

The Man of the Forest:
Mind and Instinct

This book begins excitingly. Immediately, we hear of an *overheard* scheme, through hero Milt Dale, of a big rancher trying to steal another ranch, that of the uncle of heroine Helen Rayner, whom we have yet to meet. The consequences of this attempt lead to the meeting of the two, their growing love (and setbacks), and eventual marriage. Thus goes the main story line. The book was published in 1920 (first serially printed in *The Country Gentleman*, 1917).

What adds interest are the minor plots that arise along the way—What effect will the ill feeling between Dale and the uncle have? Will Helen escape being kidnapped? What will happen to braggart/suitor Harve Riggs? What role will Helen's sister, Bo, play? Why is Roy Beeman singled out as the keenest of four brothers helping in Helen's rescue? As one issue is being resolved, another is introduced in this fast-paced novel.

And yet there is a Washington Irving feel about chapter 2, as if the story is taking place in the New England Catskills instead of the Arizona White Mountains. Dale, now thirty, seems like a Rip Van Winkle figure, coming down from his mountain seclusion to mix with simple frontier folk in the village of Pine below. He has lived a forest life for twelve years, making "only infrequent visits" with the villagers, but "welcome everywhere," for he cares about them and loves to catch the latest gossip from Widow Cass. He is good at odd jobs, like Rip, tracking a stolen horse, curing a sick cow. But he loves his life close to nature, its "solitude and beauty," most (9).

It is while roaming in his dear mountains, letting his gaze sweep along their sprucey sierra, that he is overtaken by a rainstorm and takes shelter in an old cabin. There, he learns of rancher Beasley's deal with an outlaw gang to capture dying Al Auchincloss's ranch. Beasley had once worked for the old rancher—in fact, claims to have been his partner and been cheated of his rights to the property. He wants the gang to waylay Helen until he has consolidated his position as the just inheritor and taken possession of it—possession is nine-tenths of the law.

Dale, an upright individual, has no choice but to stop this outrage if he can, hurry down to the village and alert Auchincloss. Auchincloss, however, will not let Dale even explain the situation. He is angry with the man of the forest, believing that his pet cougar had killed some ranch sheep. Dale can hardly act on his own so engages the Beeman brothers as assistants. What they do not know is that Helen, age twenty, is bringing her sixteen-year-old sister, Bo (short for nickname Bo-Peep), with her. Riggs is coming too, but not at anyone's request. He is continuing to press his attentions upon Helen—both women detest him.

Helen has a pioneer spirit and an "undeveloped love of horses, cattle, sheep, of desert and mountain, of trees and brooks" (31). She is willing to learn and will fit in well to her new Western environment. At the same time she is ever the thinker, pondering every situation, even wondering whether the need to achieve, apparent all about her, will make "thinking and pondering superficial" (42). She very much feels responsible for her sister, wanting to be a mentor for her, and *thinks* Bo will "readily adapt herself to the West" because she is "so young, primitive, elemental" (39). But she needs caring for, this "beautiful, wild little sister" (31). Bo is impulsive, loves action, and is "not contemplative" at all (74).

The differences between the two sisters has its parallel in Jane Austen's first novel, *Sense and Sensibility*, 1811, written a century earlier. As its title suggests, Elinor Dashwood, the older sister, is generally a woman of common sense; Marianne, one of excessive feeling. The latter's impetuosity ever opposes the former's rational deliberation, leaving her ecstatic one moment—for example, before a striking outdoor vista—depressed the next, should it rain. Elinor remains, for the most part, calm, matter-of-fact. How similar this is to the situation of Helen and Bo!

In *The Man of the Forest*, Dale asks how each of the sisters felt about a day's adventures out in the open, chasing a cougar on horseback. Bo's response is purely physical—the feel of wind rushing by, the smell of pines, her blood beating and burning, her nerves tingling. She, like Marianne, recognizes no authority greater than her feelings, her sensations. Helen's reaction is a mix of things, her physical response controlled by her reasoning brain. The dash and action, she says, were splendid, but at the same time she had recognized the potential dangers for herself, her pity for the animal, her "reckless disregard" of being a responsible person, a needed role model for "highly sensitive, hot-blooded" Bo (155–56). This mothering, older-sister attitude she shares with Jane Austen's Elinor, who keeps constant vigil over Marianne.

With the four women's love lives, further comparison can be made. Marianne approaches any experience, landscape or lover with feelings quivering in readiness, but without sense enough to detect the shallowness of a suitor. Bo, Zane Grey describes as a firebrand (229), also a child whose head is easily turned (215). In one instance Helen tells her to "Hush, silly!" (55), in another to "talk sense," when Tom Carmichael comes under discussion—Helen thinks he would make a fine husband. Bo admits she has been "wild about" him but hates him too. Helen replies, "Nonsense, Bo. You can't hate anyone while you love him" (225–26). She, herself, is a no-nonsense woman in affairs of the heart, like Elinor, not a Bo-like "victim to a multiplicity of moods" (251).

We see more of Helen's character in her relationship to Dale. She overhears his refusing to become the foreman of her uncle's ranch because of what he believes is his hopeless love for her. These are happy moments for her, and, she thinks, the profoundest of her life. When she, patient, comes face to face with Dale a few minutes later, she is "strong and calm, in feminine possession of her secret (and his) as well as her composure" (196). Her slow but sure romance with the man of the forest ends with their marriage on the last pages of the book, as Roy Beeman, who, we discover, is also a preacher, asks the Lord to blaze a trail for them through the "forest of life!" (379).

After many trials and tribulations, Bo gets married too, to Carmichael—in fact, a few days before Helen's nuptials. It seems that Bo, however impatient, has become something of a no-nonsense woman as well, for she accepts Carmichael's proposal in this wise: "Very well, you can make me Mrs. Tom Carmichael today—this morning—just before dinner.... Go get a preacher to marry us" (375). That preacher, also Roy Beeman, performs the ceremony, commenting later to Tom, in good fun, of course: "But I shore ain't guaranteein' nothin.' You'd better build a corral for her" (380). However, we have had Helen's earlier assessment of her sister—"Bo will come out of it true blue. She is good, loving. Her heart is gold" (215).

Although both Austen's and Grey's books end with double marriages, and happy ones, the reader feels somewhat differently about them. In Austen, we sense that Elinor may have fallen somewhat short of experiencing the emotional fullness of life, with her orderly romance, while Marianne comes out ahead in the long run. In Grey, both women are winners, for Helen's rational stance is modified when she and Bo must remain in Dale's forest camp for several weeks in order to escape the kidnappers. In the interval Dale tries, rather successfully, to get Helen to see that "blood is stronger than brain." Instinct has flourished in ancestral man thousands of years before intellect or mind came to the fore. "Don't fight your instincts so hard," is his advice. Dismissing them is being untrue to one's *basic* or *underlying* nature (156). (Dale [and Grey] unfortunately use the adjective *real* here.)

We know that mind, certainly, is as much a part of Helen's real nature as her body, for we are human and *not* mere animals (we remember Shakespeare's lines in *Hamlet*: "What a piece of work is a man! ... In action how like an angel!" [2.2.317]). True, we are animals physically, but with a veneer of civilization made by our minds. That is what makes society work; without it, we are back in the jungle. This veneer is something to cultivate, to polish, not to ignore or slough off. Still, Helen becomes more aware of her physical being, living an outdoor life and hearing Dale's insights into nature, than she had been.

Dale reveals to her the "cruelty' of nature ("red in tooth and claw" is Tennyson's phrase [*In Memoriam*, 912]), but also that that cruelty is amoral. "Men are crueler," for they "have more than instincts" (84). (Helen thinks how fine Dale's *mind* must be to know this.) The strife in nature, he continues, is necessary to keep animals from deteriorating. Although not mentioned by name, Dale is speaking of the web of life, survival of the fittest, and ecology in general. To illustrate his theme he refers to plants (141)—how they "fight" for water and sun, an "absolute and continual fight." Listening and seeing, Helen senses it all as sad and wonderful, mysterious and inspiring. She feels these facts will transform her—"even if they hurt, she welcome[s] them" (142).

Dale says she needs, at some time, to starve, be lost, face death, feel the urge to kill, and be madly in love before she can really know life. He wants her to understand the instinctual make-up that she shares with wild things, to have one wolf howl "[pierce] beyond her life, back into the dim remote past from which she had come" (179), and so better understand herself. To know something of the wild, she finds, is to be close not only to the kingdom of earth but likely to the kingdom of heaven (and the "somethin' unseen" [250]—Dale's description of God), "for whatever breathe[s] ... [i]s a part of that [heavenly] creation" (382).

Yet one more reference to Jane Austen: what she has said about her nephew's attempted authorship in her *Letters* would also apply to writers of romance, such as Grey, who were describing the vast panorama of nature. She asks: "What should I do with your strong, manly, spirited sketches, full of Variety and Glow?" (468). She was a "painter" of delicate miniatures instead. The lives of three or four upper middle-class families in a country village provide in her opinion sufficient material for a novel. This fragment of life she knows. Nature, already civilized, can be made subservient to the action of the story and to her analysis of character.

Zane Grey writes of the whole West, of all the classes of people who drift into it. His West is not yet civilized. Nature there is raw and grand, described as a force in itself, determining the action of his story and its characters. The first (extended) sentence of chapter 13 bears this out: "After more days of riding the grassy level of that wonderful gold and purple park [Dale's home], and dreamily listening by day to the ever-low and ever-changing murmur of the waterfall, and by night to the wild, lonely mourn of a hunting wolf, and climbing the dizzy heights where the wind stung sweetly, Helen Rayner lost track of time and forgot her peril" (173). Another sentence in the same chapter reveals that the setting is not only great terrestrial space but extra-planetary: "In the west, where the afterglow of sunset lingered over the dark, ragged, spruce-speared horizon-line, there was such a transparent golden line melting into star-filled blue that Helen could only gaze in wondering admiration" (175–76).

It is a West of "one succession of adventures, trials, tests, troubles, and achievements" (79), where all these events speak of the everyday work of people building a homeland in which those to come might live comfortably. "Work that does not help others," Helen tells Dale, "is not a real man's work" (202). (Yes, she has something to teach him too.)

Dale, this thirty-year-old man with a "leonine" stature (like his pet cougar), yet a "boyish simplicity and vigor" (80), is still living aloof and tranquilly in his retreat, a hidden park in what was millennia ago a volcano crater. She feels he is wasting his intelligence and manhood rather than developing the West. She does not want him to give up his wilderness ways, only realize his full potential, and he sees there is more to life than his "free, sensorial, Indian relation to existence" (263). At the end he says he will *work* all his life for her. (For Grey on work, see Wheeler, "Solitude and Work…," 9, 34).

Grey's West, wild as it is, still has its "unwritten" laws—"an eye for an eye[,] a tooth for a tooth" (260). So says preacher Roy Beeman, harking back to the Old Testament (Exodus 21:24). Tom Carmichael explains this hard fact to the sisters. They will need to live in the West for a longer time in order "to learn the ways of a country" (219). Carmichael had been a gunman in his native Texas and knows the value of a quick draw in obtaining a rough justice—as does Grey. The author gives this tribute to the men of low-slung holsters: "The pioneers and ranchers of the frontier would never have made the West habitable had it not been for these wild cowboys, these … rangers of the barrens, these easy, cool, laconic, simple young men whose blood was tinged with fire and who possessed a magnificent and terrible effrontery toward danger and death" (356).

The code of the West recognizes that as the West's wildness makes a villain's crimes possible, so it also holds him responsible (361–62). Thus when Beasley has Helen literally thrown off her ranch and Carmichael waits upon him for a shoot-out, Beasley must answer the call or be branded forever as a coward. And so the Texas cowboy shoots him, also the foreman who had deserted Helen to join him.

Jim Wilson, the best of that bad lot hired by Beasley to kidnap Helen—for he recognizes that stealing sheep, their previous activity, "ain't stealin' gurls by a long sight"—makes an astute comment: if the villains are not "wiped out by Rangers or cowboys, why they just naturally wipe out themselves" (300–301). This is what happens to the outlaw gang—they kill each other after a second attempt at capturing Helen. Actually, Harve Riggs, who is working with the gang, mistakenly captures Bo instead. He, too, is killed—by Wilson—when he tries to get Bo to escape from the gang with him. In the end only Wilson is left, and it is he who helps Dale with Bo's eventual rescue. (Dale's cougar helps as well.)

Both sisters can now marry. Bo and Carmichael will find excitement in each other—such are their characters. Helen and Dale will be tranquilly content on the ranch, with frequent visits to his forest home. It is their "Paradise Park!" (383).

11

The Desert of Wheat: I.W.W. and WWI

Halfway through *The Desert of Wheat*, 1919 (serialized in *The Country Gentleman*, 1918), Zane Grey makes this statement: "The dwelling-places of men were beautiful; it was only life that was sad" (178). The setting of this book is east central Washington, the Bend region of that state—hilly, treeless country, once sage and sand but now rich wheat-producing land, if the rains come. The beauty is in its austerity, the simplest elements of scenery only, land and sky, but comely in its checkered pattern of equal parts of cropped fields and fallow ground, the latter bare to conserve moisture for next year's planting. Individual farms run from a whole section, six hundred forty acres, to several sections.

The year is 1917, three months after the United States entered the World War of 1914–18, now in early July with the summer's heat beginning to devastate the growing wheat, although one section of crop still shows great promise on Chris Dorn's four-and-a-half sections of land. The trouble is that drought has claimed the area the last three years, and his land is not fully paid for. Thirty thousand dollars, plus interest, is owed to a Mr. Anderson, a farmer-rancher a hundred miles away who owns many thousands of acres extending into the foothills, where rainfall is plentiful—his estate is called "Many Waters." A well-meaning individual, he does not wish to foreclose.

Dorn has other worries. He is of German stock, and despite having lived in America for fifty years, still has German leanings, and is angry with the States for going to war. His old age, illiteracy, and increasingly set ideas make him an easy mark for some corrupt leaders of the Industrial Workers of the World (I.W.W.), sometimes known as Wobblies. While legitimately trying to promote shorter hours and higher wages for farm laborers, they are also disrupting wheat production, important to a country's war effort in a time of crisis. By supporting them, Dorn hopes to aid Germany.

Most affected is young Kurt Dorn, age twenty-four, the only son—the mother, an American woman, having died years before. He has been educated at the State Agricultural College, knows wheat, loves the farm, and thinks the I.W.W. to be a pack of outlaws and thieves, a power-hungry labor organization out to abolish capital and run the entire Northwest. He had wanted to enlist in the war, to make up for his father's pro-German stance, but has abandoned the idea for the moment because of the elder Dorn's anger. Another complication is that Kurt has fallen in love with Anderson's daughter, Lenore, and his father threatens to sell the land and move back to Germany (with Kurt) so that the son can marry a German girl. This, for Kurt, is the last straw, and he yells back, "If I go to Germany, it'll be as a soldier—to kill Germans!" (36).

The elements of plot, here outlined, may seem melodramatic, but Grey's overall treatment is a deep probe into the situation and the characters who play a part in it. First, we learn more of Kurt and wheat. He glories in sowing it, seeing the first tender blades sprouting, then watching the changing field day by day until its surface is like a braided rug being shaken by the wind. Finally comes the harvest, the dust and noise of it, thirty-four horses pulling a combine, and he holding the reins. He has also worked in a mill, to know how flour is made, and is the baker of bread at home, for himself and his father. He has a sense of wheat's importance, its permanence. Like the hills on which it grows, and the stars above them, it "[will] go on" (38).

Grey tells us that Kurt loves "both the physical sense and the spiritual meaning of the toil" of a farmer (32). The toil described in this instance is cultivating the fallow fields by walking somewhat awkwardly behind a horses-pulled harrow in the soil just loosened by it—as my own mother did as a young teenager in those same years on a one *quarter*-section sandy farm in Saskatchewan after her parents had moved up from Minnesota. What she did not know, apparently as Kurt does not, is that such cultivation causes erosion: the action pulverizes the soil and leaves it in a porous state, easily dried out and blown away by the winds. Grey knows this, for he speaks of the accompanying "dust as dry as powder," its " whipping back from ... the steel spikes of the harrow," enough to temporarily blind Kurt and clog his nostrils (32). So here we have Grey, who speaks for nature conservation, even in ecological terms, whenever he can throughout his books, now doing the same, indirectly, for soil conservation.

Grey also gives us, through Kurt, a three-page technical description of another concern in wheat production—smut, a parasitic fungus. Such a lengthy inclusion strikes one as out-of-place, but he probably dwells on it as a blight parallel to what Anderson has been describing to Kurt—a dark and sinister force, the I.W.W., agitating to enlist supporters but really sabotaging the wheat harvest. Kurt says to an I.W.W. spokesman, Glidden: "We've a war to fight! ... and you come spreading discontent in the wheat-fields, ... when wheat means life!" (30). Kurt has several run-ins with him. It is debased men such as Glidden and his followers that are Grey's special target. The author gives this leader "steely, secretive" eyes, and one of his men "eyes like a ferret" (29).

What we have here is a situation not really akin to that in John Steinbeck's *The Grapes of Wrath*, 1939, where workers are Great Depression migrants, picking fruit in California. There is much wage-cutting by the orchard owners because of the proliferation of laborers. We see the ensuing struggle from the side of the workers, who need to unionize to protect themselves. In *The Desert of Wheat*, we see the conflict from the side of the farmers, the owners who are also the workers, along with their hired help. There is no wage-cutting; in fact, the opposite occurs in order to keep reliable workers on hand. It is the farmers, and these workers, who need to band together to guard their crops, with rifles, from certain I.W.W. men who have marked out "independent" farmers for harassment. And this is not just fun and games. The men throw cakes of wet phosphorus into ripe crops, which when dried burst into flame, igniting the whole field.

The Dorns' one section of flourishing wheat needs to be saved. It is fall now, and the crops of surrounding farms have either succumbed to the drought or else been burned by the I.W.W. The consequence is that thirty-five farmers with their workers are free to help: "They had shown little liking for the Dorns, but here was love of wheat, and so, in some way, loyalty to the government that needed it" (143). But phosphorus fires spring up here too, and the elder Dorn, no longer an I.W.W. supporter when he is so directly affected, toils as ten men to put out the flames, overworks in a new kind of rage, and dies. Close neighbor Olsen steps in to organize a work force of a hundred men to rush through the harvest.

Kurt works at many jobs—loading bags of wheat at a combine (there are thirty of them operating) and tossing them into waiting wagons, pitching bundles into a hayrack to be hauled to one of three threshing machines, driving a wagon in a whole caravan of wagons filled with grain. A constant roar hovers over the fields, a "roar of battle—men and horses governing the action of machinery" (148). Everywhere is straw and chaff and streams of golden wheat. Always he tries to sense "all that was so beautiful and good and heroic in the scene" (150). For me, who experienced threshing days from my earliest childhood until I eventually worked on a threshing crew, Grey well captures the hubbub and excitement of the event. But the harvesters' work, after all, is for nothing; the I.W.W. burns the elevators and train cars where the grain has been stored. Then the farmers take their guns to town, confront the perpetrators, in the dark, and exchange gunfire, though no one is killed.

Meanwhile, Anderson at his huge farm/ranch is also experiencing troubles. One of his combines has broken down, and a large wrench is found inside the works, tearing up the mechanisms. The same day a threshing machine catches on fire and burns (they were made of wood in those days, not galvanized iron as were the later models). The cause?—likely a handful of matches stuffed into a grain bundle before it was pitched onto the feeder. This is outright sabotage, and one of the newly hired workers turns out to be Glidden in disguise. He is suspected of being a German agent and is thrown into jail.

Anderson, already aware of a plot against his own life, has initiated a plan to handle saboteurs—"in the good old Western way" (46). A vigilante group, all-masked figures, holds a secret ballot on what should be Glidden's fate, and it is "death." They spring him from jail, and he is hanged, from the center span above the tracks of a railway bridge. Then the vigilantes round up other I.W.W. workers in the region and put them into empty cattle-cars of a departing freight train that will cross the bridge: message sent and received. Further action involves Anderson's foreman, cowboy Jake, who hustles nearby rancher Neuman, in league with the saboteurs, back to "Many Waters," where he is forced to sell out and leave the country.

Kurt has been present at these events at "Many Waters." He had come to say good-by to Anderson and Lenore before joining the army and heading overseas. His romance with the girl has been a slow-motion affair of but a few glimpses even though its origin was sudden. Kurt's first sight of Lenore touched his "unconscious heart," his second made her an "unforgettable reality," and the third was a "realization of love" (24) toward this creature of "dancing blue eyes..., merry, provocative, full of youth and fun" (13). She herself needed one more glimpse, a fourth, to know that he had always been in *her* dreams (84).When he declares his love for her, a third way into the book (121), it is like an apology for daring to do so: he knows the immeasurable distance between them and expects nothing in return, not having the slightest notion of her caring. She is not sure how to respond—the moment passes—and it is two-thirds through the book before she can say, "Kurt, I love you just as much as—you love me.... So there!" (235).

Of course, many things have been happening all about them in the intervening time, as we know. Grey has full opportunity to delineate incidents of the developing romance, nowhere more subtly than when Lenore's father wants to know what his daughter's true feelings are (Anderson likes Kurt, will not reject him as a son-in-law, and can see him as someone to take over his estate eventually). He goes up to her room, where she is sitting in the dark. He asks if he may turn on the light, then decides not to. She knows immediately that he is leading up to something significant, some knowledge to impart or inquire about: "She could measure his mood by the preliminaries before his disclosure." She prepares herself (184).

He starts by lighting a cigar and talking about his son, and her brother, who is already training as a soldier. Jim had just written a letter home, and Anderson asks her if she sensed something from it. She wonders what he means, and he mentions "strange feelings." He himself thinks Jim will not come back, and Lenore agrees. A silence follows, but there is now a "bond of understanding" between the two. And Grey points out the accompanying stillness outside. There is an atmosphere of waiting, "of the inexplicable great world moving to its fate" (185).

Then the father is more casual. He remarks about Lenore's not being so much out-and-about as before. She reminds him that he had told her to "stay at home" (there had been an attempt at kidnapping). A bit of humor creeps in when he admits he had, but then adds: "But when did you ever before mind me?" Lenore laughs and says she always obeys him, and he responds, "Not so I'd notice" (185).

It is now time to shift the subject to what he is getting at—Kurt. He believes that her thoughts of him trying to harvest his crop (we already know what happened) is the reason for her seclusion. Anderson asks if she has noticed the smoke outside, from the Bend's wheat country. Her buoyed-up interest tells him his speculation is right, and they now talk specifically about "Dorn's desert of wheat," and what the I.W.W. is trying to do. Her outburst of "To ruin those poor, heroic farmers!" is enough for the father to state, slowly: "Lenore, ... you love this young Dorn!" He does not put this as a question; he simply "affirm[s]" (185–87). This conversation, quoted only in bits (it continues on to the end of chapter 17), attests to Grey's competence as a writer, even to his having touches of greatness.

Despite Lenore's love for Kurt (and her later revelation of it to him), despite her father's securing exemption for him from the war (because "young farmers [are] needed a thousand times more on the wheat-fields than on the battle-fields" [188]), the young man will not be dissuaded. He will be a soldier.

Lenore is understandably upset: "Why could not women, who suffered most, have some word in the regulation of events?" she (with Grey) has earlier pondered. "If women could govern the world there would be no wars" (57). But she comes to realize that by not going, Kurt would "doubt his manhood" (239). She later concludes that if men must fight, let them "forever fight their destructive instincts" (354). She can only hope that Kurt will fight his war with the ideal of protecting freedom.

There are certainly anti-war sentiments in *The Desert of Wheat*. The picture Grey paints of actual combat is not a pretty sight. Any glory won on a battle field is diminished by the appearance of the field itself. The author depicts it in a succinct five-word sentence: "The rotting dead were everywhere" (304). The surviving soldiers are "locked up in their prisons of emotion" (308). Kurt is terrified by nearby shellfire: "It reduced him to a palpitating, stricken wretch, utterly unable to cope with the terror.... [T]o be blown to atoms! It came every moment to some poor devil" (315).

There are scenes at the front line of No Man's Land with its machine-gun fire: a "rattling concatenation of quick shots like metallic cries, exploding hail-storm of iron in the air" (323). The scene at night is more uncanny with sheeted lightning showing at intervals the scrambling soldiers, wagons mired in mud, explosions of earth on high. To Kurt, repeated nights of "hellish shrieking and bursting shells [will] kill his mind" (323). Yet there is a kind of sinister beauty to it all, each black geyser of black earth is crowned with gray or creamy-yellow smoke that "float[s] away, white and graceful, on the wind" (325).

But when the enemy suddenly charges across the battle field, running low, Kurt and his comrades leap up from their trench, not in fear or anger but in a rat-like eagerness not to be cornered there, answering yell with yell, shot with shot. And at close quarters Kurt goes berserk with his bayoneted rifle. The ghastly description has images such as "one thrust at each gray form," "steel transfixed," and "ripped open in one mighty slash." He kills nine, the last a youth with the bayonet through his lungs, and a face in which he, Kurt, sees "only love of life, ... suddenly surprised at death." Then a shell-blast hurls them both into a "roaring blackness" (327–29). An odd kind of victory—we have this comment pages later: "The joy of the conquering army contrasts terribly with the pain and poverty and unquenchable hate of the conquered" (369–70).

Kurt is not killed but comes home, a stretcher-case, bearing twenty-five wounds—his left arm missing. He has raving spells, fighting again the Germans he killed, horrible to watch. A specialist pronounces that he will die, "and that really is the best for him" (349). But it is Lenore who has the words to make him recover: "Kurt, the day you're able to sit up I'll marry you. Then I'll take you home to your wheat-fields" (352).

Kurt is ever the fighter, who now battles for his health. (To paraphrase two of his earlier reflections, we can say that though the world has many defeated men, he refuses to be one of them [38]. Also, while men need not understand the uttermost meaning of life, they should live that life to the uttermost [178].)

Kurt can now think back to his harvest-time troubles with the I.W.W. and realize that they stemmed from specific agitators, not rank-and-file members, and that these same troubles in fact had brought him and his neighbors closer together. (Anderson, too, has changed his opinion, pointing out how the organization had improved conditions in Western lumber camps.) So Kurt and new wife, Lenore, together can finally experience a peaceful world, the "vast, lonely heave of wheat-slope," and be in harmony with it (350)—always "fields and toil and grains of wheat, ... the salvation of mankind, the freedom and the food of the world!" (374).

12
Wanderer of the Wasteland: Learning to Live

This is a book of raw nature—the sweep of solitary desert and stern, upright, rocky ridges in irregular pattern. Man seems insignificant here, so to maintain himself, his ego, he must react in primeval fashion, combating not only gargantuan forces of nature to stay alive but also rival man in a landscape where only a few may adequately survive. It is a place for the survival of the fittest where human combatants struggle with each other, with guns or deadly knives and also hand to hand and fist to fist. At times the battle is fought with none of these but with weaponry as gigantic as the land itself—avalanches hurled down mountainsides.

And the meaning of this struggle—the meaning of life for Adam Larey, the central protagonist, with his primogenial first name? He wanders the wasteland after enduring a kind of Cain-Abel rivalry in which he kills, or thinks he kills, his older brother, Guerd. The desert, he assumes, will be his purgatory where he can cleanse himself of this fratricidal act while seeking the true nature of God. But the journey will be a long one, of many years, for he cannot escape himself, a "murderer" who refuses to publicly admit his crime. His atonement involves rescuing women in distress, in one case killing the tormentor, always hoping to reconcile the notion of a caring God with the trying world He has created.

"Like a wild and hunted creature, [Adam] roam[s] the mountain top, halting at the old resting places, there to sit like a stone, to lie on his face, to writhe and fight and cry in his torment" (408). When his travels have brought him full circle fourteen years later, back to the scene of his crime, he discovers that his brother had not died but recovered. So what has his life of wandering meant? Has he been a plaything of the "gods" as in Greek and Roman mythology, his groundless labors but for their amusement? There is a mythic quality, of course, to the story—its huge setting and basic passions.

However, such *is* life, Zane Grey is saying, even in a lesser enactment. Life is process, where the end is found in the means, where one's development along the way is the eventual destination.

Let us now see exactly how the story unfolds, what Adam Larey's character comes to in the end, and how the author's artistic skills contribute to the overall effect. When Grey completed *Wanderer of the Wasteland*, 1923 (serialized in *McClure's*, 1920), he wrote, "I have never worked so hard on any book, never suffered so much or so long" (Jackson, 38).

When the story opens, in 1878, Adam, age eighteen, is fleeing downstream on the Colorado River, just to get out from under his hateful brother's dominance. He had always been under Guerd's thumb, had even left university shortly before to comply with his request to join him in going West. But there Guerd became a gambler and a womanizer, who stole Adam's girl; and disgusted, Adam simply fled, breaking forever the tortuous brotherly bond between them.

He comes to the wild desert "a stranger in a strange land" (11) (another Biblical allusion by Grey—from Exodus 2:22, about Moses, a Hebrew, living among Egyptians—to reinforce the notion of a great saga in a great land being told). The desert has "lilac-veiled canyons" but also the "barrenness of a dead world," beauty and terror in "immeasurable" space (20–21). Adam feels it will do something wonderful to him—or terrible. He has no choice but to work and endure.

His first job is toiling in a gold mine at Picacho, stoking fires under huge boilers, a task he succeeds at because of his giant size. His soul needs action as much as his body does. But he is not at home in the recreation of his fellow miners, sitting in a frontier bar with its smoke, discordant music, and women drinking. Still, he realizes there are two forces within him—one of fine principles and inclinations and another, newly stirring, of something wilder and strange. He feels the latter in rescuing his foreman from a disgruntled, dagger-wielding employee, feels his empowerment in the situation and glories in it.

The wilder force leads to his being attracted to the foreman's stepdaughter, Margarita, of whom the parent warns Adam: "She has as many loves and lives as a spotted cat"—"on fire all the time" (23, 19). True enough! She looks at Adam at one moment with eyes "soft with a light that had never shone upon [him] from any other woman's," and he calls her a "big-hearted girl" (28). But when he simply glances at someone else, she threatens to cut out his heart. She will slap and scratch and beat him with her "flying brown fists" another time (33), then later run through miles of thorn trees and cactus to warn him that he is being waylaid by the man with the dagger. The same fire dominates her, whether of hate or love.

Margarita is Grey's lesson number one in Adam's learning about the facets of womanhood in the course of his wandering life. She is also a kind of lesser *deus ex machina* to carry the plot forward and make Adam a true wanderer of the wasteland. For Guerd shows up, once more "to dominate and hound" his poor brother (41), and sweeps changeable Margarita from him. She is Adam's Eve, deceitful—in effect, the cause of his having to leave.

It happens in this way. Guerd flings out words "like bullets" in his haunting and taunting of Adam. He says that if their mother could see how Adam had been duped, then his cup would be full (another Biblical allusion, Psalm 23 this time—a misuse of the well-known passage, showing how morally twisted Guerd really is). He continues the patter—his hate has a terrible magnificence, and Adam, with "gathering fury..., ready to break out in destroying violence," flings out his gun and fires (58). Guerd falls backward, and Adam bolts away, climbing a mountain ridge to safety.

At this point Grey includes one more Biblical allusion. En route down, Adam slips and falls, both hands forward, into a cactus—"it was as if his hands had been nailed" (61). The crucifixion image at first may seem inappropriate, a detraction from the five preceding pages of remarkably apt, vivid prose describing the whole incident. But so Grey alerts us to the way Adam's journey, if successful, must end—as described in the last pages of the book: "trained now in the desert's ferocity to survive, [he] should use that force to a noble aim, and, climbing beyond his nature, sacrifice himself to the old biblical law—a life for a life—and with faith in unknown future lend his spirit to the progress of the ages!" Again, "he [is] concerned here with many ideals, the highest of which [is] sacrifice, that the evil in him should not go on" (411). And the overall spirit of life, "the mighty being" that initiates his renunciation, is his "idea of God" (412). It comes to him that God has been with him for his entire journey.

This is not his feeling at the start of his wanderings, on the run from the law. He confronts the great desert now before him, alone: "the stupendous loneliness and silence of that solitude ... seemed Nature's pitiless proof of her indifference to man and his despair. His hope, his prayer, his frailty, his fall, his burden and agony and life—these were nothing to the desert that worked inscrutably through its millions of years, nor to the illimitable expanse of heaven, deepening its blue and opening its cold, starry eyes" (62). He can do nothing but "take up his burden and go down the naked shingles of the world" (62), down to the very basics of existence to work out his salvation.

Adam begins his new life by buying a miner's outfit (including a burro) but has to abandon it when a sheriff appears. He crosses the Colorado River into California and wanders the desert there. A sun's rising effects a "wondrous transfiguration" of the scene making it a marvel (74), but soon that same sun burns hot. Grey's careful analysis of the stages of Adam's near thirsting to death is detailed over four pages. At the end, tongue black and hanging out, he staggers in a circle and passes out.

Thankfully, he is discovered by another miner, Dismukes, to whom he gives his name as Wansfell in order to hide his identity. Then recovering from a body-weight loss of seventy pounds, he insists on his "need to live—to suffer—to atone" (85). Dismukes's wants are not so spiritual: he simply wants to prospect for gold till he has accumulated half a million dollars, then see the world and enjoy life.

The two men part, Dismukes directing Adam to a Native American band fifty miles distant, where he can fully recuperate and learn to live a desert life. But along the way Adam nearly dies again even after being more resourceful, fashioning a slingshot from pieces of his own clothing to kill quail, ground squirrels, and a rabbit. In trying to kill a large snake with a rock, he trips and the snake bites him. Again he collapses, and is rescued and nursed back to health by a Native girl.

Days pass into months, and months into years: Adam counts time now by the coming and going of snow on the mountain peaks. He is learning much about nature. Each wild animal, he realizes is perfect in its way, "each fulfilling its mysterious destiny of sacrificing its individual life to the survival of its species" (126). Even plants, with their penetrating roots and leafless branches, "know" how to catch and conserve water for survival. "The simplicity and violence of life on the desert [pass] into Adam's being" (126). He glories in the world about him, appreciates the adaptation to life of its varied constituents. His own senses gain greater competence.

And the rescuing girl, Oella, is Grey's second lesson for Adam in gaining a knowledge of womankind. Her father, the chief, offers her to be his wife. Adam, however, cannot be dishonorable. He is a criminal and may someday be arrested. Oella's piercing, level gaze searches his soul: everything about her is "eloquent of woman's love." "Stay," she says, for she is not afraid. Her "deep-toned passionate voice" shakes Adam's heart (133). She will wander with him. Her appeal is simple, direct, touching, but he cannot accept, and departs. Grey wisely uses only a few words in this scene—just half a page of writing—and in so doing presents a stronger picture of what women can be than he did delineating Margarita's tantrums over several pages.

Adam and Dismukes meet again after eight years. Nature reflects their joy at seeing each other, with a brilliant sunset: "Clouds ... colored into deeper glory.... The dark purples had an edge of silver, while golden rays shot up from behind the red hazed peaks" (136–37). Adam is pleased to learn that strangers to both of them speak his name "Wansfell" with respect and wonder because of his little "unremembered" kind deeds (142). He himself remembers only that he has lived mostly alone, working sometimes at freighting posts or gold diggings. But other deeds, like his killing a woman's tormentor, have given him a reputation as a retributive force. Although still young, Adam is "old with the silence and loneliness and strife of the desert" (142). He has an eagle's overview of things, and is able to be helpful when called upon. In contrast, Dismukes is a lone wolf, by his own admission, looking out for himself only.

Dismukes so far has accumulated only half the gold he wants, but to Adam "a gold-pan, a dish-pan, and a wash-pan" (157) are all the same—his wanderings have not been for wealth. He likes to spend much time "watching the living things of the desert, or listening to the silence" (154). He is like both a primitive man "in harmony with nature" and a meditating priest "who has begun to divine [its] secrets" (159–60). Has he found God there? Dismukes wants to know (the two friends have talked of this before). To the miner God and nature are one and the same, but Adam answers that God must be something more, something involving immortality.

Thinking thus, the two men go their separate ways, one to find more gold, the other to seek out, at Dismukes's bidding, a man and wife on the edge of Death Valley. Something is terribly wrong with the couple, she standing alone before his gorilla ways. Basic man can be worse than a wild animal, presumably because he has more brains to deliberately make himself worse. Such seems to be the case here. Maybe Adam can help.

Adam finds the couple living in a rude hut in a most perilous location, under a mountain with unstable rocks. They can roll down at any time, killing the occupants. To make matters worse, the husband, Elliot Virey, seems to have come unhinged and is deliberately loosening stones to roll down *near* the hut to terrify his wife, Magdalene. At first, she appears to have a martyr complex: she wants to stay in the most hellish location in the country, where her husband has brought her, and there be stoned to death. What's going on? Is a false bravado keeping her from the simple practicality of getting away?

She certainly does not want to exert herself and is surely impractical: she cannot even boil a potato. She is beautiful, a cultured woman, used to luxury, who once had had the world at her feet. Now it is literally going to come toppling down on top of her. She calls Adam *Sir* Wansfell meanwhile, as though she likes to have someone paying court to her, a knight fulfilling her every wish. And Adam with his wish to serve humanity—doing so is part of his atonement—cannot see that she may be subtly manipulating him. To him it seems that he has met "a wonderful woman who [is] going to love him, and a despicable man whom he [is] going to kill" (195).

Here is Grey's third lesson for Adam, about women and their ways. It is more difficult than the others, almost "a riddle beyond solving" (196). In his effort to understand this complex woman, one of "mind, passion, nobility, soul" (196), he tries to come to grips with her husband's motivation and gets an inkling that she must have terribly wronged him. This, in fact, is so: she has loved another man during their marriage and borne his daughter, Ruth, whom Virey for several years had thought his own. Then, his love became hate, and his vengeance horrendous. Magdalene, for her part, reveals her vein of iron: she will not have her husband underestimate her strength. She will accept all the punishment he can hand out with a "sublime effrontery" (198).

Adam ponders the situation and determines to aid Magdalene—to teach her "the victory of life [is] not to yield" willingly to death (199). She responds by desiring "to work" (200), that wonderful remedy in the Zane Grey medicine chest, and finds by enduring toil and pain as much as her frail self allows, she becomes no longer frail at all. She tells Adam the story of her life: that she broke her husband's heart and ruined him, that she had to give up her daughter, now age fourteen, to her father for safe-keeping. She herself is thirty-eight and still a "she-creature" of "illimitable emotion" (217, 210), but, he now knows, not the right woman for him.

A few months pass. The tension between Virey and Magdalene worsens, then flares up with the midsummer furnace winds from Death Valley. The deranged husband rolls enough rocks to start the whole hillside into an avalanche, burying and killing Magdalene. Adam escapes the landslide, but Virey tries to kill him too by sliding down individual stones, which Adam sidesteps while working his way around and above the vengeful killer. Then *he* rolls down stones to kill the killer, without success, though their actions cause the whole slope of stones to thunder down in a second avalanche, crushing Virey.

Sir Wansfell, the knightly wanderer, takes his weary way from this valley of derision and death, valor and victory. Before he leaves the region entirely, he comes across Dismukes prospecting for gold in a most grievous way. Five claim jumpers have taken over his operation and harnessed him to an *arrastra*, a treadmill machine that pulverizes rocks to free their veins of gold. He is the motive power, pacing round and round, whipped so that he will not slow down. Adam surprises and kills the jumpers (some being crushed in the mill) and releases Dismukes, squaring his debt with the miner, who had rescued him when he first began his desert sojourn.

Dismukes regains his full quota of gold and will begin his world travels. Adam is left to his wanderings. It seems to me that Grey could have ended the novel here. There is a sense of completion, a debt paid, and Adam has greatly fulfilled his earlier vow to "rise above wrongs and hate and revenge"

(91). Over the years he has discovered, as he recently told Magdalene, that what "helped [him] most was not to pass by anyone in trouble" (177). Perhaps the author might have used Dismukes's later return to the desert as an ending, for it supports Adam's estimate of the miner: "It's the gaining of gold—not what it might bring—that drives you" (138). It would also bear out the theme that one's journey through life is an end in itself.

Grey, however, has more adventures for the "wanderer," completely different ones, gentler ones, perhaps to reflect a fuller picture of humanity. Adam comes to rescue a fourteen-year-old girl, Genie Linwod, from kidnappers, and when her mother dies, raises her. They continue to live on the desert, at an oasis with cottonwoods and palms. Nature is attuned to Adam's new role of providing tender loving care to an orphan. It is springtime, the breeze is soft in the rustling palm leaves, flowers are blossoming, and the sky is a "velvety" blue. This is all so different from the "violent, harsh, and bitter" roles that destiny had previously given him (307).

Three years go by and Adam realizes he should settle Genie in a happy home in San Ysabel. He finds one with the Blair family, on a poor ranch run by kind Mrs. Blair and her twenty-year-old son, Gene. Adam, through Grey, learns yet another facet of the opposite sex: "Goodness [is] the commonest quality in the hearts of women" (391). He helps the Blairs financially. And here is a happy ending. Genie and Gene are attracted to each other—a romance is in the offing.

As for Adam, it is at San Ysabel that he meets Ruth Virey, daughter of Magdalene, now nineteen. They are also attracted to each other; he sees her as a "dreamful" girl of wonderful potential. "Be a woman!" he advises her, and she replies, "Stay—stay, desert man, and make me a woman!" (398–99). Unsure of himself, with fratricide still on his conscience, he responds by fleeing back into the desert, ponders his state, then heads to Picacho, the scene of his "crime," to take his punishment. Well, he finds his brother alive, we know, and on that note the story abruptly ends. Presumably Guerd is still able to cause more trouble for Adam and any relationship he has with a woman, this time passionate Ruth, and Grey needs another whole novel, *Stairs of Sand*, 1943, to definitively resolve the situation.

13

To the Last Man:
A Feud Mentality

Zane Grey carefully researched an actual family feud as background to his novel *To the Last Man*, 1922 (serialized in *The Country Gentleman*, 1921). It occurred in Arizona's Tonto Basin and was known locally as the Pleasant Valley War fought between two families, the Grahams and the Tewksburys. He first heard of it from a cattleman in New Mexico, then started asking old-timers about it, but they were rather noncommittal. His next step was to visit the area. This he did in 1918 but learned next to nothing from the Texans living there—it was among these people that the feud had occurred. A further visit, the next year, at least gained for him their friendship. It was only the following year, on his third visit, that he began learning the details. However, no two of his informers agreed on them, apart from the fact that only one man actually survived the fighting—hence, Grey's choice of title for his book.

The differences of opinion probably account for Grey's way of retelling the events, now described as a feud between the fictionally named Isbels and Jorths. There are two main "battles" involving all the male members, and a few neighbors, and some smaller skirmishes or shoot-outs among the survivors. We see them at firsthand through the author's omniscient perspective but then also as retold by a member of either faction, or both, and/or a bystander. In other words, we are getting different versions of the happenings as well as Grey's own psychological probe into them.

The original dispute goes back to the boyhood days of the principal combatants, Gaston Isbel and Lee Jorth, in Texas. We hear Isbel's version first, related to his youngest son, Jean. The two men were lifelong enemies, getting into scraps even when playing together as children. Then as young men they fell in love with the same girl, Ellen Sutton. Isbel won out but, when engaged to her, had to leave to join the South in the Civil War. During his absence, Jorth continued his courtship and married the girl. After the war, Isbel caught Jorth rustling his cattle. Gambling troubles between them led to Isbel's settling in Oregon, where he married, twice, and then moved to the Tonto Basin. Jorth later drifted into the same area but as a sheepman, trying to graze out Isbel's cattle range. The Hash Knife Gang riding up from Texas augmented the sheep faction. With no law in the valley, Isbel predicts a war between "honest ranchers against rustlers maskin' as sheep-raisers" (59).

Jorth's account, told to his daughter, Ellen, is that Isbel won over her mother at first because of his wealth ("but she loved me"); then charged him, her father, with rustling, made him out to be a cardsharp, and hounded him to ruin: "An' so help me God, it's got to be wiped out in blood!" (115). Grey's assessment is that Jorth's "morbid hate" had eaten into his heart like a parasite "that battened upon the life of its victim" (191). Really, this opinion applies to both men. But it is the women who suffer most. A daughter-in-law of Isbel complains that he is "draggin' in every relation" and "leav[in'] a lot of widows an' orphaned children!" (186). Jean's sister says simply, "It's awful! It's wrong! Wrong! Wrong!" (193).

The novel starts with twenty-four-year old Jean, a son who grew up in Oregon, heading to Arizona in early spring at the request of his father. Born of Isbel's second wife (with some Native blood), he is known as a crackshot and expert tracker, someone who can be of great help in the pending warfare. Almost at his destination he meets a sheepman's daughter, carrying a rifle—already a sign of forthcoming hostilities. But he is taken with her, and says so. She exclaims, "In these rags[!]" (13). This might be a typical feminine response to get further compliments, as Huck Finn would say, but the manner of her saying the words—"with a ... passion" (13)—shows her to be a caring and competent young woman: she does sew up tears in her outfit when she has anything to sew with. (Incidentally, *Huckleberry Finn*, 1884, also considers a prolonged deadly dispute between families, in which the two factions take their guns to church!—a comparable exposition of feud mentality.)

The woman is also fair-minded in saying that she thinks cattlemen in the local dispute with the sheepmen have the better case, although she adds, with spirit, that she will always be on her father's side. Jean wants to come round and see her again, so they introduce themselves before parting and find they are on opposite sides. She is Ellen Jorth, and "no Isbel can ever be a friend to [her]" (23). However, the two have a common bond, a profound affinity to nature. Ellen has just shown Jean a favorite view, a glorious spectacle of the Mogollon Rim; they both seem "under the spell of a vastness and loneliness and beauty and grandeur that could not but strike the heart" (19). Will they be "star-cross'd lovers" (*Romeo and Juliet*, Prologue) or deadly enemies?

Grey, so far, has a lighter, perhaps more natural, touch than usual, in recording the conversation of Ellen and Jean. He does not analyze the speech as he sometimes does but lets it "speak" for itself. We can make our own assessment of what lies behind the words; we do not feel forced as we read by being told what everything done and said *means*, no matter how apt or pertinent that information is. The author in effect is letting us use our own literary acumen—he has faith that we can and thus wins us over as readers. No matter how thorough and good his other writing is, these opening chapters of *To the Last Man* may be even better.

In them Grey also captures a person in just a few words in a Dickensian manner (cf. the portrait of the friendly waiter in *David Copperfield*, 1849–50). After Jean's homecoming we see the elder Isbel, competent and unshakable, in this phrase—"bareheaded, ... striding with long step." We see Jean's half-brothers, Bill and Guy, both "lean and rangy," and their wives, one a "stout, comely little woman, mother of three," the other, "young, a strapping girl, ... with wonderful lines of pain and strength on her face" (her family had been murdered when she was a child). Then there is his younger sister, Ann, engaged now and hugging Jean "in a way that took his breath," and Aunt Mary "delight[ed]" at his appetite at supper. The children, too, are portrayed, "all shy, yet all manifestly impressed by the occasion" (33–35, 39).

There is the wonderful scene after the meal when the children push the smallest of them to Uncle Jean to deliver "the question of tremendous importance": what presents did he bring? Jean plays along to add to the fun and makes them guess, then calls for his pack. When deposited, it jars the room, giving forth "metallic and rattling and crackling sounds." "Everybody stand back," he cautions and then, keeping them in suspense, gives nearly a one-page account of the history of the pack—being stolen on shipboard; carried by burro, stage, and freighter; bucked off by a mountain mule.... Finally the treasures are spilled onto the floor, where they lie, "too magical to be touched at first, [while] the two little boys and their sister simply kne[el]" (36–38) (here, cf. the Cratchits in *A Christmas Carol*, 1843). Of course, there are presents for the grown-ups too, and Jean reserves one package, of the several he had planned to give Ann, for Ellen. (It contains something to wear.)

The joyful family gathering is not out of place in the book. Grey is showing us what family life can be, should be, when a member's selfish, rabid hatred has not corrupted it into the horrors to be revealed shortly.

Meanwhile, Jean calls on Ellen with his gift. Isbel has called her a hussy, but Ann has mollified that appraisal by claiming she is lonely and unhappy, living with rough men: "Maybe she's wild. But she's honest" (70). Her wildness is shown when at the agreed-upon meeting place, a high promontory on the Rim, she remains hidden, concealed by a pine thicket nearby. Her ears are those of a listening deer as she waits, intensely curious to see whether he will come, yet ashamed of her eagerness to see him.

When he arrives, he waits till sunset in vain. Grey has ample time to describe Ellen's changing feelings (in ten pages), her self-examination regarding them, her assessment of a possible relationship with an Isbel. She, at eighteen, feels "very young, very shy, very strange" in turn. She hates Jean because he obviously expected her to come, softens toward him from "an intangible something ... that was too deep for her understanding" (82), then feels repugnance again at his very name. And yet "What's in a name?" we might ask, recalling those other lovers of feuding families, Romeo and Juliet (2.2.43).

Jean eventually departs, leaving the gift behind. Ellen's first reaction is "What effrontery!" and she kicks the package about, toward the campfire where it can burn up, but she has second thoughts and goes to bed without destroying it or opening it. There will be time enough after she gets home with it from the sheep station. On the way she stops to chat with old John Sprague, a onetime prospector—they like to confide in each other. Indeed, Sprague is one disinterested bystander who provides updates on the developing feud. Now he tells Ellen how Jean badly beat up a sheepman, Simm Bruce, at the Grass Valley store for speaking disparagingly of her. This knowledge prompts her to open the package and cherish its contents—two pairs of fine shoes (and four pairs of stockings), hardly a gift to *kick* about. She also calls Bruce a liar when we get his own account of the fight later, although she is still determined to stand by her father, whatever happens in the feud. In the meantime, she keeps busy at many tasks, "thus earning the poise and peace of labor" (123), a theme Grey emphasizes in most of his books.

But Ellen's poise cannot be maintained with a new course of events. Her father presents her with a horse that he claims he traded for. It is actually Jean's stolen horse, and Jean *gives* her the animal later. However, words between the two of them lead to other words, to yet harsher words, to his bursting out that Lee Jorth is a horse thief. (Grey is excellent in depicting the "righteous and terrible scorn" of both of them in this rising argument.) It is then that Ellen feels a "wild, fierce passion to hurt" him because she knows he is right—"to rend, to flay, to fling back upon him a stinging agony." She takes a ruthless satisfaction in trying to kill his faith in her, and lies that she has had many men as lovers (128–138).

The first battle of the feud occurs in late June. Jorth's men—including his two brothers, the Hash Knife Gang, and storeman Greaves—ride out to the Isbel ranch. There are eleven of them. The Isbels are supported by two neighbors. They take shelter in the main cabin. When the sheepmen invaders set out to steal some horses from the nearby pasture, Guy Isbel and neighbor Jacobs rush out to bring them in but are shot dead. Their bodies cannot be recovered because of the steady gunfire. That night under cover of darkness, Jean evens the score by getting behind the enemy line and shooting one sniper and knifing Greaves. All is described in raw and grisly detail, particularly the death of the storeman. Jean stabs him twice, the first time for insulting Ellen. He cannot believe in his heart of hearts that she is but a hussy.

The next day the Jorths get revenge by breaking a fence so that the enclosed hogs can get at the bodies of Guy and Jacobs—a horrifying scene. When the Isbel men do not rush out, the two wives do and bury their husbands. The men of both sides, stunned, cease their fire. Grey scholar Carlton Jackson says that the true heroic characters of the book are women (75).

Ellen, meanwhile, had been left alone when the Jorth men had ridden off. The solitude was a relief for her. She had taken to the woods, where a storm came up with clouds "clustering and darkening at last to form a great, purple, angry mass that ... burst into dazzling streaks of lightning" (221). It had no terror for her, for it eased the turmoil within her. Her storm consisted of the remembrance of the dastardly lie she had told Jean.

So it is with some relief that she sees Sprague again, with more news for her. She hears, and we hear again, about the first Jorth-Isbel fight. She is most concerned about Jean, and when she hears what he said on killing Greaves, and what her father said when he heard about it, that "there's one Isbel who's a man" (226) (something we didn't know before), she is dumbfounded. Then when Sprague, with his old-age, far-seeing wisdom, says that Jean must love her "terribly" and believes her good, she has a sensation of being lifted by an invisible power.

She has to fly, to sail, to run, and she flings herself onto Jean's horse and is off, flying down lonely wilderness trails. The ensuing seven pages to the end of the chapter (227–34) are an amazing portrayal of a young woman's re-awakened feelings in relation to the man of her life. She needs the fast movement, the wind fanning her hot face. Is she escaping from her scornful self? The sky is now "gloomed by purple and silver cloud, shadowed by gray storm, and in the west brightened by golden sky," reflecting her changing emotions. The brightness is hers, she loves Jean, and she rides on—to the promontory, her favorite view, where she once waited for him in secret. She crawls again into the covert, face down, hands clutching pine needles. Her life is "sensorial..., elemental, primitive"; she abandons herself to nature, to an "intense and exquisite preoccupation of the senses, unhindered and unburdened by thought." But when thought does break through, she thinks she again is under gloomy skies; she has killed this love with a vile lie. She falls flat once more upon her pine-needle bed and grovels there "in agony that can[not] bear the sense of light."

Later that night after Ellen has returned home, she is awakened by three fugitives from the return engagement of the Isbel-Jorth feud. We already know that it took place at the store, of stone construction, where the Jorths had holed up. There Isbel challenged Jorth to come out and settle the whole affair by themselves, man-to-man. They attempted to do so but someone in the store shot and killed Isbel. Isbel's men decided to create some diversion at the back entrance (by Jean outside) while the others crashed into the front. Most of the Jorth group were killed, including Jorth himself, and several Isbel supporters too.

The fugitives force Ellen to flee with them to a secret hideout in the forested canyon country to the north, where another escapee awaits them. Only now does Ellen learn about the second battle—another version, this from Colter, the most devious of the group. He tells her, falsely, that Jean brutally killed her father. She wonders what life can have in store for her, what misery, but knows that she cannot help loving Jean Isbel.

Days go by. Colter is always bothering her—making advances, wanting her to ride off with him. He and the others are also scouting the territory for signs of the trailing Isbel force. When it draws near, Colter grasps a violently struggling Ellen, swings her onto his horse, and gallops off. There is a barrage of gunfire and the horse is shot, but Colter, dragging his hostage along on foot, escapes into denser timber. Now there are separate skirmishes; more are killed, including Jean's half-brother Bill, whom Ellen sees alone before he dies. He gives her a true account of Lee Jorth's death.

Individual manhunts follow, vividly described. Finally, the Isbel faction is down to the last man, Jean. He has no ammunition left but still carries his knife, and has a bleeding left forearm wound. Colter is also alive as is his buddy, Springer. They still have horses to ride and chase Jean. Much weakened by lack of food and sleep these last days, he stumbles upon the empty hideout cabin and, hearing hoofbeats, climbs up an inside ladder into the loft for refuge.

Colter and Ellen arrive, she still holding off his coarse advances. Grey has a penchant for being overly graphic in gruesome scenes. The author seems called upon in such instances not only to indicate what is happening but also, so to speak, to twist the knife's handle, as if he, the author, does not know when to stop. This is what critics blandly call his overwriting, readers his "overkill." Please, Zane Grey, leave something for the imagination: the happenings you have so carefully built up into a wrenching climax are dramatic enough—as what ensues in the final episode of *To the Last Man*.

Springer rides up and Colter goes out for the latest news of Jean. Ellen, inside, rests her hand on a ladder rung and, horrified, sees a bloody smear on that hand: Jean is above, waiting, but in what shape? Colter returns, notices Ellen's bloody hand, looks about slowly, then whips out his gun and starts climbing the ladder. Ellen screams, snatches up her rifle and shoots Colter, twice, the second time when he catches hold of the rifle barrel. Springer hears the shots, rushes in to see what is the matter, and Jean, above, with a tiger's spring, lands on top of him. There is no knife-handle twisting here. Grey concludes this final skirmish and the whole Isbel-Jorth warfare with just ten short words: "Jean lunged forward with a single sweep of his arm" (310).

Ellen rushes outside, in shock really, and falls on her knees. Jean joins her, but cannot lift her up with his crippled arm, so drops to his knees too. It is fit posture of thankfulness for the end of the horrific feud, and for the beginning of the smooth course of their true love. As with the little children, earlier in the book, and the wondrous moment of new gifts before them, they "simply kne[el]" (38).

14

The Call of the Canyon: Going Home

In 1940 a Western song by Billy Hill, "The Call of the Canyon," made the Hit Parade (it was a follow-up to his hits of "The Last Roundup" and "Empty Saddles" from the previous decade). Before that, in 1921, Zane Grey had written his novel of the same title, had it serialized in *Ladies' Home Journal* that same year and into the next, and published as a book in 1924. (Titles cannot be copyrighted, hence Hill's capitalizing on a name already known to the public.)

The song, like most Hit Parade tunes, is essentially a love song, and Grey's book is essentially a love story with a Western setting. But the author depicts no cattle-range disputes, no gunplay, and just one fight, the loser being knocked into a sheep-dip. What is dramatized are themes Grey felt important—the treatment of World War I veterans and loss of old ideals and values during the subsequent Roaring Twenties.

The story begins New Year's Eve, 1918, in New York. The heroine, Carley Burch, age twenty-six, and Glenn Kilbourne, returned from the war at age twenty-seven, shell-shocked and gassed, are watching the holiday celebrations from a high-rise apartment. Grey describes the crowds below as "thoughtless," like "contending columns of ants," crying out their "strife and agony" (2–3). At least this is Glenn's reaction: continuing to live in such an environment will not help *him*. Although he and Carley had become engaged before the war, he now tells her he is leaving for the West (the red rock country at Oak Creek in Arizona) to recover his health, body and mind. They will keep in touch.

Out West, he fights another kind of battle, on his own. He finds that he is good for something, that hard physical work is a mender of souls— even if it is just raising hogs, the first work offered him. After all, the government he had fought for had left him to starve, to "die for all it cared" (4).

Grey refers to this situation throughout the book—he will not spare the government—but nowhere stronger than in Glenn's own outburst much later. "I came home a wreck," he says, and what did the government, the employers, his fellow citizens do for him?—"nothing!" (169). The author treats the case symbolically too, when a bald eagle, "the regal bird you see with America's stars and stripes," flies off with one of Glenn's suckling pigs, "degrad[ing] [it]self to the level of a coyote" (173). Strong words, indeed!

From Arizona, Glenn writes to Carley that his love for her when they were first engaged was selfish and immature, but he has found himself in the West; his love for her has grown better. Carley's concern, really the plot of the whole book, is whether she can develop her love correspondingly. She lives a life of luxury, excitement, glitter, and gadding about, her aunt tells her (and that is exactly the lifestyle that Glenn was trying to get away from). Nevertheless, she resolves to go West herself, to bring him back to her world.

Her observations en route are interesting to the reader; for example, she sees a lot of flat land and muses that it would be great country for automobile roads—yes, to speed around on at sixty miles an hour, we learn elsewhere, in 1919 model cars. She still lives in the fast lane. But she has some detached self-awareness too, seeing herself as a "spoiled doll of luxury!" (16). Grey also uses her trip for some of his own comments about forests despoiled by money grubbers.

Carley looks at the wild surroundings of Oak Creek Canyon: the bare rock walls, towering pine trees, and rushing water. It is the first time she has ever taken note of anything natural—but not much, for she reflects that these things really have nothing to do with her. When she sees Glenn, Grey shows us the difference that has developed between the two as his strong work-worn hand grasps her soft little one. Can their two worlds really come together? All that is wrong with her, she thinks, is that she needs to be loved. She thinks only of what someone else can do for her, not what she can do for that someone. When Glenn asks her how she expects to please her husband, she replies, "Why—by marrying him, I suppose" (70).

Yet she is a good sport, puts up with some of the typical Western tomfoolery played on her, and agonizingly sticks on her horse over a twenty-five-mile ride. All the time she is becoming more aware of the awesome beauty around her. European scenery now is like "operetta settings"; even her native New England landscapes are but "pastorals." Here, the "immensity of the West seem[s] flung at her," and she feels "uncomfortable," although recognizing it as wonderful and glorious (110–11). She is beginning to feel, somewhat, "the call of the canyon."

She later buys a section of land nearby, in secret, a future present for Glenn, who favors the location, knowing that he will always love the West, will want to visit it occasionally once they are living happily married in the East and that she herself could stand Arizona for a month or so "at long intervals" (167).

Meanwhile, she has Flo Hutter to think about, a Western girl who also loves her constant, persevering Glenn. Flo had recognized the wreck he was and helped a little to save him, a good enough reason for loving him. For Carley, it is a "humiliating shock" (133) to realize that she has been thinking of herself all along, instead of the man she "loves." Glenn is patient with her: sometimes seeing depths in her, possibilities under her "idle attitude toward life" (153); at other times only a little "kid" (171).

A more brash assessment comes from a brawny sheepman, aptly named Haze Ruff, who bluntly tells her, "You're not what a *hombre* like me calls either square or game" (151), and rides off. His judgment, apparent before, has for her "some peculiar, unanswerable power" (148). Grey keeps showing the workings of Carley's mind—her thoughts that "germinate subconsciously" (162), tides beating at the "gate of her intelligence" (164), "miasmas" fading away (175). Now, he lets her realize that it is "self, self, all self" (178) actuating her.

However, she cannot reconcile herself to living in the West permanently; Glenn, on the other hand, will never leave. Hating herself, she goes back East; Glenn remains behind, hoping…. Grey writes: "Stumbling and breathless, she hurried on" (182). It is stumbling not ahead, but backward really, to the "damned round of things [she] was born to" (181). The author is just excellent in describing this breakup, in dialogue and commentary.

It is true to human nature that once Carley departs, is on the train and traveling away, she appreciates even more the beauty of what she is leaving, in her case the western sunsets. The first night she sees: "Banks of broken clouds hung to the horizon, like continents and islands and reefs set in a turquoise sea" (183), and the next night "clouds … like thick, heavy smoke, mushrooming, coalescing, forming and massing …—a vast canopy of shell pink, a sun-fired surface" (165).

Yet her first statement to her friends on the station platform back home is "I—I hated the West. It [is] so raw—so violent—so big. I think I hate it more—now" (189). The hesitant start to her declaration, her pauses, her use of "think," and the add-on of "now" all point to a hasty rationalization of her position or perhaps a hiding of her true feelings or, most likely, an accurate exposition of very confused emotions. She needs to settle into some routine.

Her plan is to keep busy—and forgetting, glad of the fight ahead to occupy her body and mind. She steels herself with all the "pride and vanity and fury" of a defeated woman who scorns defeat (192). But she has no illusions about herself, not about the people she associates with. She sees them as having no real work nor any ideals—time wasters, all of them. And she—she loves Glenn still—"Oh, my God! If I were honest, I'd cry out the truth!" (202).

Then she gets a letter from him, urging her to see a fellow veteran, Virgil Rust, lying sick in a hospital in New York. The tone of the letter tells Carley that her hog farmer still cares for her, however apart their worlds are, and now at least she has something worthwhile to do. And she changes her mindset. She will give herself up to remembrance rather than useless months of trying to forget. What she does not realize is that in visiting Glenn's friend, and the other sick veterans in the hospital, cheering them up, she is taking her *first* step in thinking about the welfare of others.

A complication arises, however. In her visits over several weeks, Rust brightens up and continually praises her for standing by Glenn, unaware that she has broken up with him. She becomes unstrung, knowing she has let him believe a lie, and tells him the truth. Through Rust, then, she has to admit publicly, and not just to herself, how selfish she has been. There is now only scorn in Rust's eyes, and Grey's fine writing depicts her feelings: "Carley fled. She could scarcely see to find the car. All her internal being convulsed, and a deadly faintness made her sick and cold" (219). At last she knows that she cannot escape from herself, that she will have to change. This is a step, too, in accepting Glenn's world.

The Grosset & Dunlap dust-jacket blurb about this book says immediately: "This is Zane Grey at his best." Readers of the first half of the volume might disagree, feeling that the plot drags somewhat, that the descriptions of nature are overlong. As an amateur naturalist myself, I glory in the descriptions, and forge ahead, but will acknowledge that in these last episodes, and subsequent chapter 10, we have some of Grey's most powerful writing.

Carley's world, what the author calls her "edifice of hopes ... and struggles," has to fall; a "passionate repudiation" of self must occur before she can become a new Carley (220). Rust has thrown "a white, illuminating light" (221) on what is really her desertion of Glenn, and Grey uses a Biblical image to describe this returning of nothing to a man who has given all in the war: "Stone for bread! Betrayal for love! Cowardice for courage!" (221) (see Matthew 7:9).

And so Carley begins to be haunted by recollections of Oak Creek Canyon, the sensuous appeal it had in sights, sounds, and odors to awaken her primal self, to renew her being. She sees again the turreted canyon walls, hears winds moaning, and smells wet earth and wood smoke. All this is background to her "contending passions [giving] birth to vague, slow-forming revolt" (221).

Although she has returned to her old life, it provides no forgetfulness nor any pleasure. She is restless and critical. The upshot is a blunt rejection of a new suitor, some straight talk with her best friend about women's role in society and the dominance of fashion in their lives (Carley speaks for free will and idealism as determinants of women's lives, not chance and materialism), and finally an avoidance of the high society crowd.

Hence, she reads, with winter's coming, devouring books on the war. This gives Grey an opportunity to make a final comment on the subject, on war itself, and not just the veterans' welfare: "It was monstrous and hideous. If nature and evolution proved the absolute need of strife, war, blood, and death in the progress of animal and man toward perfection, then it would be better to abandon this Christless code and let the race of man die out" (240–41).

When spring comes, with the whole atmosphere of awakening life, Carley happens to fall in with her old crowd again. One of the women taunts her by saying there is nothing wrong with life in old New York. And Carley blows up. Her rant, building up in her over the long winter, lasts a full two pages. "Nothing wrong when...," she explodes and goes on to list a dozen wrongs, all beginning with the same three-word opening. She mentions crippled soldiers, inadequate education, mocking of prohibition (Grey was a teetotaler), sex exploitation in movies and magazines, and the god money. She finishes with another half a dozen wrongs listed directly. "You doll women," she calls her audience, "you parasites, ... you painted idle, purring cats" (249).

The next day, if not the same, Carley bursts into her aunt's quarters, with a "Look at me.... I'm going back West to marry Glenn and live his life!" (250). The aunt tells her she has found herself at last. And that could be the end of the book, but Grey wants to show whether she has really changed and is indeed thinking of others as she should. There is a hint that she has not, for even in this instance she, at first, has not given any thought to her old aunt's welfare in her absence. With that resolved, Carley is off.

When she arrives, she finds Glenn gone to the Tonto Basin on business, away for a month, and decides to have some work done on her own section of land to make it more livable. By June, with its "vast creamy-white columnar clouds roll[ing] up from the horizon, like colossal ships with bulging sails," she feels rejuvenated, her pulse quickened, her senses intensified. She is one with the earth, a product of it, a woman no longer "blind to her meaning, her power, her mastery." And she senses an "unutterable happiness" (270–71).

Then she gets the latest news from a grinning ranch hand: Glenn has married Flo Hutter. She is shocked, almost out of consciousness, wandering dazedly about for most of the next night. But the strength she has gained from her transformation remains to bolster her in the depth of her disappointment. She has to face the issue at hand—not without, however, an initial burst of hateful female energy at her fate, an unreasoning primitive passion.

The next morning she faces herself in a mirror and, in contrast to her former breakup with Glenn, tells herself, "Go on! Not backward—nor to the depths—but up—upward!" (278). Riding out to the height of land, she sees her new world and takes heart at the mass of mountain, its strength a kind of defiance to things. She resolves to endure and rides down to Oak Creek Canyon to congratulate the new couple—and finds Glenn alone, *un*married, warmly welcoming, waiting to be *her* bridegroom. The false news had been the ranch hand's queer joke, just another bit of Western tomfoolery for her to put up with.

15
The Vanishing American:
A Thoreauvian Native

The Vanishing American represents Zane Grey's strongest pro-Native stance. Some critics, such as Carlton Jackson, consider it his finest novel. Certainly it is the book that Grey wished to be remembered by. In fact, the author was so sympathetic to Native Americans and correspondingly so scathing of Federal Indian Agents, inept and/or uncaring in looking after their charges, that there was considerable controversy in even having the story published. Furthermore, Grey sketched such a horrific picture of the treatment provided by missionaries, working hand-in-glove with the agents on the Navajo Reservation in northeastern Arizona, that after the story was first serialized in *Ladies' Home Journal,* 1922, public furor dictated that Harper & Brothers demand that he make changes before they published it in 1925. The principal alteration was that the Native hero, Nophaie, not marry Marian, a white woman, at the end of the book. Fortunately, Grey's original manuscript was published fifty-seven years later, in 1982. It is this version presented here (and quotations stem from the Pocket Books edition).

The story opens with young Nophaie, age seven, tending his father's sheep. Such responsibility is not beyond him, for he has already shown remarkable bravery and fortitude, his heritage being that of a chieftain. He is also "unconsciously and unutterably happy," living in simple harmony with nature, where he feels the "infinite beauty and poetry of his life" (5). He is like a very young Wordsworth, "trailing clouds of glory" ("Ode: Intimations...," 187).

Into this idyllic state come white people—first, some ruffians, who kidnap him; then, some do-gooding tourists, who "rescue" him and place him in school and college, the Carlisle Indian School in Pennsylvania, for eighteen years, where he becomes an exceptional student and sports star (shades of Jim Thorpe) and where he meets and falls in love with Marian Warner (and she with him). Upon graduation in 1915, however, he does not follow up his studies with some scholarly or athletic career, but returns to his home reservation, dresses in plain buckskin and corduroy, speaks no English, and is again a Native American.

He writes Marian from there the next year and knowing that she longs "for wild and lonely places" (13), asks her to come out and teach on the reservation. She, always yearning to do "something different, unusual, big" (20) and hating the breakdown of society's morals during World War I (although the United States is not yet a participant), heads West. Nophaie has already told her of the missionaries sowing "fear, doubt, distrust, and hate" among his people (14). She will learn of worse things—rape and the misappropriating of Native land.

Marian first meets Mr. and Mrs. John Withers, trading-post operators, at Kaidab (Grey's name for Kayenta). They are fictional representatives of John and Louisa Weatherill, from whom Grey obtained most of his information about conditions on the reservation. In his general criticism of the missionaries at that time, he feels that their efforts to convert the Natives to Christianity have been futile: not one has become truly Christian. The faith is just too different from their own, developed over the centuries to fit their lifestyle. They are "children of nature" (41); their own religion "is best for [them]" (103). However, the *caring* missionaries have done some good, and he singles out the Catholic priests in this category. (Perhaps, the rituals of their religion are something the Natives' own faith allows them to appreciate.) Only one other missionary faith is mentioned, when a Mennonite demands payment for a service not rendered.

From Kaidab, Marian leaves by mule train for Nophaie's home, a difficult two-and-a-half-day trip through desert and canyon country. Two chapters are needed to describe the journey, giving Grey ample opportunity to describe the intervening landscape, which he does well, although some readers may think this description to be overly long. The author is really emphasizing the long *cultural* gap that needs to be bridged between the two main characters: "The splendid spectacle, the fragrance of sage, the cold air, so untainted, the marvelous purple of the undulating desert, ... naked expanse of rock ...—these stirred in Marian the emotion of [awe].... How wild and free! ... [L]oneliness and solitude reigned" (87). Can she adapt to life in such surroundings? Nophaie is living in poverty.

Their greetings are amiable but somewhat reserved. "Must we get acquainted all over?" she asks (80). Actually, their love has been seasoning into a maturer kind of happiness in each other than when they were a year or two younger. She feels she should help him, but how? She must move slowly. Her first "adaptation" is loping beside him on the gift horse he has given her (that instead of the plodding journey of the past few days). And she finds the new pace has "changed everything, her sensations, the scenery, the colors and smells, the feel of the wind" (89). So far, so good. She wishes to range the countryside and "forget the world" (89), that is, leave behind her former life.

Marian is gaining something of Nophaie's sensuous awareness of place. She begins to understand something of Withers's comment: "places have more to do with happiness than people." Nophaie adds this further explanation: "Human nature is imperfect. Places are true. Nature itself is evolution—an inexorable working for perfection." His words reveal something new in the make-up of the man, the "strange combination of his Indian nature developed by white man's intellect" (90), and Marian divines that such a combination may create difficulties for him, and for her too.

Nophaie has taken to living in a red-earth and cedar-branch hogan furnished only with an Indian blanket and sheepskin for a bed. His work is tending a small flock of a few hundred sheep and goats across a sage-cedar upland. Will such occupation be satisfying for him over time? And how will she fit in? She strips some leaves from a sprig of sage and presses them to her nose and lips—her growing sensuousness. Their sweet fragrance and bitter taste are symbolic of her status—this simple life is sweet at present but may be bitter to experience if prolonged into the future.

She resolves to teach in the Native school at Mesa (Grey's name for Tuba City, seventy miles southwest of Kayenta). Headquartered there are missionary Morgan and Indian agent Blucher, the two villains of the story. Morgan is a sexual predator of the young girls at his school, ever masking his actions with the "Old Book" (131) (Bible); Blucher is a dispenser of federal funds in running the reservation, ofttimes withholding a large share for his private use. Nophaie says they run their affairs, not for Natives or government, but for "themselves" (105). Marian, without intending to, becomes a kind of spy into their activities, reporting on them to Nophaie by letter or in secret meetings.

He is strengthened by this white woman's love for him and her work to help his people. But he still has his own major problems: his religious status of infidel. He cannot accept the Native American God (his white upbringing killed it), and he will not believe in white man's religion (not when propounded by such corrupt missionaries as he has seen). One and only one thing of sanctity is left him—"a love of all nature" (115).

For this love he can thank, in part, his Native heritage and its closeness "to elemental life, to primitive instincts" (285). He is akin here to naturalist Henry David Thoreau, who ever sought to inculcate more of an instinctive, western life into his conscious, civilized one; he spoke for "anything that implies a simpler mode of life and greater nearness to the earth" (14:88) (all Thoreau quotations are from his *Journal*, 14 vols., unless specified otherwise).

A further look at the many parallels between Grey's title protagonist and the Concord naturalist is called for. There is no evidence that Grey ever read Thoreau and so could have been influenced by him, but he, like his predecessor, felt the same nearness to the earth, the outdoors. Frank Gruber, author of Grey's official biography, refers to nature's "abnormal attraction" to the novelist even as a boy, his liking nothing better than a tramp through the woods amid the solitude there (10, 18). Jean Karr, another biographer, says that Grey never lost his sense of wonder over the outdoor world (xvii), and Carlton Jackson is more explicit in affirming that that world gave him "a sort of transcendental experience of unity with nature" (133).

There may be a common literary source for Grey's and Thoreau's similar ideas on the concept of man's unity with nature (and on the mystical experience leading to this oneness, to be discussed later). Both were readers of Wordsworth, to whom, we know, "the meanest flower that blows can give / Thoughts that do often lie too deep for tears" ("Intimations Ode," 191). With Wordsworth, sensuous perception could lead to an experience of suspended *being*—a part of the natural world. In *The Excursion*, 1814, he wrote of a boy holding a seashell to his ear; by listening "intensely," he feels "mysterious union with the native sea." Such experience makes one "brightened with joy" (4.1137–40).

Jackson discovered, through a perusal of Grey's diary, that the author wished to read any book "until thoroughly imbued with the power and thought of the writer" (136). And one of the writers that he believed should be read every day was Wordsworth. That Grey read him regularly is suggested by his saying that he experienced a "Wordsworthian uplift" during a change of weather (136). It seems likely that he was "imbued" with, or at least attuned to, some of the poet's thoughts, shared also by the Concord naturalist.

Much of their joint feeling about nature is delineated in the character of Nophaie. Nophaie's white man's education enables him to see how modern progress is destroying the rugged simplicity of his people's customary life, a life of peace and contentment where "wants [are] few" (115). "Superfluous wealth can buy superfluities only," Thoreau would have remarked, as he does in *Walden* (329). Nature is what they need; in fact, they can never have enough of it.

And Nophaie's Native heritage has made him "singularly acute," like Thoreau, "in all his sensorial perceptions" (115). Frequently he surrenders himself wholly to sensations—"watching, listening, feeling, smelling perception that engender[s] happiness" (313). For instance, he notes the "pink glow" suffusing a "steely, blue sky," hears the "song of a mockingbird, the yelp of a coyote, the scurrying of a cottontail," and smells the "wood smoke" from Native hogans, all while climbing up a "wind-scalloped and rain-carved" rocky slope (309). (Thoreau typically "imbibe[d] delight through every pore" while outdoors [*Walden*, 129]).

One natural phenomenon singled out by both Nophaie and Thoreau as something particularly to be excited about is what the Concord saunterer termed the "drama" of a landscape (4:78), its kaleidoscopic cloud cover. The Indian, charmed as Grey describes him, gazes at "soft clouds, creamy and silver where the rays str[ike], ... and shading to purple where the thick mushrooming, billowy rolls [reach] to the blue zenith" (8); or at clouds, "fleecy, like wisps of coral in a turquoise sea ... — clouds of pearl and alabaster, and higher in the intense blue, smoky wreaths of delicate mauve, and bossy beaten masses of burnished bronze" (203).

Both men are so overwhelmed by the grandeur of nature that man seems, that they themselves feel, dwarfed by its magnificence. To Nophaie, the "silent [canyon] walls, ... the deep shadows, ... the vast heave of the mountain rock, and the infinite sky above, ... [bring] a sense of littleness of all living things" (201). He feels like Thoreau, who suggested that man with the (snow-covered) earth beneath and the whitish winter sky above him seemed "but a black speck inclosed in a white egg-shell" (11:445). And each observer has a sense of doubleness, an ability to stand apart from himself and see that self in the scene. Nophaie imagines he is a soaring eagle whose strong vision clearly sees the world below, even a "lonely statuesque figure of man — the Indian — Nophaie — strange, pitifully little" (206–7); Thoreau, in peering at an insect in *Walden*, was reminded of a greater force looking down at him, "the human insect" (332).

But Nophaie's reaction, unlike Thoreau's, is unsettling, for he sees himself as "the mystery of life thrown against the stark background of age-old earth." The word "stark" has grim or desolate overtones — as does a further description of his continued gaze. He is "like a shipwrecked mariner on his spar-strewn sinking deck." "Spar-strewn" suggests disorder, and "sinking" a hopelessness. Nophaie is left alone in his "abasement," with "burden unlifted" (207). Thoreau, on the other hand, could see himself as "drift-wood in the stream"; being so was not debasing but an opportunity to attain a desired closeness to the natural world. "I go and come with a strange liberty in Nature," he wrote, "a part of herself" (*Walden*, 135, 129).

Nophaie longs for such freedom, lost during his upbringing in white society. But by relegating himself to prolonged isolated sojourns in the wilderness, he is able to confront his primal self and re-establish the feeling of kinship with nature, as befits his Native heritage. The earth again is his "mother" and he a "comrade" of the rocks as he sees with "renewed eyes" (221, 317). He senses a comforting familial connection, just as Thoreau did in the previous century when he exclaimed, "Of thee, O earth, are my bone and sinew made; to thee, O sun, am I brother" (3:95).

For Nophaie, and Thoreau, there is an opportunity to gain mystic insight. Thoreau's particular nature mysticism I have elsewhere termed a "super-sensuousness" (*Spirit*, 107): a state in which an intense steeping in sensations, visual or otherwise, gives way to visionary perception. There are obvious parallels in Nophaie's experience, which may also be termed super-sensuous. Author Grey says his character attains a kind of "thoughtlessness": he lies "with the absorbed senses of the Indian tranced in their singular capacity of absolute thoughtlessness. He d[oes] not think. He fe[els]" (146).

"Unconsciously" he still *sees* the dome of sky, the pale gray obscurity of sage and hills; *smells* the fallen leafage, the hint of rain; and *tastes* the breath of living things. His ears *hear* "the sounds of silence—nothing but the vast low thrumming of nature" (Thoreau, we note, heard "the unspeakable" [4:472]—the grand rhythm of the universe). He *feels* the "immortality around him, the ... life all about him in stones and woods, ... fe[els] the vast earth under him." And he is "unutterably happy" while the trance lasts (146–47).

Nophaie, like his real-life counterpart, is here not overly concerned with philosophizing about this deity. His prime concern is to *experience* nature— and the spiritual presence, however manifested. This fine passage from *The Vanishing American*, describing a Native's sensuous response to sunrise and sunset, would also have been Thoreau's reaction: "From the invisible center of his surroundings breathes the potency of creation, the divine essence, the secret. At sunrise the Indian stands entranced in adoration of the renewed burst of light, facing the east, with his prayer on his lips. At sunset he watches the departing glory of the lord of day, silent, rapt, his soul absorbing that golden effulgence" (157). Thoreau himself wrote that the sun rises with a clash of cymbals to tell him the world is newly created ("A Winter Walk," 58); the sun sets as the "most gorgeous sight in nature" (2:296).

Nophaie, then, in his character exhibits many traits that Thoreau admired or embodied himself. Nophaie represents in part that "Wildness" in which, according to Thoreau's famous pronouncement, "is the preservation of the world" ("Walking," 202).

As we see in the course of the novel, Nophaie does his utmost to preserve a sane world. He rescues a fourteen-year-old girl, Gekin Yashi, from the clutches of Morgan by stealing her away from the mission school and hiding her among some faraway Natives. It costs him all his sheep to engage them in this service so that he becomes a "wanderer of the sage" (141). The plan ultimately fails, but Nophaie is heralded as a hero by reservation inhabitants for defying white corruption. When the girl is recaptured by the missionary's henchmen, Nophaie bursts into the school and subdues Morgan, and Blucher, and exhibits his superb athletic skill by kicking them about like so many footballs. He scorns "to soil [his] heathen red hands on such dirty beasts" (196). Even mild-mannered Marian is held in thrall by the spectacle, but she prevents Nophaie from outright killing them. He must go into hiding in any case.

On April 6, 1917, the United States declares war on Germany. Nophaie comes out of seclusion to enlist, encouraging many able-bodied Natives to go overseas with him. There he wins the Distinguished Service Medal before the war ends. On coming home, he meets one of his former Carlisle teachers, who declares how "Indian soldiers," having served their country so well on the battlefield, should now be better treated. In this man's authoritative words, Grey presents his own opinion: Native Americans should have the right to live among white men or on "unmolested" land of their own; no more bureaucratic reservations—they are obsolete! Make the Natives free with full citizenship (283–84). Nophaie adds—and let their religion alone (285).

Nophaie's return home coincides with the influenza epidemic sweeping the country. Three thousand of his people die, and he himself contracts the disease though his strong constitution withstands the "wind of death," and Marian whispers, "Oh, thank God" (304). After sufficient recovery he rides off to be alone with nature, a healing time physically, also a spiritual quest to dispel his atheism, a pilgrimage to find his God. There he hopes to gain peace, lose his bitterness about, and desire for revenge against, such men as Morgan and Blucher.

Nophaie rides for seven days in order to reach Naza, the great stone bridge, "rainbow hue[d]" (319), god of his people. His education makes him at first see it as "only a ... scarred masterpiece of nature." True, his earlier revealed nature mysticism had led to "some acquaintance with the All," in Thoreau's words (9:246). He had pondered the question: "might there not be a spirit in nature infinite and everlasting?" (190); he had seen its "soul" gleaming through the "painted windows" of natural phenomena (207–8). On the one hand, he seems to be a pantheist in (literally) sensing a presence or deity everywhere about him (the notion of immanence). But to him, and Thoreau, this presence is also something distinct and apart (the notion of transcendence), "an invisible spirit hovering over all" (146). Then, he could be considered a pan*en*theist, like Thoreau, in entertaining a two-faceted view of "God."

Now, at Naza, Nophaie spends a twenty-four-hour vigil. He comes to realize that the great sandstone bridge is "not imperishable[,]" that it "must in time pass away in tiny grains of sand." Just so, some of his old ideas (of the heart) must also change, incorporate some new ideas (of the mind), leaving him a feeling of being "free, all-satisfied." His devotional watch at the bridge has allowed him to close the gap between the faith of his fathers and that which would supplant it (really, keeping the best of the old and merging it with the best of the new), and heir to both, leave him a stronger individual, at peace with himself and able to go on to a fulfilling future. He sees but one "Universal God of Indian and white man," leading him to an acceptance of Christianity and its brotherhood (316–19).

He begins his ride home, but many signal fires warn him of a Native uprising. He changes course, just in time to prevent a real skirmish by a gathering mob and save the lives of Morgan and Blucher—because of the peace within him and his constant love of Marian. Still, he is shot for his pains by one of Morgan's men. It is this wound that ends his life in the first edition of the book. In the original manuscript he survives. Here it is Native Americans of the uprising, fresh from their mob scene, who "ride into the sunset" and "vanish" (341–42).

It is Nophaie who stays behind, with Marian, his soon-to-be wife. In time he will vanish too, he tells her: "I shall be absorbed by you—by your love—by your children.... It is well!" (342).

16

Tappan's Burro:
No Greater Love

After Zane Grey had published *Desert Gold* in 1913, he received a letter from an interested fan, Sievert Nielsen, a Norwegian sailor who had now become a prospector in California. He wanted more particulars about the lost treasure described in the novel so that he could look for it, promising to split the fortune with the author. Grey had to inform him that the gold was fictional, like the rest of the book, but asked him to drop around—he seemed like someone worth meeting. He was so, a giant of a man, age thirty-five, who had once walked one hundred fifty miles through desert country. Now he agreed to accompany Grey on some of his exploring adventures.

In March of 1919, Grey interrupted his writing of *Wanderer of the Wasteland* to hike across Death Valley in California with Nielsen. Grey knew how the region had received its name. In 1849, a Mormon caravan had attempted crossing it after leaving Salt Lake. It tried a shortcut, got lost, and perished amid dust storms, sinkholes, and unbearable heat. Only two of the seventy members survived (see Karr, 124). Grey thought a walk over the seven-mile course in spring would be feasible and, who knows, maybe provide background material for a story. Well, the result was *Tappan's Burro*, a three-part novelette, 1923, also published in *Ladies' Home Journal* the same year. The first part describes a forced journey through Death Valley.

The title character, Tappan, is a giant of a man, age thirty-five, so one can see that Grey used his companion, at least in part, as a model. The story starts with the birth of the other title character, a poor little donkey, "not a vigorous offspring" (3). Tappan—we never learn his first name—cannot leave her to die, and she is not strong enough to follow her mother while their master continues his vagabond travels prospecting for gold. He is described as "more of a naturalist than a prospector, and more of a dreamer than either" (5). Like most of Grey's characters he is given to staring across the surrounding countryside, in this case the desert wastes, observing the hues of rises and valleys, and gazing at nearby wasteland flowers and smaller animals.

At times his mining seems almost incidental. He is not an expert at it; the best he can do is usually just grub up enough gold to stake another sortie across the desert elsewhere. Thus he comes to know most of the arid Southwest, from the magnificent views about the Rio Colorado in the Arizona uplands, with the sawtoothed mountains "notch[ing] the blue sky" in the distance (4), to the Pecos River in the east, and back to the Chocolate Mountains in California. This is where he is now, making a permanent camp for two weeks until the baby burro, which he names Jenet, can follow her dreamer-naturalist-prospector's course each day. When Tappan discovers a pocket of gold, just as they are about to leave, he praises the little animal for bringing him luck.

So the months progress, summer and winter, the baby burro learning patience and endurance at the side of her mother, eventually replacing her as Tappan's one beast of burden. Jenet grows to the size of an ordinary mule and can carry a three-hundred pound pack without trouble. Other prospectors want to buy her, but Tappan would then lose someone to talk to, a requirement to keep him human. She is his ship of the desert, going where no horse nor man alone can go, and he is her friend. He starts each day energetically saying to her, "Look at the mountains yonder callin' us," but sometimes ends it "older, wearier, sicker" (7), tired of living like a desert rat, moving from hole to hole. On his plodding, brooding days he predicts that eventually his bones will grace the sands and no one will care. We sense here a habitual wanderer yet one with an inner longing for home and stability. Grey, in fact, is preparing us for events in parts 2 and 3.

Meanwhile, Tappan relies on Jenet. She can follow a trail blown over with sand, avoid treacherous quicksand, scent a faraway spring, and survive on greasewood, cacti (mashing out the thorns first with her feet), and willow leaves. She endures all weathers, has no wish to stray away from camp, but never refuses any trail that is possible to climb or descend. Tappan has the perfect travel companion; however, he has not *really* appreciated this complex animal—so far.

Then one August, with extreme drought and heat, Tappan is working a promising claim in the Panamint Mountains above Death Valley. He has saved up six small bags of gold when he discovers boot tracks about his camp, from several men. These will be claim-jumpers, murderous desperadoes who will stop at nothing to secure his gold. His only direction of escape is down through Death Valley; making a start is the immediate problem. It is Jenet that saves him. While he is fetching the gold, she remains in camp, and from a distance he sees her with tall ears erect, alert. The men are trying to ambush him, but he instead shoots them, killing one and injuring another. Their comrades are too far behind to be of real trouble, particularly when Tappan and Jenet turn the last corner into the Valley.

Grey's description now is of firsthand experience: before them is "a ghastly, glaring level of white, over which a strange dull leaden haze drooped like a blanket" (18). "Leaden" is an effective word, suggesting not only color but a heavy weight pressing them down. And the heat!—Tappan feels he is "being pursued by a furnace," its temperatures reaching 145º F. When Grey says the heat is "blinding," he is using synesthesia, describing one sensation in terms of another sense (here sight for touch) in order to convey the extreme *total* effect (20).

The coming of twilight hardly lessens these conditions, for man and beast have descended into levels of silt and borax and "a sluggish belt of fluid" (20), hardly a stream, which they cannot cross because it is so strongly acidic. The wise burro skirts the edge. Night falls, a night "without stars or sky or sound, hot, breathless, charged with some intangible current!" (20–21). Jenet finds a place to cross, on broken salt crust "like the roughened ice of a river" (21). Here the comparison is merely visual and taunting—the heat is still oppressive. Tappan cannot keep his bearings. Just as all sensations seemed to be just one—heat, so seem all directions—overwhelming darkness, with "silence a terrible menace" (21).

Death Valley has endured for millions of years without man's presence. What need then for puny man to be there for even a day? Tappan and Jenet are now three hundred feet below sea level. Their last hope is to rely on primitive instinct, the beast's being stronger than man's. For the air begins to move, the dreaded furnace winds of midnight. There is moaning, then roaring—a hellish blast, drying up creatures' organs. Tappan's lungs heave "like leather bellows" (22), his heart pumps like a fuelless engine. All senses fail but touch—he still grips Jenet's trailing rope. He stumbles on, and on, and falls into oblivion.

When he regains consciousness, he is lying on grass, with a babbling stream nearby. Jenet has led him into the mountains and to an oasis. She is none the worse for the adventure. Tappan exclaims that she has saved his life and that he will never forget; unfortunately he does, in part 2.

Here is a change of scene and a change in action. Tappan and Jenet are traveling leisurely through southeastern Arizona. He has traded one bag of gold for supplies in Globe, then travels into the Superstition Range to look for the Lost Dutchman mine, sees the black forests of the Mogollon Rim to the north, and heads to them instead. Such are the meanders and byways of a lone prospector. There, a swarthy middle-aged man and younger woman, she of a "possession-taking gaze" (30), ride into camp, presumably brother-

and-sister ranchers. They invade his "privacy and solitude" (31), and though he does not find the man, Jake Beam, trustworthy, Madge inveigles herself into his good graces.

She takes over his attempt at baking biscuits: "close to him now, smiling in good nature, a little scornful of man's encroachment upon the house-wifely duties of a woman" (33–34)—a nice way of describing her advances. Tappan goes with her, and Jake, to see their quarters, a beautiful ride through lush mescal and cedar, pine and spruce, oak and maple—so different from desert surroundings, and preferable. Grey deliberately describes these woods as thoroughly as he does in showing that they are no longer the prime attraction for Tappan. He is indeed smitten by Madge and imagines her a wifely companion in this luxuriant setting. The quarters, however, are pitiable, never mind that she assures him they are but a *winter* home; the real ranch house is farther away. Tappan, in his state, will not inquire into anything too closely. He does think that the pair may be associated with rustlers but rationalizes that thought away—she is surely a good woman.

After three weeks of companionship, enchanting fall weather sets in—autumn is Tappan's favorite season and for him the perfect time to turn a lonely, middle-aged man's fancy to real thoughts of love: "What riot of color! The tips of the green pines, the crests of the silver spruces, waved about masses of vivid gold of aspen trees, and wonderful cerise and flaming red of maples, and crags of yellow rock, covered with the bronze of frostbitten sumach.... From below breathed up the low roar of plunging brook; an eagle screeched its wild call; an elk bugled his piercing blast" (40–41). The author is at his sensuously descriptive best, and Tappan feels boyish again in this bright, surging world. If he needed any justification for his feelings, it is here. Nature seems to call him, to support his romance.

But he is still reticent in declaring himself. He has never been much of a talker. So Madge uses a more sophisticated ploy. She confesses that Jake and she had really planned to trick him out of his gold by selling him a worthless ranch, but she cannot, not now. Simplicity and humility seem to be part of her true character. She cannot deceive. She wants only to be taken away and throws herself into Tappan's arms. He will take her away.

She has a plan all ready for their escape, by horseback that night. When he insists that he must take his burro too, she persuades him otherwise. They must make a quick getaway, and he agrees. (My review of events here are highlights of what is happening; Grey's account captures all the subtleties, nuances, shadowings, of any man-woman relationship of this kind.)

She has led him astray mentally and emotionally. Now in their flight she does so physically. The trail grows rougher, disappears, and they appear to be going around in circles—at one point, possibly hearing another rider nearby. Tappan has some uneasy feelings but again rationalizes: Madge is a moody creature, hustling at one moment, weary the next. When they come to an abandoned shack, he suggests they halt till dawn. They dismount, something frightens the horses, and Tappan takes after them, but can catch only one. He returns, to find Madge gone, along with his pack containing five sacks of gold.

Her note says it all. She is Jake's wife, who really tried to escape with him but was followed. Her chasing away the horses, and he after them, was done to save his life. The reader is left to ponder what, if anything, is true, what are lies. For his part, Tappan takes after the thieves—to Globe, Phoenix (where he learns his gold was cashed for twelve thousand dollars, a small fortune then), and on to Yuma and San Diego, from which Jake, alone, had fled into Mexico. Tappan spends the winter in the latter city searching for Madge. He feels only love for her, not resentment. Does he believe her innocent, in a way? Does he not want to give up on the only love affair of his life? Is it the idea of love, the abstraction, that he is trying to recapture? Who knows? Grey wisely lets the reader come to his own conclusion.

In spring, Tappan wanders back into Arizona. Something has died within him, something lost, perhaps just his earlier boyish feeling, for his mannish strength of a giant remains. And then he remembers Jenet, his burro. What has happened to *her*? Once more he is driven, to find the animal; once more it is autumn. His camp near the Mogollon Rim is much the same as before, iron pots standing around, even the canvas tarpaulin used for packing and sleeping outdoors more or less intact. And there are small hoofprints leading away. Tappan follows and finds his Jenet, staying around the camp, as usual. He is beside himself, realizing it takes a beast, not a human, to be faithful, and vows again never to forget her or to leave her. We will see, in part 3, whether he keeps his word.

Tappan's wandering days are over. He finds comfort in staying in the Tonto region where he had once known love for Madge. But now it is directed solely to Jenet. He stays up near the Rim each year as long as possible, into early winter, and then comes down for a few months because the snow can pile up to fifteen feet on the heights, and he would never get out. What he likes best, again, is the autumn season, even the transition into winter with the brown and green forest land transfigured into dazzling white, the dark tree trunks stately in contrast.

Years pass. One November another giant of a man makes his appearance, Jess Blade, on the run from justice. Tappan is hospitable and shares his camp. Blade, a mountain man, points out that the wind presages a storm, and, at that time of year, a blizzard—they do not want to get trapped in the high country. But Tappan is not interested in this fellow man and his advice; he prefers to live in a dream world, caring only for his "lop-eared, lazy burro, growing old in contentment" (58). The next day Blade repeats his warning. Even Jenet seems waiting to get packed. They all ought to go, but Tappan lingers. Then snow comes, melts half away the following day. Blade's continual prodding makes the aging prospector ever more defiant. Then a three-day blizzard sweeps the Rim, with gale-force winds unabated. Their only hope now is to wait even longer, till a crust forms so they can walk out, but what about Jenet then? She cannot don the makeshift snowshoes that Blade improvises from old boxes and strips of sacking.

Blade suggests he shoot Jenet for meat, and thus the two men become out-and-out enemies. Tappan insists on her coming along, somehow, and straps his tarpaulin on her back. Blade grabs Tappan's rifle, tries to shoot the burro, and a terrific fight ensues. The rifle breaks in two, and Tappan cracks Blade's skull open with the rifle barrel; the luckless criminal plunges back, out of sight, into the deep snow, but one boot showing, holding aloft a homemade snowshoe.

Tappan and Jenet take their leave, slowly. He has his snowshoes, but she is now dependent on him to show her where to walk with her sharp little hoofs. The situation is reversed from that other trek in Death Valley years ago. For three days they so continue at the easy pace of five miles each day. The fourth day the going is too difficult—he must carry her at places, and their food is almost gone. The next day he hits upon the idea of using the tarpaulin as a sled for her. The next three or four days so incommoded are very tough going and thence even impossible. The crust fails for Tappan himself, and he is forced to plunge and stamp a roadway for his companion, yard by exhausting yard: "The pangs in his breast [are] terrible—cramps, constrictions, the piercing pains in his lungs, the dull ache of his overtaxed heart" (76). Grey is excellent at detailing this day-by-day ordeal, the symbiosis of man and beast. Jenet helps Tappan in giving him a reason to struggle on, to live.

Finally there are patches of bare ground. Tappan "pluck[s] and pluck[s]" (77) at the tarpaulin now to cover himself before falling asleep (the repetition of "pluck[s]" effectively reveals to us the man's feeble state). Jenet grazes all night. The temperature drops, and the stars, the eyes of nature, look down "without pity or hope or censure" (78). The next day Jenet hears another burro braying, and she answers with a call "clear as a bugle blast.... But this morning Tappan [does] not awaken" (78). He has proved faithful this time, even unto death; he has sacrificed his life for her. His atonement is complete; greater love hath no man.... Any Biblical overtones (John 15:13), consciously felt or not, will further enrich the story.

Tappan's Burro stands among Grey's best work.

17

Code of the West: Growing Up in the Twenties

Readers of the first few chapters of *Code of the West*, 1934 (first serialized in *The Country Gentleman*, 1923), may think this novel is a somewhat superficial look at Western life, and possibly an embarrassing attempt at trying to be funny. But a further perusal reveals a well-crafted story with memorable characters. Yes, the story begins in a light fashion, a departure from Zane Grey's typical Western where we sense at once that life is real and earnest, with a full share of turmoil, and violence too. Here, the "humor" of the ranch hands seems barefaced and immaturely obvious, but that is their reactions to situations, not the author's. They are simple, rugged, backwoods people of the Tonto Basin in Arizona. The author remains an omniscient commentator, with subtle asides and revelations, wonderful insights into masculine egos and feminine ways.

The story begins with an introduction to Mary Stockwell, a thirty-something teacher at a log schoolhouse in the Basin. She boards at the Thurman ranch, six miles from school, to which she walks each day. Hailing from the East, she has adapted herself to country life in the years following World War I. In fact she has her eye on the oldest Thurman son, Enoch, and hopes to settle in the West, permanently.

Mary, however, is not the principal female character. It is her seventeen-year-old sister, Georgiana, who is coming for a lengthy stay. A letter from the mother reveals that she is a thoroughly modern Millie—"whatever the modern girl has developed, Georgie has it" (2). She knows more than her hopelessly out-of-date parents, must have her own way, and is forward in anything she does. In a forced effort to be an individual, she becomes less so and more a prototype of the Roaring Twenties, an audacious flapper, with bobbed hair, short skirts and all; also a precursor of someone more directly familiar to most of us—a post World-War-II baby boomer.

Landon Y. Jones gives a detailed analysis of this latter generation in his saga, *Great Expectations*, 1980, referring to its "prolonged adolescence," its hundreds of major demonstrations staged and so becoming a kind of "loose cannon on the deck of society, rolling and smashing whatever stand[s] in its path" (68, 80). Well, Georgiana becomes a one-woman demonstration herself, much to her sister's consternation. Grey, it seems, delights in placing such a phenomenon not only in the West but in an old-fashioned corner of it. What will happen? The mother's wish is that it be the girl's "salvation" (3).

The action starts with some tomfoolery. Mary wants one of the hands to get Georgiana from the stage, eighteen miles away. The cowboys are happy to oblige. However, to get back at them for the many tricks they have played on her, she shows them a photo of her homely aunt as the one to be picked up. All but Cal Thurman, nineteen, have excuses now not to go. There is more tomfoolery, for the rest are going to show up at the stage to razz Cal as the youngest brother—he is always the butt of jokes. But taunts will turn to envy when they see the lovely sister, who, it turns out, is also an "outrageous flirt" (2).

Cal drives the ranch's old Model T Ford to get Georgiana and on the way stops to give a lift to a down-and-out young man looking for work. What he looks like, we are told, is a giraffe—he is so tall and lanky, and to get into the "Lizzie" (28), he needs to fold himself in (16). It turns out he is a former marine, a boxing instructor, and one-time sparring partner of heavyweight champion Jack Dempsey. His name is Tuck Merry, and he earned his nickname of "Tuck" because whenever he punched somebody he tucked him away, that is, to sleep. Cal realizes this is the kind of buddy to have—to protect him from jibes, friendly or otherwise, and from whom he can learn something of the art of self-defense. He has treated him to a meal, now promises him a job on the ranch.

There is a glorious mix-up in waiting for the auto-stage. The other ranch hands have come, dressed-up and clean-shaven, already kidding Cal and, apparently, having jimmied the old Ford so that it will not run. They, in the ranch's bigger, newer car, offer to take Georgiana, as does Bid Hatfield of a rival ranch. He, the villain of the story, is the most courteous of all, and Georgiana, if she could, would prefer to go with him. Naturally, she is enjoying all the attention. Cal asserts that he is the one assigned to drive her to the ranch, but a phone call from sister Mary is required to finalize the original arrangement. The ten or so pages of conversation—the jibes and compliments, courtesies and snubs, misunderstandings and explanations—are deftly written (the flow is well-paced), revealing that Grey has some playwright skills, however unsuccessful he was at the deliberate writing of theater drama.

What is nonetheless apparent is his sureness with dialogue. When the car fails to run—Cal, his passenger, and Tuck already seated in it—we are *treated* (double meaning intended) to another ten pages of back-and-forth bandying humor, now with Georgiana joining in. When Cal whispers to her to stick with him and "be game," no matter what happens, she replies, "Game is my middle name.... [W]e'll give them the merry ha-ha." Young as she is, she understands the male ego. When Cal's cousin says she had better ride with him or she might have to walk, she replies, "That would be lovely. I adore walking" (54, 63).

Tuck gets into the fun by jumping out of the back seat and, in his droll manner, offering his expertise on getting the car started: "Buddy, let me give this can the once over.... I used to run a cheese-cutter." In looking at the engine, he orates: "The carburretor has been detached from the ventriculator and the trolley wire is off. The ignition has been jammed in the midriff. Then the juice no longer coincides with the perambulator.... Outside of that the engine is all right" (55, 56). It is all jargon—Georgiana thinks "he's just too funny" (56) (she understands Tuck too)—but he gets the engine running and they are off, with the disappointed ranch hands saying they will drive behind to pick up any falling parts.

Cal is struck by the "vague sweetness" of Georgiana's presence beside him. "Please don't call me Mister," he tells her (66). But he begins to have some second thoughts about her. She is Eastern, after all, and he does not understand *her*, let alone her slangy talk. He drives faster to keep himself aloof, and she loves the speed. He himself is somewhat frightened by cars altogether (he'd rather be on a horse, and a wild one at that). She, on the other hand, has no worries at all—"If you're going to get it in the neck, you'll *get* it, that's that" (68). She is definitely an "I-don't-care-girl."

Grey says this is a "wholly new species of girl to Cal." And when he addresses her as *Miss* Georgiana, her response is so different from what his had been, in expression, that he does not catch her meaning. "Cut the formal stuff, for tripe's sake," she says, and at his dumbfoundedness has to add, "Can the *Miss*, will you? I'm not an old lady" (68). He is shocked, and not pleasurably. This feeling is reinforced when he purposely stops so that she can admire the sunset. He cannot envision anything more glorious (nor can Grey), but her comment is dismissive: "Oh, it's nifty, all right, ... but too wild and woolly for me" (70).

The growing impasse here can lead only to harsher words, about her flimsy dress, and soon they are back to being more formal. She is once again Miss Stockwell, and he Mister Backwoodsman, then she, in retort, Miss New York. She has the last word in this exchange, and eternally feminine, says she wishes she had come with *Mr.* Bid Hatfield. The situation is saved by the jimmied car going out of control and slamming into an embankment.

Cal thinks Georgiana is hurt when she presses close to him but then discovers she is doing so out of "pure feminine deviltry" (75). She is a game girl, all right, and they both realize they have a common enemy to dally with, the "jimmiers" in the follow-up car. The two plan to fool them by pretending she is seriously injured. The others will be sheepish then, crestfallen, instead of gloating over the crash. Cal and Georgiana, now in "cahoots," play up their ruse even to their arrival at the ranch house, where she exclaims sweetly to everybody, "We put it over on them, didn't we?" (87).

Later that evening, Cal is pacing the pasture outside the ranch house, alone. A few hours before he had been the usual Cal Thurman. Now his reasoning powers have gone into eclipse; his heart is stormed; he is madly in love, a new experience for him, and with "not the kind of girl he wanted to love" (90). How this situation will resolve itself is the plot of the book.

Grey describes nature well, and his ecological concerns give this description a philosophical depth; he knows the cowboy life and writes of it realistically, and his appreciation of all that is Western gives his writing a gloss that makes a reader feel satisfied with the portrayal; but what, I think, he does best in so many of his books is to probe the female psyche, its varied manifestations as revealed in women's dialogue with men, as we have already glimpsed, and with each other. (A prime example of woman-talk is Mary Stockwell's discussion with her much younger sister in chapter 6.)

There is much need for the big-sister conversation that occurs shortly after Georgiana arrives because she has upset the whole Tonto world in just three weeks, with her Eastern clothes, manner, and speech. She oppugns and sets at naught the code of the West, which speaks for forthright and steadfast behavior, ultimately for respect and dignity. For Georgiana is a trifler, glorying in the sensation of young men drawn irresistibly to her, of young girls heralding her immodesty, of older women (and men) thinking her a menace and intruder. She can be sweet and lovable when not crossed, but entirely another creature otherwise—when bossed, she seeks to do the thing forbidden. Work, she abhors, and as Grey says, is simply a product of her times, a "shallow, selfish, thoughtless" girl (94).

Mary dearly loves her sister and must try several tacks, for the little sister senses a big sister "getting after" her, and she has had enough of that back home. Georgiana knows that the talk will sift down to just one thing, her relations with men. But Mary senses something too, with her older wisdom, understanding that the crux of the matter is not just men but more specifically her sister's bitterness toward them (for their seeming mastery, freedom, and independence). There is always so much behind what is being said, which Grey hints at subtly and which become shadowy, embryonic flutterings in the back of the reader's mind, enriching the prose on each page.

Mary gets down to brass tacks, as she says, and makes her point: if Georgiana loves her sister well enough to spare her anguish, how will she continue to trifle with men, yet spare *her*? Georgiana is unfazed: "Simple as ABC, sister darling.... I'm far too wise"—"I'll not take any chances" (101). Mary realizes that her sister is no fool. Grey maintains this lightness of touch in presenting the serious matters discussed. These come round to the question of understanding Western men. Mary sees them, we have been told before, as "manly young giants ... full of latent fire and reserve force" (5). They do not understand Georgiana's flirting—and Mary says bluntly, "they believe you are cheap, easy, open to light advance" (102).

She can see trouble ahead when one man will genuinely fall in love with her sister. Thus the discussion comes round to Cal, who in fact has already proposed marriage. Georgiana says: "I liked him fine until he began to get serious, sort of bossy, and jealous. Then good night." Mary assures her that his proposal proves "how fine and earnest he is" (103). "Why do you have it in for Cal?" is a question for the younger sister to ponder, relating to the reference to "bitterness" earlier. Georgiana's provocation just will not do in this Wild West. Men like Cal have a natural strength, "a code of honor that no woman can risk breaking" (104).

The sisters remain on pleasant speaking terms, even good-humored: a few days later, when Georgiana dons a dainty apron, Mary asks blandly, "Georgie, are you wearing the apron because you're going to do housework, or doing housework because you want to exhibit the apron?" Georgie smilingly replies, "There you are with your hammer again.... It's a lead pipe you have me figured, Mary. You ought to be tickled if anything made me work" (105).

The badinage continues: "Georgia, you *might* make some man a good wife, after all"—and—"Sister, old dear, get this.... I'll make a darn sight better wife than..." Mary laughs and gets in her final word, "Oh, so you have really condescended to imagine you might marry some day" (105). "Condescended" is the key word and gets to the heart of things. Really, the sisters' conversation here is the heart of the book, Zane Grey at his finest in delineating character, and forwarding the plot too. Mary has some advice for Cal as well before the chapter ends: "If you must go on [with this romance], why, do it with all your heart" (111).

There is much action to follow, typical of any Grey novel: Georgie's trail ride with Cal, a flirtation with Bid Hatfield at a schoolhouse dance..., the course of true love never running smoothly. In the midst of the turmoil, Enoch (who has eyed Mary all along, as she him, but without ever having courted her) quietly proposes and she accepts. It is a peaceful contrast to the ups and downs of the Cal-Georgiana relationship. Georgie, in fact, after her schoolhouse fling, tells Cal that she is not worth his respect, and they drift apart. Meanwhile, he has been busy, working at his new homestead, building a cabin: "This was pioneer work..., blazing the path for civilization" (200).

It is at the homestead that Cal realizes what must be done regarding his love life. He must have Georgiana—that is all there is to it. In accepting her no matter what she may have done, he is following the code of the West, both claiming his mate and ending her dangerous trifling with men. It is his duty to do so. And it is his buddy, Tuck Merry, who tells how exactly this can be done. Cal must simply waylay her—kidnap her, in fact—and *marry* her. Not only will such an act solve his problem, it will be her salvation (as her mother had stated) and a blessing for her caring sister. Tuck will look after all the arrangements, having a minister handy and leaving the impression that what is to happen is an elopement.

Somehow the marriage comes off—Georgiana seems to be in a trance-like state after the abduction. But will she not run off when she comes to her senses? She and Cal live in separate rooms of the cabin, being together only for meals, which she prepares. She is still too stunned to plan an escape. Then Mary arrives for a visit—the mothering older sister is so bubbling over with good wishes and excitement over her own upcoming marriage that Georgie is tongue-tied. Again, Grey is excellent in his writing of this one-sided conversation.

The author's coverage of Georgiana's ponderings when the bewildered girl is once more alone is also well done. Her thoughts are interspersed throughout the narrative of her daily activities, cropping up in every free moment she has—what should she do, what *can* she do? The activities, meanwhile, the work she feels obliged to do as long as she remains "under Cal Thurman's roof," are a kind of panacea for her: the homely chores ease her mind—"she must work for her *own* sake" (emphasis added); otherwise she would "brood herself sick" (262). Thus, she soliloquizes, again and again. (The necessity of work in one's life is a constant Zane Grey theme.) She begins to take an interest in the homestead livestock; she responds sensuously to the natural world around her: the piny smell of the forest, the cloudy mantling of sunset skies. But she and Cal still live their separate lives.

It is Bid Hatfield's spreading false rumors about her character that changes things. Cal, true to his code, fights Bid but is badly beaten. Nursing him, Georgiana realizes she cannot desert her husband. She is "chained ... by her conscience, by her longing to make amends" (294). And, steadfast and forthright, she seeks out Hatfield her individual self, publicly denounces him, and finally gains the respect and dignity affirmed by the code.

18

The Thundering Herd:
A Buffalo Saga

At age thirty-five, Zane Grey met the man who would change his life. Though he had already written his Ohio River trilogy (*Betty Zane*, *The Spirit of the Border*, and *The Last Trail*—the final book still needed to be published), he had not yet written a true "Western"; in fact, had never lived in the Far West. His fortuitous meeting with Charles Jesse "Buffalo" Jones in 1907 (in New York) led to his going there and eventually to his writing of *The Thundering Herd*, 1925, an epic story of the great slaughter of the bison and the tragedy of the animal's decline.

"Buffalo" Jones had been a hunter of the huge beasts himself until he realized that they were becoming extinct. It was then that he began devoting his life to their preservation, going so far as to crossbreed them with black Galloway cattle to produce "cattalo." When Grey met him, Jones was showing wildlife films in the East to raise money for his ventures. Grey journeyed with him back West, to Arizona, to write about their experiences on this frontier.

The resulting book, *The Last of the Plainsmen*, came out the following year, 1908. Carlton Jackson has called it a "foundation work, ... inspir[ing] many of Grey's later settings and events in his western novels" (29). It would be another seventeen years, however, before Grey published the book specifically detailing the near extermination of those animals which Jones had worked hard to save. The account was first serialized in *Ladies' Home Journal*, 1924.

The author hoped to educate his readers with the tale of *The Thundering Herd*. In a note to *Boy's Magazine* (cited in Jackson, 78) he stated his wish that his "true picture" would give them "the impulse toward conservation of what wild life still exists in our great country." He termed the departed buffalo one of the "most wonderful of our own American animals."

Grey's opening chapter is a truly magnificent evocation of the great plains of the American South and West and the vast buffalo herds upon them. Presented are three pictures—that of an olden time before man came on the scene, then one with Native Americans on hand, and a final picture including the first white men, Spaniards under Coronado, who encountered the herds of "crooked-back oxen" (12).

The author adopts an eagle's viewpoint for the first scene, fittingly not only because man is absent but also because a panoramic view is needed. Many words and phrases suggest the immensity of what is shown below. The slope of a valley is "endless," its floor "boundless," and yet the "black mass [of buffalo], creeping with snail-like slowness," is "as long as the valley is wide." It reaches far away to "the dim purple distances and disappear[s]." The main flow is fed by tributary "dark moving streams," encroaching "always" upon new areas of grass and "cover[ing] them." The herd has "no end"; there are "leagues and leagues of buffalo, millions of buffalo!" (1–2).

The scene is as boundless in time as in space, for Grey speaks of a "living heritage of a million years," the "wild, primitive, grand" picture being "eloquent of the past" (2). Even as our view narrows to focus on two huge bulls fighting for dominance, the battle is described as "relentless as nature itself," a nature where the only law respected is the age-old "survival of the fittest" (5, 4).

After the battle, the herd breaks into a run, and now from our nearer vantage of "miles of bobbing black backs," we also hear the "rhythmic pound" of hoofs. The sound seems to be planetary as it sends back "such thunder as now [rises] from the shaking earth." It is "one long continuous roll," an "avalanche" of sound, and the running buffalo a "tidal wave," a "thundering herd" (7–8).

The remaining two pictures are described more briefly. With Natives present, the buffalo are still seen in "leagues and leagues": "all was a dense black that merged into the haze of distance." The waiting hunters, armed with primitive weapons, killed only what was needed for their own food, raiment, and shelter. It did not occur to them that the buffalo might some day vanish: "They had always been; they would always be" (8, 10).

In the final scene appears a "straggling" band of white men. Its numbers seem miniscule compared to that of the herds, and the men resort to piling buffalo chips, found aplenty, as markers to guide them. But these Spaniards, some on horse and carrying "strange weapons" (guns), have with them that which, when augmented by lust and greed in future generations, can all but wipe out the species. In Coronado's day such extinction was not thought of. The party's historian reports that the "foul and fierce beast" frightened the horses and could even overtake and kill them (11, 12).

So ends Grey's evocative portrayal of buffalo in the past—this before he takes up his own tale of their mass slaughter on the Llano Estacado (Staked Plain) of Texas in the 1870s.

Grey is quite right in describing buffalo alone on their grazing grounds at first, with man nowhere in sight. Paleontologists and archeologists tell us that earlier forms of buffalo (or, more correctly, "bison") came over the Bering Land Bridge in prehistoric times from Eurasia (a close relative is the "wisent" of Poland/Russia). They may already have arrived in the mid–Pleistocene epoch, some one million years ago and well before humans, with further waves appearing later when access was again available: the land bridge surfaced and submerged several times during this epoch's great Ice Age. The animals could occupy stretches of ice-free central Alaska/Yukon, then with succeeding recessions of the glaciers, migrate down an open corridor between the western Cordilleran and eastern Laurentide sheets to the plains in the south. (For an account of bison distribution and development, see Wrigley, 242–45.)

One of the early species of migrating buffalo evolved into *Bison latifrons*, the giant of them all, carrying six-foot horns. It was generally a northern parkland animal. Also large but smaller horned was *Bison antiquus*, a southern grassland species. When the famous site discovered in 1926 near Folsom, New Mexico, turned up a stone projectile point amid bones of an extinct buffalo, they were found to be those of this latter species.

Man was definitely present, then, to hunt buffalo, 8,000 years ago, according to the radiocarbon dating of the bones. Some other sites with these points dated even earlier so that buffalo of one kind or another have been game to man for at least the last 11,000 years.

Meanwhile, buffalo were evolving into, or being supplanted by, smaller specimens of their genera. In time, about 5,000 years ago, they had developed into the buffalo of historic times, *Bison bison*, yet more diminished in size. This only remaining North American species is still fit "monarch of the plains." Grey described it as "twice the bulk of an ox" and "high as a horse" (3).

While the size of buffalo decreased over many millennia, the total number, until white man's arrival, did not. Buffalo ranged all the way from northern Mexico, through the United States from New York to California, across the Canadian prairies and into the Northwest Territories. The population when settlers first came has been estimated at sixty million, seemingly unaffected by Natives' continuous hunting.

Grey's second picture shows Natives waiting in ambush for the animals to come down to drink at a river. This was one of the several means by which the hunters could outwit the hunted. Aboriginal hunters might also stalk buffalo, doing so covered in a complete wolfskin. At other times a hunter in a buffalo's hide might imitate the actions of a buffalo and so entice a herd into a wing-like funnel, constructed of branches and dirt, which led into a pound or corral where the trapped animals could more easily be killed. With horses, re-introduced to America by the Spaniards, the Native Americans could more readily panic bison into entering the pound, or, better yet, over a jump or precipice. Such a site at Great Falls, Montana, covered five acres and contained 25,000 tons of bones.

A final method of killing buffalo by Natives on horseback was racing alongside a herd, or into it, singling out an animal and spearing or shooting it at full gallop. The Native and horse became Centaur-like in oneness, their combined skills bringing success in this fast-paced action, and many Western artists—including George Catlin, Alfred Jacob Miller, Paul Kane, Frederic Remington, and Charles Russell—have depicted such a pursuit.

It was this method that was adopted by Métis communities in the first half of the nineteenth century during their yearly prolonged hunts for food and robes, anticipating on a smaller scale the mass slaughter described by Grey. Some summer's outings yielded as much as 500 tons of meat, a lot of which would be cut into strips, dried, and pounded into pemmican by the women. Besides feeding the Métis, it helped provision the fur trade to the north.

In the 1860s, transcontinental railway construction launched a new assault on the buffalo, to feed the builders. Here white hunters stepped into the picture—none more celebrated than "Buffalo Bill" Cody. (It was reported that he alone killed more than 4,000 buffalo in a year and a half.) As construction was being completed, railways could transport some of the rarer cuts of meat back East. Buffalo became a profitable business on the plains.

What had occurred by the 1870s, the time of Grey's *The Thundering Herd*, was an "industrial revolution" in the manufacturing Eastern states, following the Civil War. There was a demand for pulley-belt leather to drive factory machines. And it just so happened that as railways were opening the West, parallel developments occurred: a tanning process was developed to turn buffalo hides into the best of such leather, and the repeating rifle became widely used to kill those buffalo supplying the hides.

The fate of the "monarch of the plains" was more or less doomed in the face of such market demands and improved ways of meeting them. That the government policy of the day favored the slaughter of buffalo as a means to subdue the Native (for they were his food base) and make the land open for settlement simply speeded the animals' demise.

Grey's book chronicles the slaughter by hide hunters when the Great Plains herd of some ten million buffalo was killed in the space of a decade, marking the virtual extinction of the species. Over the Santa Fe Railroad alone 200,000 hides were shipped East in 1876, and more from Fort Worth. And an old photograph in Jules B. Billard (ed.), *The World of the American Indian*, 1974, shows 40,000 hides, a "month's supply from one shipper," waiting to be loaded at Dodge City, Kansas (330). It is suggested that up to five buffalo might be shot for every one skinned.

The hunters in Grey's book, true to real life, also use the chase technique, usually as a second course after the herd begins moving. First, there are repeated firings and killings from a "stand." Buffalo are often slow to move, even when fired upon. A buffalo will drop, and its neighbor will keep on grazing. Thus hunters may deliberately position themselves, perhaps using a gun rest for their heavy .50-caliber Sharps rifles, or blazing away with one of the new repeating rifles. Cody had once killed sixty-nine animals from a single stand in his day, and Grey reports someone with 126.

In the southwest, specifically in an area near the Texas Panhandle, there were still herds fifteen miles long by three or four wide in the mid-seventies, according to Grey. His main character, Tom Doan, "throw[s] in" with a hard-working "outfit," led by Clark Hudnall and scout Jude Pilchuck, to kill the animals (20). Tom kills 360 bison in twenty-four days (not an excessive number) but skins 482, for skinning is his chief activity. An average of twenty skinned a day (at thirty cents a skin) represents a solid day's work—with the skin "an inch thick, tougher than sole leather—an' stick! Why it's riveted on an' clinched!" (52). The very best skinners, however, may average nearly double that amount, and a companion hunter kills 286 buffalo in a single day!

Troubles arise when a rival outfit, headed by Randall Jett, appears. He and his henchmen, Andy Pruitt and Hank Follonsbee, are really hunter-pretenders, accumulating their several wagon-loads of hides by—theft! A further complication is that Tom has fallen in love with Jett's step-daughter, Milly Fayre. The situation is resolved when an argument breaks out among the thieves about divvying up the spoils: Pruitt shoots Jett, and their teamster, Catlee, concerned about Milly's welfare, shoots both subordinates but is killed himself.

Milly Fayre, never involved in the hunt directly, has looked at the buffalo slaughter objectively and voiced, it seems, the author's view of the actual events in history: "If the meat was to be used, even given to the hungry people of the world, then the slaughter might be condoned. But just the hides!" (98–99). In another place she tells Tom—"You are stealing [the Natives'] food.... Their meat—out of their mouths. Not because you're hungry, but to get rich" (160).

Finally, we see through Grey's dramatization and in his own gripping narration the carnage of the buffalo herd on the Brazos River in chapter 18—thirty miles of hunters in a relentless day-by-day extermination: "These hunters stuck to a job that in a worthy cause would have been heroic. As it was they descended to butchers." The details are exceedingly graphic—"hundreds of newly skinned carcasses over ... miles. Buzzards were as thick as bees. And the stench was unbearable" (371).

Then Tom is caught in a stampede of the remaining animals. The superb description of some dozen pages is an echo of an earlier, similar, admirable account (and of equal length), when Milly with a team and wagon was caught up within an immense slower-moving migration of unharassed buffalo. Then, the movement had lasted a whole day, the woman's ears being filled with a "continuous trample, at first a roar, then a clatter, then a slow beat, beat, beat, of hoofs" (307). When the motion and sound had eventually passed her by, she could not become accustomed to the silence.

Tom's involvement in the stampede is another matter. It lasts only an hour or so, and things are ominous right from the start. A thunderstorm is brewing, with mushrooming clouds moving toward Tom and scout Pilchuck, who halt their horses to see the "heavy changing forms" merge into a "purple-black mass." Lightning slants down in "zigzag ropes." Yes, it is thundering, but the older scout says, "Listen." Tom hears nothing special, even dismounting and walking away from his horse in order to hear the better. Then the scout says, "Try again" (379–81).

Just thunder as before, but now, under it, "another fainter sound"! (381). In this manner Grey composes his prelude to the coming stampede—the thunderstorm and the thundering herd complementing each other, the latter eventually drowning out the noises of the competing storm, as the buffalo take on a kind of cosmic significance.

The men remount, wheel about, and try to outrun the herd, this "terror of the plains, more appalling than a prairie fire," in order to gain a rocky eminence which can split the "black bobbing line" that has appeared along the horizon. The horses, excited, simply fly in this headlong race—and reach the goal. Safe, Tom "whirl[s] in fear and wonder" (384–87). He is spellbound.

He speculates on what can happen if the buffalo too somehow scramble up the rock, and senses an impending justice meted out: "What an end for hide-hunters! Killed, crushed, trampled to jelly, trampled to dust under the hoofs of the great herd! It would be just retribution.... How magnificent and appalling!" (388).

Grey orchestrates more lightning flashes, "in vivid white streaks," and has the "thunder" no longer heard from above but rather along the ground. "[A]n army of maddened beasts ... [are] shaking the earth," the buffalo seemingly controlling the very planet, for they *can* make it tremble. Tom's ears stop functioning. "He [can] no longer hear. The sense ha[s] been outdone" (388).

A deluge of rain follows, after which the sky lightens and the sun breaks through. But the stampeding herd still pounds by, a storm that seems not to end. Its persistence, in contrast to the brevity of the thundersquall, seems to magnify the glory and splendor. Yet the thundering herd at last passes out of sight. "And the thunder be[comes] a roar, the roar a rumble, and the rumble die[s] away" (391). The passing of the sound foreshadows the extinction of the herd.

"The last herd!" the scout exclaims. "The storm of rain [is] like the storm of lead that'll follow them." Then an old buffalo appears, "forlorn, alone, lost," and heads into the "melancholy gray of the prairie" (392). Tom vows to end his buffalo slaughter. In the next, and final, chapter, he meets Milly again, proposes marriage, and her "Yes!" (400) ends the story.

Zane Grey was not completely satisfied with his book, despite the extraordinarily fine writing of the preceding chapter. The characters, he felt, were not strong enough to make it the great epic he had wished to write. Yet it is surely a well-reasoned and moving saga of the buffalo—really, the *main* "character"—and we can learn much from the novel.

Conservation measures before and after the publication of *The Thundering Herd* in 1925 have ensured that the population is once more increasing. From a low of thirty-nine wild buffalo in the United States in 1900, a total of about 2,000 now roam freely in Yellowstone National Park. In Canada, the world's largest park, Wood Buffalo (straddling the Alberta/Northwest Territories border), was established in 1922 to protect the species. More than 5,000 live there. Smaller numbers live in game preserves throughout the continent.

The days of hunting these wide-ranging creatures by methods that served the early Native hunter so well, individual stalking or the wild chase to pound or jump, are long past, of course, as is the color they provided. And game laws and park regulations, thankfully, have cut short any wanton destruction as once practiced by the market hunters.

But like those early Native Americans, whose whole culture was dominated by the buffalo, and those early white men too, like Coronado, who were the first of their people to see this magnificent animal—we today can feel a sense of awe in beholding it. It is as if we are experiencing the wonder felt by Tom Doan at the close of Zane Grey's book: he had "seen and felt its overpowering vitality, its tremendous life, its spirit" (392).

19

Wild Horse Mesa: One Grand Spectacle

"Days passed. The beautiful Indian summer weather held on, growing white with hoarfrost in the dawns, rich and thick with amber light at the still noons, smokey and purple at sunset" (177). So begins one of the chapters of Zane Grey's *Wild Horse Mesa*, halfway through the book. This Western was first published in 1928 but had been serialized by *The Country Gentleman* in 1924.

The mood expressed here in no way reflects the plot, for much has already happened to a raft of characters, and as much will happen later. The book is a real "actioner." Perhaps this quiet time anticipates the ending when strife has been resolved, or maybe the author himself (or reader as well) needs a respite from the galloping run of events. The yarn, of course, is a horse story, about wranglers of the animal; there is not one *cow*boy present. Cows are generally placid but what we have here describes a time before ranches were established in the area.

The locale is the extreme southeast corner of Utah, where the San Juan River flows into the Colorado, and if not exactly Grand Canyon country, it is the adjacent region, a canyoned wilderness. Present are Native Americans—the Piutes, bands of wild horses, and temporary camps of wranglers out to capture the mustangs. Where there are horses and money to be made catching them (thirteen dollars a head), there will be horse thieves too, general skulduggery and murder. This is the Wild West. The overall plot is already apparent. What Grey does, however—through splendid description of the varied natural scenes, subtle delineation of characters, particularly the women, and pointed disclosure of base wrangling practices and treatment of Natives—is to write a novel that holds our interest throughout, despite a somewhat stereotyped plot—and hero too.

The very first sentence is arresting: "The mystery and insurmountable nature of Wild Horse Mesa had usurped a thoughtful hour of Chane Weymer's lonely desert life in Utah" (1). Thus the book's title is presented as a lofty, seemingly unclimbable, tableland, yet—as the next paragraph makes clear—a refuge for a great wild stallion, Panquitch, and the mustangs he leads. And Chane, who covets this horse, is a "loner," as many of Grey's heroes are (cf. Lassiter and Lin Slone)—like the writer himself, standing alone among American "literary" contemporaries in choosing a super-man for the central character. There are such people in real life, Grey would argue, people always principled, unflappable, in their decisions and actions. Who, after all, better for a hero in a story?

Chane, age thirty-four, expert at his job, not only has admiration and respect for the horses he wrangles; he also longs to experience their wild freedom. In fact, his attitude extends to all of nature: he glories in the band of cloud "canopying" the mesa, sees the changing light in it as the sun sets— "white clouds turning to rose, with centers of opal, like a coral shell" (5). It uplifts him, this "evanescent power" (6), what he senses as atmospheric freedom. He is given to meditation on things, emboldened to act manfully whatever may happen.

The horse he rides is to horses what Chane is to men, a superior individual. Taller than average, he has a massive chest and sound legs, enabling him to outrace other horses and to do so at long distances. His look is questioning, with his fine head raised up whenever his owner approaches, and "pride and fire" (24) are there too. Man and beast appreciate each other— Chane talks to him as if he were another person—and Grey names him Brutus after his own horse, this dark brown, mottled with black, stallion.

As for the well-characterized women, the first to appear in the story is Sosie Nokin, the sixteen-year-old daughter of Piute Toddy Nokin, Chane's friend and supplier of captured wild horses. She has been to a government school and is quite eloquent about the "tragedy" of her situation. Her trying to upgrade her own people now in any way makes them accuse her of being too good for them, while if she were to seek work elsewhere, the only job open would be that of a housemaid. Grey here is critical of what white society has done: "schooled and missionaried" the Native religion "out of her" (261) so that she does not feel at home anywhere.

Chane tries to advise her, but she is determined to get away even if it means riding off with a no-good wrangler, young and handsome Bent Manerube. She thinks he will marry her. When she starts to leave, Chane steps in, beats up Manerube, and sends him packing. The two men, in keeping with the progress of a Western novel, will meet again.

The next chapter introduces us to another horse-wrangler camp, that of "Mel" Melberne and Jim Loughbridge, and their families. Here we meet two other young daughters, Sue Melberne, almost twenty, and Ora Loughbridge, about eighteen. There are interesting comparisons and contrasts between the two (and between each and Sosie) in their backgrounds, outlook and demeanor—and their relations with Chane and Manerube (also with Chess, Chane's younger brother, who works for this outfit).

Sue, like Sosie, has been to school but chooses now to fit into the nomad world of wrangling. She responds well to a "primitive life in the open" (44), and finds the "colorful stone-monumented" desert to have a "strange, impelling beauty" (44–46). In this she is like Chane, whom she has yet to meet, and also in her love of wild horses. For her the attraction is watching these free animals, not capturing them. When she sees Wild Horse Mesa, that "red-walled black-tipped, flat-topped mountain" (71), her first thought is that there these horses must be safe. Overall, she appears to be a soul mate for Chane, but we should know that in a novel the course of true love never runs smoothly.

Ora is flashingly pretty with her dark eyes (similar to Sosie in this regard) but somewhat spoiled and snippy—the men in camp enjoy giving her a little dig every so often. She is smitten by Chess, but he thinks her spiteful, only to be reminded by chestnut-haired Sue that "any jealous girl is that way, you know" (56). Sue herself has no romantic interest in Chess— she is looking ahead to sometime meeting his older, much-spoken-of brother—but when he and Ora are away together, Grey cannot resist saying that she felt "a tiny feminine twinge of pique" (74). And we will see her jealous, too, when she meets Sosie. Finding romance, being courted, is a learning experience for her, a total maturation process of understanding others, and herself as well—she is growing up, becoming more fit for marriage.

In the meantime Sue gives herself up to the loneliness and solitude of her surroundings: "the whole sweep of valley and stone barriers beyond slumbered under a haze of purple, ethereal and mysterious close at hand, dark and heavy and enveloping in the distance" (70). These lines may comment on things still to occur in Sue's life, unknown events light-hearted and somber, but they also point to her growing sensuous approach to nature, common to so many of Grey's heroes and heroines. She loves the sight of "stars, the moon, ... the smell of the cedars, the pines, ... the feel of the rocks" (73).

Then a stranger appears in camp—Manerube. He will be hired as foreman to catch the mustangs in the valley. Sue and Ora both feel called to primp up for the evening's outdoor meal, what with this new worker present, and prolong their eating of it. Sue, however, is soon put off by his bragging, then greatly upset when he recalls his fight with Chane, and himself as winner and defender of Sosie!—all this with a "deprecatory gesture" (85). Chess immediately calls him a liar and strikes him. There would have been blood shed had not others separated them. Ora runs off crying, and Sue seeks her own tent, carefully pondering the incident. Whom should she believe?

Despite Manerube's playing up to both Sue and Ora over the next days, the business at hand is catching mustangs. The new foreman suggests that the men use barbed wire to fence off one end of the valley and drive them into it. This is a most brutal method, for the mustangs have no acquaintance with such fencing and will run headlong into it, cutting themselves badly, even becoming disabled. There is not enough wood nearby to make a more humane fence, and using wire makes for an easily constructed trap. Loughbridge is all for it, thinking of the quick money to be made; Melberne is eventually convinced to go ahead with it against his better judgment.

Two events happen first. One is another kind of roundup. The men have spotted some wild mules, not nearly as great a number as that of the horses. The wranglers think they can merely ride up to the mules, cluster them together, and herd them away. Grey inserts this kind of drive as a bit of comic relief before the barbed-wire horror to come. For the men cannot catch them. The sure-footed animals lead them a merry chase, up one unguarded slope and down another, outsmarting them really, and it is the men who are "mules." Sue is delighted to see Manerube's discomfiture—"Oh, what fun! I wouldn't miss this for worlds" (145). Ora is offended by Sue's laughter.

The other event is the arrival of another stranger in camp that same evening. He is completely worn out and starved, as is his horse, from escaping some outlaw wranglers trying to kill him. The horse, in effect, has saved the man's life. It is led away, while he just lies there, limp, in his ragged clothes and beard, with Melberne and daughter looking on. The chapter ends with this splendid sentence: "Sue recognized a man she had never before seen" (151). He is Chane Weymer, her Prince Charming, Western style.

She has more to ponder, but is lost. What good is it to think, she reflects, when her feelings seem independent of her thought? Hers is a mind-heart struggle that will not be resolved quickly. Meanwhile, she (and Ora) takes extra pains to dress up for next morning's breakfast, to the hardly hidden amusement of her parents. "Girls will be girls," says her father (165). Meanwhile, Chane gets hired as another hand for the outfit. He will not quarrel with Manerube, barring some immediate provocation, and the foreman, like most braggarts, is too much a coward to start anything.

Up to this point we know about Sue's feelings mostly through Grey's description of her thoughts. Now we see her act out her feelings, by playing up to Manerube, whom she despises! What is happening here? Is hers a perverse spirit? Of course, she cannot shake her doubts about Chane's past—it is rumored (falsely) that he had once lived with a Native woman—but that is not the prime motive for her action. Nor is it what we typically might believe—a wish to get Chane's attention by making *him* jealous. Rather, it is an attempt to hide her love for him from him. But more than that! It is to *hurt* him for making her, "unsought, unwooed" (184), smitten. She is not consciously aware of her full motive, and only comes to understand it a hundred pages later (276). (Thus Grey probes her psyche.) Her father, meanwhile, smiles knowingly.

Now the "barbed-wire" roundup begins. It is even bloodier than first imagined, and Chane takes part, knowing that the others are going ahead with it anyway, and his skilled participation may lessen the suffering of the captured horses somewhat. It is a huge operation: five thousand mustangs in a valley three miles wide and nine miles long. Seventeen hundred of them are corralled—a din of shrieking animals, barbs covered with hair and bits of flesh. Chane shoots many, mercy killings all, and cannot estimate how many other break free to die lingering deaths.

The worst is yet to come the following day when almost two hundred are "prepared" for herding to the railway. Every horse must be thrown, then hobbled with a front leg bent back at the knee and tied up in that position. That is the only way the frantic creatures can be readily driven along. Even so, wild with fury and terror, plunging and falling, forty are lost or killed en route. Half that number need to be put down at the stockyards before shipping. Still, a profit is made, but only Manerube and Loughbridge are pleased with the day's work. The others dread having to repeat the horror, tackle the same "bloody" job, with another two hundred horses the next day (and in the ensuing days after that).

Grey is more graphic than here depicted in exposing this example of man's inhumanity to fellow creatures. Mercifully, there need be no further such description: Sue frees all the horses left behind when the men are away, that thirsty mass of mustangs with dust rising in a "pall" (244) over them. Her father is secretly overjoyed; Chane compliments her on her courage. Then Toddy Nokin and Sosie arrive to see Chane. From them Sue and her father learn about the latter's stalwart character, while Chane hears, for the first time, about his brother's tussle with Manerube—causing a near showdown with the foreman, stopped only by the intervention of the other hands.

The upshot is that Manerube and Loughbridge part from the outfit, leaving Melberne, his family and hands, free to head to "the most beautiful place for a ranch in Utah" (261), recommended by Chane himself, somewhere near Wild Horse Mesa. In the vicinity they can catch mustangs for their own use through individual chases, something best done by one of the riders, a Mexican vaquero. Melberne soon decides that he has enough horses. It seems that the horse-wrangling life will be succeeded by the less hectic one of ranching.

Chane has more time now to examine the country, especially the unique mesa where the one wild horse he yet covets, Panquitch, still has his domain. One November day he comes back with the news that he has discovered a way to the top. He, Melberne, Sue, and Chess plan to ride out on an exploring trip of a few days to investigate. Once camp is made, the two older men set out on different courses, Sue and Chess following a third. There is always a playful banter between these last two, Chess knowing that his brother and Sue love each other. The trick is getting them to come to their senses, as he puts it.

There is another matter at hand: Panquitch. Chane, once more a "loner," sees the "tawny black-maned beauty" (317) and because of a pool on the escape route, is able to rope him. The chase and capture, excitingly told, with Brutus and Panquitch matching their superb strengths, run for half a dozen pages. The fleeing horse had no chance at all, he realizes, and feeling pity and remorse, wonders what he wants with this creature whose heart "would ever be wild" (325), when he has his splendid Brutus, devoted to him. Sue arrives, who has also seen the "leonine" horse and sung out, "Fly! Oh, Panquitch fly!" (316, 318), having earlier released some thousand trapped mustangs. Her conversation with Chane some readers may find overwritten. The gist is that she will marry him if the great horse is released. He is.

The story could end here, but readers of Westerns know that one other matter needs squaring. When Sue and Chane return to camp, they are met by Manerube and the outlaw wranglers. Chess, who had already gone back, is tied up. So is Panquitch, who, exhausted from his former capture, has been easily lassoed once more. Another prisoner is Loughbridge, who finally has recognized the true character of his previous foreman. The situation is an impossible one for Chane to resolve—till some shots ring out, and Manerube falls dead, the other outlaws skedaddling. Sosie's Piute kin, including her new somber-eyed husband, have been tracking the hoodlums and had their own account to settle.

The story now rightfully ends. Melberne and Loughbridge will both homestead in "this most beautiful place for a ranch" (261); Chess and Ora will be reunited too. Panquitch is freed, again: he has come to symbolize the grandeur of wild spirited things, even the freedom-loving vitality linking Sue and Chane. The happy couple watch him seek his Wild Horse Mesa for the night while sunset marks the day's close: "above the corrugated world of wind-worn stone[,]" the "massed clouds [float] in the west, dark-purple, silver-rimmed, golden-edged, in a sea of azure blue.... All the forces of nature [seem] to have united in one grand spectacle" (362).

20

Under the Tonto Rim:
A Backwoods Tale

Lucy Watson, a city girl graduated from normal school, decides not to be a regular teacher but a welfare worker among the isolated farm families in Arizona's pine-woods back country. Such is the setting for *Under the Tonto Rim*, 1926, serially published in *Ladies' Home Journal* the year before. The book has something of the feel of John Fox, Jr.'s earlier *The Trail of the Lonesome Pine*, 1908, and Marjorie Kinnan Rawlings's later *The Yearling*, 1939. Thus we have sentences such as "Lucy sat under her favorite pine, her back against the rough bark," and "lifted face and arms to the green canopy above..." (272) and "Then rose a chorus of barks and bays.... Lucy began to be conscious of qualms when a sharp voice rang out.... 'Hyar, you ornery dawgs, shet up!'" (27). Lucy might well be Fox's June Tolliver in the Kentucky/Virginia Cumberland Mountains or Rawlings's Penny Baxter visiting his neighbors in Florida's hummock country.

That Lucy is successful in instilling a better home life is due in part to her special situation. She grew up without a mother, her father a saloon-keeper, and a younger sister who had eloped with a no-good cowboy: all casting a shadow on her teenage years. Leaving home for her is a relief, a thrill, and a hope for better things to come. She is determined that deprived families under her charge will be happier, cleaner, more gainfully employed, more engaged in cultural things. She has developed a new golden rule—"to do for others what she had been forced to do for herself" (145). She had to pull herself up by her bootstraps; she will help others to do so too. And enduring her own past experiences has given her the strength to go ahead.

To her mind, there is much need for her work. She thinks these backwoods folk are "many generations behind city people in their development" (80). Here she is stating Grey's notions of the evolution of mankind. Early men were cave men, concerned only with survival. They hunted to live and wandered in tribes for protection from fierce animals, adapting themselves always to their surroundings, which changed over time to forest and prairie, and finding in each new locale their food and clothing and shelter. Throughout the ages, their ways had progressed according to a "law of life"; her charges were but closer to an earlier primitive lifestyle "than their more fortunate brethren of civilization" (81). Her attitude may sound condescending, but Lucy cannot help wondering also whether the backwoods children may not be more spirited than their city counterparts: it would be a shame to rob them of their instinctual joy in things. In her new environment, she recognizes something of the primitive in herself: "the early progenitors from which her people had sprung had lived thousands of years in the forested wilderness, barbarians, nomads. She felt it all so intensely. The giant seamy-barked pines, rough and rugged, were more than trees. They had constituted a roof for her race in ages past, and wood for fire. The fragrance, the strength of them, were in her blood.... [S]tronger than education, this passion claimed her" (164).

Yet she knows that advances of the mind are ongoing, inevitable. She is a teacher, rather in a home than in a school, and is called a "backwoods Samaritan" (241). She will guide both parents and children into a more fulfilling life. But how to start? The state government is paying her a small salary, with a budget for local home improvements; it leaves her on her own in what is an experimental program to set up as she thinks best. All she is told is this word of confidence: "We would not trust every young woman with this work" (2).

She is fortunate in being able to confer with the local regular teacher. He tells her that the community has no church, no doctor, no amusement (except what is self-made). As for the school, it does not operate in winter because of the weather—most students ride burros to school for a distance of half a dozen miles or more—and they are aged four to nineteen. At first he thought the situation tragic, but has learned that "a good many of our necessities are not really necessary, after all" (13) (this could have been a statement from Henry David Thoreau's *Walden*, 1854). The teacher concludes that she will be a blessing to both the overworked mothers and the children.

Lucy is fortunate, as well, by starting off in the Lee Denmeade household and helping that family. He is the most influential and welcoming of the backwoodsmen, and word of her good works there will quickly spread. Her first sight of his farm is not encouraging—pine trees chopped down to make a yard had been left where they fell and that yard now full of pigs running at large. I have already referred to the dogs barking a warning (or welcome). She likes Mrs. Denmeade, who tells her she will be one of the family, rather than company.

The family consists of nine children, from Edd and Joe, men really (Edd is a wild-bee hunter and keeper, making an independent living), and Allie and younger Mertie, grown women (Mertie is sixteen and ready for marriage—girls marry from fifteen up), to school-age children and twin girls, aged five—all living at home, in a two-room cabin! Uncle Bill, Lee's brother, sleeps in the attic with the older sons. This arrangement is considerably better than the neighbor's, where eight people live in *one* room, "with one door an' no winder!" (31).

There is a hillbilly element here. The oldest children have three or four years of schooling, vain Mertie but two. She is the only one who shows any neatness in her dress. The men and boys sleep in their clothes. As for their speech, the father drawls; the boys use words like "yep" and "disremember" (shades of Huck Finn); Uncle Bill greets Lucy with "Right pert this mawnin'" (49). The teenage children like nothing better than standing around, partaking in a "remarkable exhibition of banter and absurdity," breaking at times into a "primitive pleasure in tormenting" each other (71, 72). When a neighbor boy talks to a couple in a buggy, putting his foot casually on one wheel while doing so, and the team starts away suddenly, the onlookers let out a howl of guffaws at the boy's falling down. Yet Lucy feels in them a kind of natural hardiness. What she does not like is some families' addiction to "white mule" (31), a moonshine whisky brewed locally.

So that Lucy does not rob the parents of their own bed, the teacher loans her a tent with a board floor to set up outside (and extra wall boards and a little stove for winter). Thus she has independent living quarters that can be moved to other households later. Her job is to survey each situation, then buy things or make things for each home (or better yet, help the family to do so)—she has taken a course in manual training. At the Denmeades', she buys a sewing machine for the women to make sheets and pillowcases, which are lacking, also curtains, tablecloths, and clothes. For the men she buys carpenters' tools so they can put up shelves and closets and make needed furniture. Her *pièce de résistance* is having the father and Uncle Bill put up a pulley and bucket over a gulley so that the family can haul up fresh water from the stream below instead of running down and carrying it back along a steep trail. Edd is impressed, reckoning the women must be ashamed of the menfolk for not thinking of such a thing themselves.

The other aspect of Lucy's work is developing the children's minds, and those of the adults too. She finds a tendency among these backwoods people to more or less hibernate during the winters, just waiting for planting time to come round again, when they could instead be learning about the outside world. ("The universe is wider than our views of it," Thoreau has wisely said [*Walden*, 320]). Otherwise, they will simply do what their parents have done before them. She admires Edd for being a bee hunter in addition to being a backwoodsman like his father. She would like to see his future son as a forest ranger and his grandson as possibly a city worker. Lucy's efforts bear fruit all around, for when she returns to "civilization" for a month's respite, she is highly commended by her government employer, has her salary raised, and is asked to advise new welfare workers.

All the time she herself is learning, whatever obstacles encountered stimulating her growth. She realizes she does not know as much about her own self, her feelings and motivations, as she had thought. Her biggest jolt comes when Edd questions her purpose, her teaching his younger brothers and sisters a lot of things fitted for the outside world, when they, he says, "got to grow up an' *live* here. They might be happier knowin' less" (80). She will have to "learn as much as she t[eaches]" (46). This is particularly true in her trying to upgrade Edd's own life. She had not recognized his forthright individuality, had "denied him an intimate personal sense of himself" (122). She will have to learn about him through his interest in wild bees, his work in the forest "lin[ing]" them (172). Being a woman, she likes him as he is, his manliness, yet strives to change him too. Grey adds, in another chapter: "Perhaps she had given too much thought to herself. Vanity!" (165).

The plot takes on further complications when Lucy's sister, Clara, asks for refuge with her. Her cowboy lover, Jim Middleton, had not married her but absconded. Clara, the incorrigible flirt, now appears a "pale frail flower" (144). What she needs is love, and Lucy, the super-woman, is prepared to give it. What Lucy does not know is that there was a baby, now cared for by an older woman in the city, expecting regular payments. Clara cannot tell her sister of this because Lucy seems so big herself, so strong, that she *will* not see the littleness, the weakness, of her younger sister. Because Lucy has resolved to welcome Clara *now*, she will not let her speak of the past; her idealistic mind will not accept realistic consequences. Clara could have told a less self-sufficient person.

Meanwhile, having gained physical strength from her new life in the outdoors (she sleeps in Lucy's tent), Clara becomes the regular schoolteacher in the district when the previous one leaves. She and Joe Denmeade, who, like brother Edd, is working on his own homestead a few miles off in the forest, seem to be gaining each other's affection. Actually, they get married secretly.

For her part, Lucy takes up Edd's offer to spend a bee-hunter's day with him. Grey aptly describes the scene with a Keatsian/Tennysonian sensuousness: "The air seemed murmurous and melodious with the hum of innumerable bees. What a sweet, drowsy summer sound!" (177) (see "Ode to a Nightingale," 279, 281; *The Princess*, 7.207). Lucy learns the origin of the word "beeline," meaning a direct route: bees fly in a *straight* line to their hive after gathering nectar and pollen even though the distance is a mile or two. A bee hunter will note the flight and find the hollow tree with its honey.

She enjoys the adventure, floundering through brush and over rocks, up and down gullies and cliffs, all to stay on the beeline, but she tells Edd that he cannot make a wild-bee hunter out of her. He drawls back, "Shore, but you might make one of yourself" (181). This is an Emersonian remark on self-reliance, a trait characteristic of them both. They do have something in common. And it dawns on Lucy that the crudeness she had seen in Edd on first acquaintance is no longer there. Grey asks the reader: "Was it because of change and growth in him—or in her?" (190).

Back at her tent at sunset, Lucy, utterly exhausted, falls on her bed and says to Clara, "I'm dead! ... Walked, climbed, slid, and stung to death! ... What a glorious, glorious day!" (198). It is the sister who tells her, gently, that she, Lucy, must be in love.

A year has passed since Lucy began her home-teaching. She is visiting Clara at the school after class. It is here that Clara reveals her two secrets—about her having had a baby with Jim, and her marriage now to Joe. Before Lucy can really react, other than wringing her hands, a man rides up and rushes in with a letter, threatening some kind of blackmail. It is Clara's dissolute cowboy. She faints. In the overly melodramatic scene that follows, Edd comes to the rescue, grappling with Middleton, who tries to fire his revolver. A shot rings out and the cowboy falls dead. Edd had heard him raving about a baby, and Lucy, to protect her weak sister, still fainted away, says the baby is her own.

Days go by. There is no closure for anyone. But when Lucy tells Clara that she has claimed the baby as her own, the real mother is distraught. A horrific quarrel ensues, with Lucy winning the battle. Then comes the calling down. Lucy describes Clara as miserable and wicked: "But you are my sister—all I have left to love. And I'll do what you cannot!" that is, be a mother to Clara's child. Clara moans, "Oh, Lucy—Lucy! ... God help me!" (270).

On this distraught note the novel might have ended, but not for Grey. In the next chapter, Edd steps up and tells Lucy that he reckons she has had her own way long enough, then philosophizes: "Life is a good deal like bee huntin'. You get stung a lot. But the honey is only the sweeter ..." (276). He proposes to her. Clara, meanwhile, has told Joe of the baby and can atone for the past; they will rightly care for the child. Edd, on hearing this, says, "It's all in the family" (279).

A romance novelist might end the novel here, but not Grey. In the final page we find Lucy alone in the forest that same evening at sunset. Nature is always a strong influence on a Grey hero or heroine. Lucy finds a healing strength in the woods after all the turmoil, feeling at harmony with it. She is soothed and sustained. Earlier she had felt its lesson unfolding, spelled out by the eternal sounds of night birds and crickets, low winds in the pines, and the weird patterns of needles overhead "all studded with stars of white fire—these taught her the littleness of her life and the tremendousness of the spirit from which she had sprung" (259–60).

Now she understands that "life [is] real and earnest, beautiful and terrible, inexplicable as the blaze of the setting sun"—with love, suffering, and nature combining "to burn out baneful selfish weakness" (280). She returns to the clearing, knowing that her own stature, just one instance "in a vast world of struggling humans, [is] like a little pine sapling lifting itself among billions of its kind toward the light. But that lifting [is] the great and beautiful secret" (281). And with this prose echo of Longfellow's "A Psalm of Life," the book ultimately ends.

21

Forlorn River: Prolonged Drought and Money Madness

Forlorn River, 1927, was first serialized in *Ladies' Home Journal* the year before, one of eight books by Grey this magazine carried. It is also one of his most tightly plotted novels. The story is a variation of Lord Acton's dictum: "Power tends to corrupt and absolute power corrupts absolutely" (see Mathew, 185). Power is often related to wealth, and here it is wealth that corrupts, and sudden wealth does so hugely.

That is the fate of two ranchers operating at Tule Lake in northwestern California. Hart Blaine and Amos Ide have been poor all their lives, to the point of outright poverty. Their lands are but marsh country along the lake, but when the government drains the lake, they each immediately gain property that had been under water before. What they do not need, they can sell at an enormous profit. Also, their holdings are such that they still have access to good water, while other ranchers in the vicinity are cut short and have to sell out, particularly when the area is experiencing a six-year drought. Blaine and Ide in fact can increase their acreage by cheap purchases as well and have dreams of becoming great ranch barons. Blaine expects to "be a millionaire some day" (27).

Wealth has certainly affected most of the Blaine family. Hart, a once likeable farmhand in Kansas, now struts about, pompous and seemingly important, telling his teenaged daughter whom not to associate with anymore. His wife, a former milkmaid, is lost among all the newfangled things bought for her household, unhappy that she can no longer do the homely tasks she was used to; she is altogether pathetic. These two people are among the best drawn characters in the book, maintaining our interest in the course of events, for he over time grows befuddled while she, at first dominated by him, gains self-assurance.

The four oldest children, three brothers and a sister, are already putting on airs, with two of the boys "leaning away from farm work to white collars" (24); the girl, jealous and haughty, is engaged to a city lawyer. These characters have inconsequential roles. The heroine, a teenaged daughter, Ina, now nineteen, has been away the past four years, at school in Kansas, and so has remained unaffected by all this new wealth. Then there are two youngsters—Marvie, a bright fourteen-year-old who likes nothing better than horseback riding and fishing, and who takes on the important role of Ina's confidant (not too often does a boy have a fairly major role in a Grey novel). The youngest family member, Dall, a gawky twelve-year-old girl, is simply there.

The Ide family has changed too, but in a different way. Amos, a stern religious figure, has caught the same money fever as his friend and neighbor Hart, yet his actions are not so out in the open—his land deals are quietly made and not talked about, and he has spent no extra money on his home. We sense a rivalry between the two men, an animosity, with Amos thinking Hart's liberal spending a showing off. Mrs. Ide suffers, though not because of her husband's stinginess. Rather, something had happened four years earlier, before they became wealthy, a confrontation between Amos and their oldest offspring, Ben.

Ben, a young man of twenty then, was tired of being tied down to the grubbing life on his father's farm; he wanted excitement, roaming the nearby hill country and catching wild horses—he loved horses. To Amos, such an occupation was nomadic and disreputable, a wild life not a suitable calling for his son. So Amos gave Ben a choice: stay and remain a sound family member or leave and be disowned. He left, and so doing broke his mother's heart—thus a letter from his sister, Hettie, informs him. Mrs. Ide's health is failing, and he should return, at least for a visit. The plot thickens. Ben Ide and Ina Blaine had been "kid sweethearts" (16); now they will meet again.

At this point it is useful to know something about the region where the story unfolds and about Ben's recent life. He has taken up bachelor's quarters at Clear Lake, the source of Forlorn River (identified on current maps as Lost River—its aboriginal name). The river indeed seems to be lost, for it wanders northwesterly into Oregon, then swings back into California toward Tule Lake, having taken a somewhat circular hundred-mile course that ends on the other side of the Sage Hills/Mountains from which it started. To go home, Ben has but to make a good half-day's ride along a bridle trail over the mountainous terrain. (Today, both Clear Lake and Tule Lake are National Wildlife Refuges for thousands of geese and ducks.)

Ben has come to love the gray slopes about him, the bands of wild horses roving upon them, accompanied by the sounds of honking geese and the smell of sage. For it is spring, and there has been a reawakening of spirits.

He had hibernated like a bear the whole winter, and must now be up and doing too—if only to impress his father that he has a worthwhile occupation. He already has a large barn and a huge corral with some wild horses for sale, if not as many as he might have had: he "loved the horses, not the money." Grey says that "he would rather catch one beautiful wild mustang and keep it for himself than sell a hundred common horses" (5). (And there is just such a wild horse, California Red, whose capture by Ben at the end of the book is almost his complete undoing.)

When we see Ben alone, on the porch of his weather-beaten cabin set picturesquely on the shore of the lake, rapt in the beauty of the natural world about him, we might well think of Henry David Thoreau in reverie at Walden Pond. But Grey says: "Ben Ide was chasing a rainbow and he knew it" (5). He needs to have "something more significant to live for" (6). Perhaps his companion can rouse him from his lethargic spring fever.

This unattached cowpoke had ridden up to Ben's campfire some years before, wounded, exhausted, starved. Ben's only concern had been helping him, nursing him back to health, never questioning his circumstances, except for one query: "Where are you from?" With the one-word answer "Nevada" (10), the stranger gained a nickname and a lifelong friend while revealing nothing of his mysterious past. Now he is just back from Tule Lake, having made "a jim-dandy deal" for the horses (7), bought a six-month grubstake, and, best of all, brought the letter from Hettie, telling of Mrs. Ide's condition. Nevada has been enchanted by Hettie's soft-voiced manner and stirred by her personal message for both Ben and himself to make something of their lives and dispel rumors that they are the wild-horse wranglers who are rustling cattle: "Chase wild horses, if you must, but *ketch* them. Sell them. Buy cattle. Homestead land. Study an' think an' plan, an' *work*" (14). Nevada does his best to convince Ben of her logic and warns him that a Less Setter is around, a trouble-maker from his own Nevada days. Ben rides off to Tule Lake to see his mother.

Meanwhile, Ina Blaine opens her eyes on her first morning back on the ranch. She hears wild geese honking, and cries rapturously, "I'm home" (22). Her response is significant. It is not just being with her folks again (in a strange new house), but hearing a familiar bird call that brings back sweet memories of former days. She is a daughter of nature, another Thoreauvian, and responds sensuously to ducks "dot[ting] the rosy sky, ... geese head[ing] toward the dim blue swamp land," and old Mount Shasta, "sunrise-flushed," fifty miles to the southwest (25). She "breathe[s] it all in, color and fragrance and music"; what she learned while away "only strengthen[s] her hold upon the simple natural things" (31).

Yet what greets her on going outside is her self-important father introducing her to "one of [his] pardners" (33), Less Setter, whom she distrusts instantly. When Setter says that Ben's wild-horse chasing is a cover for cattle-thieving, she bursts out, "You lie!" (35). The battle lines are drawn up quickly. She visits Hettie and says that the two of them need to be "archplotters" (49) on Ben's behalf.

Then she secretly sees Ben after his arrival and says that she is sticking up for him even to her father. Before she can say more, Ben's own father appears. Ben steals away into the shadows—and returns to Clear Lake. He cannot face his father yet. Once back at his cabin, he mulls over the brief meeting with Ina and decides he cannot see her again until he has proved himself worthy of her.

And Ina?—she has to put up with one Sewall McAdam, son of a big merchant in Klamath Falls with whom her father has big transactions. Hart Blaine wants her to marry Sewall to further these deals. The thought is absurd to Ina: Grey has brought the young man into the story for comic relief. Dall calls him "Mr. Blondy Pop-Eyes" (149).

What follows is a ten-page conversation between Ben and Nevada about what has transpired so far, really a dialogue between two lovelorn cowboys that is both humorous and serious as they plan their strategy. Grey presents the scene very well, and here is just a snippet of it. Ben speaks first:

> "You don't trust me?"
> "When a fellar's in love he ain't reliable."
> "See here, Nevada, I believe you're in love, too. With my sister! That's what changed you from a lazy, good-humored, don't-care cowboy to a regular devil with highfaluting hunches" [91].

The hunches are to catch another batch of wild horses, buy out three neighboring ranchers who cannot make a go of it in the drought, and possibly dam up a canyon to make a permanent lake.

The two cowboys secure the three extra quarters of land and set off with a third companion, Modoc, a Native befriended by Ben. He is an excellent tracker whose ability will prove invaluable in catching horses. They are in luck. In the lava beds to the southwest, they discover a large depression, more than an acre in size, having precipitous sides. It is a natural corral, and what is more, there is water in a cavern at the bottom, where wild horses come to drink—accessed by one narrow trail that can be gated. All the men have to do is wait for a band of mustangs to enter. They trap 150 prize horses, then break them enough so that they can lead them back to Ben's pasture at Forlorn River. Doing so takes the men well into the summer.

That same summer Hart Blaine and family move for a kind of summer outing to an old ranch that he has acquired about forty miles south, across

Clear Lake from Ben's home. The elevation is higher there, the weather cooler. Blaine has been foreclosing on mortgages and buying more property throughout the area, with Setter making the deals and he himself supplying the money. Setter's highhanded methods have not added to the reputation of either man. Now tents will be set up on the deserted ranch for the family, and Ina for one is delighted with the change, as is her mother: she has "fallen upon old tasks, the habits of a lifetime that sudden wealth had denied her, and she be[comes] another woman" (138).

Ina's delight is changed when, after a week, Setter arrives, for he had begun to make preposterous advances to her. Not only that, but Setter and her father seem to be plotting something, for no good, she is sure. Marvie is her "spy" to report what is going on. Her mother becomes quite outspoken about her husband's activities: "We were poor so long that money when it came set him crazy" (147). Later, she says: "An' pretty soon I'll give [him] a piece of my mind" (149). Blaine's response (to Setter) is—"I ain't as keen about this ranch buyin' as I was.... My wife, too, is worryin' me" (153). While Blaine wants to buy Ben out, Setter wants to *drive* him out—this is their scheming. More headache for Blaine—and rising friction with Setter!

Setter is a man possessed. He rides out to Ben's place with some of Blaine's cowboys and threatens young Ide: "We're on to your shady deals!" (165), then gets the beating of his life. When Blaine hears of this, he is afraid to think of what lies ahead: "I'm up to my neck in deals with Setter. He has my paper for thousands. I can't back out..." (107). Ina says her father is "so deeply mixed up that he doesn't know whether he is riding or walking" (215). To add to his discomfiture, he knows that Amos Ide is in a similar position.

Things begin happening quickly. With Nevada's intervention and Marvie as go-between, Ben and Ina come together, pledge their love for each other, and become engaged. But there is some business to be taken care of still. Setter has literally *hired* lawmen—they may be bogus officers—to arrest Ben and his two friends as rustlers, for many ranchers have been missing cattle. The three decide to hunt for the real rustlers and thus be away so as not be apprehended and just maybe catch the cattle thieves themselves to prove their own innocence.

This is no wild goose chase. Modoc had previously spotted one Bill Hall and his gang of four. The pursuit is much like the last roundup of horses all over again. The rustlers have taken to a cave in a lava bank where there is water at hand. They are spotted by the pursuers, who rush to the entrance and have them trapped. Now the waiting begins till the "cave men" are starved out. There is a lull in the action: the rustlers cannot get out safely; Ben and his buddies will not let up on their watch. Days pass. September comes with its cold nights at the high elevation. Finally the rustlers give up, are bound and brought back to Ben's ranch.

The story could end here, but there on frozen Clear Lake, drinking at the open water in the center, are California Red, the wild mustang coveted by Ben all these years, and six other horses. Unshod, they cannot run fast on the ice to escape from the men, but they also cannot be cornered by just three men. Ben loses his head, offering the prisoners their freedom if they will help him catch the great sorrel stallion. The work is then no trick at all, and when accomplished the rustlers ride away, without guns, on their jaded horses.

Grey is ever the horseman. Although he has already described California Red's capture in six graphic pages, he tells it once more over four pages as seen by Ina across the lake, through field glasses. And what a dramatic finish to the incident it is. For the horsemen where she is, Setter's hired sheriff and deputy, leave to arrest Ben, Nevada, and Modoc! They come back with Ben and Modoc only; Nevada gets away.

While a kind of informal court is being held, Nevada races up on his horse, and leaping from the saddle, shoots both the "sheriff" and "deputy," then turns to Setter, saying he has just helped the county's real sheriff capture Hall and his gang, who are all coming down the road. Hall will give evidence that he was also in Setter's employ.

Setter jerks for his gun, but Nevada is too fast for him. Two shots ring out, both drilled through the villain's heart. Then looking at Ben, Nevada leaps on his horse, says, "So long, pard. We're square" (317), and rides away—not slowly into a sunset, but like a bolt, a lightning flash, allowing no chance for his apprehension. And the shocked bystanders now can guess what his mysterious past has been—the life of a deadly gunman, not easily given up.

Then comes the calm after the "storm": Hall tells the ranchers at large, "You fellers must have been locoed" (332); Blaine admits his stupidity and blindness, hopes to save at least his Tule Lake Ranch out of the mess; Amos Ide says he had been headed to ruin or worse. He really is the one suffering inwardly the most, having judged his own son a rustler. Blaine looks at him with "mingled pity and scorn" (324), and Amos stands motionless, dazed. Then the son passes by, and Grey is at his finest in depicting the utter pathos of the situation in these few words:

> "*Benjamin!*" called his father, in a tone Ben had never heard. Nevertheless, he rushed on.
> "*Ben!*"
> But Ben went out, deaf to that voice [327].

It is Ina who will bring father and son together later.

Ben tells her, "And now if it'll only rain." She replies that it will—"An old wild goose honked it down to me not long ago" (331).

It does rain, for a week; the unparalleled long, long drought is over; the madness occasioned by sudden wealth has ended. Ben and Ina are married; Ben forgives his father. Only the fate of Ben's sister, Hettie, and of Nevada is unresolved, but there is a sequel (see chapter 23).

22

Valley of Wild Horses:
A Cool Reckless Spirit

Many of Zane Grey's Westerns begin with a page, or several pages, of a description of the locale of the story. Grey as a close observer of nature believed that setting determined character. Some of his books, more so those that are sequels, draw the reader immediately into the action. *Valley of Wild Horses*, serialized in *The Country Gentleman*, 1927, but published only in 1948, after his death, does not follow either pattern. It begins, in Dickensian fashion, with the birth of the hero (cf. *David Copperfield*, 1849–50, where the first chapter is entitled "I Am Born.") Grey's central character is born on a plowed field after his mother had brought his father a noon-day lunch where he was breaking land in the Texas Panhandle. The boy is named Panhandle and called "Pan" for short.

There is a great deal of charm in the telling of his pre-school years and his elementary schooling. We hear of his climbing into a cupboard, falling out of it, and getting blood over his "dress" (1). He is still very young. Then he finds some tobacco in his father's coat pocket, chews it, and becomes seriously ill. His distraught mother rushes to the nearest neighbor for help, but he recovers meanwhile and is into more mischief. He runs away from home one day, on his short legs, and falls asleep in an irrigation ditch. A hastily organized search party cannot find him, but freshly flowing water in the ditch does, and the little boy, wet and bedraggled, toddles home on his own.

The family, Mr. and Mrs. Bill Smith and Pan, moves to a ranch, where the boy's playmates are a litter of baby skunks, found under the house porch. When his mother engages a neighbor's son, Dick Hardman, age seven, to get rid of the animals, Pan immediately dislikes this swaggering, inept bully, who in trying to rout them out with a lighted torch, burns down the house. Dick remains Pan's nemesis for most of the book, his actions being very much part of the plot, thwarting Pan's own attempts to succeed in life.

The family is now forced to live in a quickly built one-room shack through a cold and lonely winter. When spring arrives, young Pan's joy is sitting at a small window and watching real cowboys ride by—or running to the other side of the shack and glimpsing the cowboy world through a knothole! He is enamored of their sombreros and bright neckerchiefs, their spurs and lassos. His mother makes him a little riata, with which he constantly plays. Then one day his father brings home a pony for him. He is enraptured; he "live[s]" on the back of his horse (6). There is no doubt he will be a cowboy when he grows up.

But he is still a pre-schooler when he rides out to his first roundup. Grey, with the reader, takes enjoyment from the experience in which the little boy feels that his only hindrance in taking part is that he does not have a saddle. He bears the cowboys' good-natured jibes and learns, from one of them, how to twiddle his fingers at the others. When he is asked to ride in and help out, he is "breathless and radiant, beside himself with bliss" (8). Being asked to eat with the cowhands—"Stranger, did you fetch your chuck with you?" (8)—makes his day complete. At the "mature age of five," he continues his cowboy life back at home, now playing roundup all the daylight hours and dreaming of bucking horses and bawling calves at night.

On one of his real rides on his pony, past neighbor Jim Blake's home, he finds Mrs. Blake lying in pain on some hay in a cowshed. She asks that he go for his mother, and he replies that everyone is away, in town. She says: "Then you must be a brave little man and help me" (12). In this manner he is present at the birth of Lucy Blake, someone to play with through the next years, eventually becoming the one woman in his adult life. Thus, the author tells us, three links—his pony, the cowboys, and Lucy—have been made in the forging of his life.

School starts for Pan when his mother moves into town for the winter, as do several neighboring mothers and their children. There he has to endure the barbs of an older Dick Hardman. This continues for two winters, until the ranchers build their own country school, and Pan can *ride* there, "another red-letter day in the life of Panhandle Smith, cowboy" (17). And, a few years later, Lucy joins him. Unfortunately, Dick is there too, with more taunts, and now fisticuffs. Finally, the day after Pan's fifteenth birthday, a prolonged fight takes place between the two boys over Lucy, a running fight across the schoolyard and into the classroom, with the teacher sending for help to stop it. Pan is found stabbed by Dick, while Dick lies unconscious on the floor from a wallop by Pan.

Pan leaves school the following spring, and for him, and his neighbors, times are a-changing rather quickly over the next while. He joins a roundup in earnest and starts riding the range over much of Texas, joins a trail ride to Montana and drifts on to Cimarron country and the Platte. Meanwhile, the Blakes and Lucy move west to New Mexico, and the Hardmans leave as well—who knows where. Apparently, the father, Jard Hardman, has come into some money, and Dick, who has been in a "serious shooting scrape" (33), has to get away.

At age twenty, Pan has experienced all the hard life of a typical American cowboy, acquiring his virtues, such as self-reliance, and vices too, such as an eager handiness with a gun (his reputation in this regard is spreading). But his vices have not involved the opposite sex: he has "never lost the reverence for women his mother had instilled in him, nor his first and only love for Lucy Blake" (35). With this in mind one sultry night, riding herd to the rumble of distant thunder—a "weird yellow moon" above (35)—Pan senses an emptiness in the world and in himself. He is homesick, quits his job, and rides home.

Other Westerns might start at this point, for here real complications arise that need to be resolved. Pan's parents, he now discovers, have moved straight west of their panhandle home to Marco, New Mexico, after losing their cattle and about ten thousand dollars in a bad deal with Jard Hardman. Actually, the father trailed Hardman there, hoping to get back some of his money, and it is where the Blakes moved—a boom is taking place in the area. Pan realizes he has allowed the wild range to hold his fancy for too long.

A three-week stage journey takes him to this rugged promised land, and he immediately learns that Hardman, Sr., a saloon-operator, is king here, also owning a huge ranch, with his son, Dick, running it—or, as Pan's informant tells him: "Old Hardman makes the money an' Dick blows it" (47). Jard, in effect, "owns" Sheriff Matthews, while Dick drinks like a fish. These will be Pan's combatants as he tries to help his parents. Before even seeing his loved ones (they live out of town), he meets a friend of his cow-boying days, Blinky Moran, and *his* friend Gus Hans, and decides to throw in with them, wrangling horses. He prefers that to punching cows, any day.

His father, he soon finds, is reduced to working in a wagon shop, his mother is physically ill from worrying about her lost son, and Lucy lives with them. Altogether, things could be worse; however, there is a problem. Lucy's father is being held in jail because of some early-days rustling. Hardman/Matthews will let him go if Lucy marries Dick, whom she despises.

Grey describes his hero as having a "cool reckless spirit" (77). These few words sum up his approach to the new situation he faces. We also know that in spite of his relative youth his rambling life has given him a keen insight into human nature. He understands men of the West—their motivations, their reactions. This unconscious psychological bent, if you like, combined with his seemingly brazen unconcern for possible consequences, gets him to the core of an issue at once and a fit resolution.

His first meeting with Dick Hardman in Marco illustrates his tack (84–85). "Howdy, Skunk Hardman" is his greeting before Dick even recognizes him. When Dick says that he himself is as good as married to Lucy, Pan's fast reply hardly gives the other a chance to finish his statement: "Nope, you're wrong.... I got here just in time to save her from that doubtful honor" (84). He is as quick with his words as he is with his gun. Dick stutters out a countermand: "I'll have—you—run out of this country" (85). Pan's response is immediate *and* comprehensive: "Bah! don't waste your breath. Run me out of this country? Me! Reckon you never heard of Panhandle Smith. You're so thickheaded you couldn't take a hunch. Well, I'll give you one anyway. *You* and your crooked father, and your two bit of a sheriff pardner would do well to leave this country. Savvy that! Now get out of here pronto" (85). He knows how to play his cards: meet his adversaries boldly, menacingly, to get an advantage. Later, he reflects: "It wasn't much to be excited about. I didn't expect any fight" (110).

Pan admits that he does not know women that well, but adds this insightful comment: "I reckon they live by their hearts" (89). So he sums up Lucy's need to marry Dick in order to save her father: she is thinking of basic practicalities here, forgetting that she must *care* for the man she marries. "[I]f you marry him you'll be crooked. To yourself! To me!" (82), he tells her. When she affirms she loves just Pan, he says the four little words, "Be honest with me" (83). Lucy can only reply, "Oh Pan, you have saved me from ruin" (86). (It is highly likely that the popular song of 1940, "The Call of the Canyon," was named after Zane Grey's earlier successful novel; one cannot help wondering whether a popular song of the following year, "Be Honest with Me," made famous in recordings by Bing Crosby and Gene Autry, also stems from Grey.) Really, the mood of the whole Smith household changes—happier and more confident about things—just because of Pan's appearance, words, and actions. His father laughs again, his mother is cured, just like that, and a much younger sister and baby brother idolize him (Pan hadn't even known he had a brother). He announces further plans. His father can quit his job; he himself will spring Jim Blake from jail (which he does) and head him to Arizona, where they all will be going shortly.

"So much is settled," Pan says matter-of-factly, as if there have never been any problems. He, after all, like the typical cowboy, is "warmhearted, simple, elemental" (100), partial to ordinary things. The natural beauty of the "purple distance" awaits them, while Marco, "a hideous blotch on a fair landscape" (93) can be left behind (this, both the cowboy's and the author's comment on nature compared to man's creation).

To complete his "meet[ing] the issue in this way of the West" (116), Pan deliberately returns to the Hardman saloon (where, the previous day, he had knocked down the owner, then insulted the sheriff), has a drink, and calmly walks out, pausing in the doorway to light a cigarette, with his back to the bar. Such is his collected effrontery. He knows he has made the sheriff the laughing stock of the town. Most of the town, he feels, is with him. That advantage may be useful later.

Right now, his task is to join his horse-wrangling friends and head to the Valley of Wild Horses to make a decent grubstake (and more) in catching the mustangs. Grey tells us there are two kinds of cowboy, those brutal with horses and those who are gentle. Pan is definitely the latter kind. We see this in his careful making of fences and corrals that will have no broken branches extending inward to injure milling animals. And the group's success is phenomenal; it catches about 1,500 horses. Grey devotes nine pages to describing the final drive, and once again we sense his love of horses.

But Jard Hardman and his men are waiting as the corrals fill up. They intend, with a superior number of men, to claim the drive, or at least a good share of it. In the ensuing showdown, one of Pan's outfit outdraws Hardman and kills him, then is shot himself by Jard's gunman, but Pan downs him. With the two evil leaders killed, their cohorts skedaddle. Pan and company are able to sell the horses to a professional buyer at ten dollars a head (making some $15,000); moreover, they find on the dead Hardman and his gunman a huge store of cash almost equivalent to what Pan's father had lost to the big rancher. Of course, Pan will keep a few mustangs back to break and take along to Arizona.

Zane Grey now feels called to sum up events so far. Pan has accepted responsibilities he should have taken up long ago. At last he can dream of a more stable future—love, home, and children. Yet, Grey points out, that dream could not have come true without this moment of violence: "That [is] the bitter anomaly" (179). Later, he suggests that nature is pleased with the outcome: "The sky was as blue as the inside of a columbine, a rich and beautiful light of gold gilded the wall of rock...; and the wide sweeping expanse of sage lost itself in a deep purple horizon" (201).

There are still a few matters to deal with back in Marco. When Pan gets there, he sees Lucy just having boarded an outbound stage for Frisco, and *married* to Dick. (Her father had been apprehended again, and she'd heard that Pan had been shot by Dick's father.) Dick, about to board the stage himself, Pan flings to the ground, his wedding high hat spinning off in the dust (a symbol, surely, that Dick will no longer "high-hat" Pan). Pan tells him to get a gun before he shows up again. Lucy he tells to go to his mother (we feel there's some hope in the situation yet).

That afternoon the crooked sheriff lies dead on the street. No description of how he died is given, but we learn later that the town's citizens forced him out of the saloon to meet Pan in a customary shoot-out. Dick is too cowardly also to confront his rival and is hiding behind a curtained-off closet in one of his saloon girl's quarters. He had lured her to Marco with a promise of marriage but then (unbeknownst to her) had married Lucy. There is a further complication. Pan's friend Blinky is in love with this girl, Louise Melliss, and both cowboys hope she will leave her sordid life, marry Blinky, and join them on the journey to Arizona.

Pan calls on her. What follows would be high drama in any Western movie. She is dead drunk, and their labored conversation of several pages finally comes to the point of Dick's duplicity and Pan's wanting to kill him. Her response is to leap up, snatch a knife from under her pillow, sweep the curtain aside, and stab the two-timing Dick Hardman. Pan seizes the swaying girl and tells Blinky, who has just arrived, to shoot out the saloon lamps. The turmoil of patrons rushing out somehow sets the whole building ablaze, and the three of them make their getaway in its burning light. Next stop—Arizona!

While *Valley of Wild Horses* does not have the complexity of Zane Grey's great Westerns, the vivid straightforward treatment of people and events in this old-fashioned cowboy yarn will not disappoint its readers.

23
Nevada: Life of a Gunman

Nevada, 1926 (serialized in *Ladies' Home Journal* the same year), is a sequel to *Forlorn River*. The earlier novel ended with a nameless cowboy, known only by the name of the state he came from, shooting a ruthless swindler and his two bogus lawmen. This book begins with the gunman plunging down the road on his goaded horse, fleeing anyone who might try to stop him, the "blue smoke from his gun ... rising slowly, floating away" (1). Such graphic detail describes an event that saves the life of his only friend and solves the economic troubles of the friend's father and future father-in-law. But it initiates the travail of Nevada, who, although able to conceal his past life in the first novel, cannot escape from it any longer.

In *Nevada*, Zane Grey examines the life of this gunman/vigilante. How did he become one? How can his character change? Will he be able to leave off and live a normal life? Nevada himself would like to know some of the answers.

While escaping, he feels that the elation gained from meting out a kind of Wild West justice is soon replaced by a mood terrible and grim. His mind is whirling, matched by the swift pace of his horse, but deep inside is a "cold and horrible sickness of soul" (2). He is in fact trying to run away from that self. When the running is over, another agony sets in—he knows he must return to the wilder border country of his home state, Nevada, where he will again fit in, a gunfighter with a quick draw. But he detests the sordid life of the crooked men there, where he must ever be alert, never "wear a glove on his gun-hand" (4).

His situation is even harder to endure because in his peaceful days at Forlorn River in northern California he had fallen in love with his friend's younger sister (and she with him). Because of his pride, he cannot bear to shame her, now that she has some inkling of his past deeds. So he is driven to be alone, his campfire his only companion, "something alive that wanted to cheer him" (7). But he cannot forget her and sees her face in the embers, a shining youthful face that bids him be true to his finer instincts, his best self. It all seems so hopeless. At times he thinks he should crawl into a hidden den and die there like a wounded animal; or else revert to, and lose himself in, his old gunslinger days. But no, he must be true to Hettie Ide.

As he continues his journey, to Lineville, a community on the border of the two states, he senses that the barren ranges are like his future, and yet this wild country speaks to what is "raw and deadly" within him (12). Banish such thoughts! He must not brood, but be busy, even mingling with others, however evil, to save himself from that whelming shadow darkening his mind. So he takes up lodgings with a bustling Mrs. Wood, whose kitchen has the homely smell of baking bread, and does handyman chores for her. They had known each other before, but he assures her that his life has changed, that he is not looking for trouble.

Their conversations allow Grey to voice some of his opinions about gunmen. With some, an obsession to kill grows on them over time. They get a "mind disease," and if another killer comes on the scene, they are forced to go out to meet him, "just to see if [they] can kill him!" (26–27). So says Mrs. Wood. She also speaks of young punks developing their shooting skills and satisfying their own blood lust by killing a seasoned gunman, solely to build up their own reputation. Jim Lacy—she knows Nevada's real name only—better be careful! Nevada/Lacy says he learned to draw a gun quickly for self-defense but not for the sake of killing. True—she later describes him as "the quietest, nicest, soft-speaking fellar," but also says that "he was hell when he got riled" (113).

To himself, he admits he is really two men in one—quick-draw Jim and peaceable Nevada—and Jim should back down. Nonetheless, he oils his holster so that the gun will come out more easily. And he takes to going to the town's saloon, not to drink, but to show people there, particularly the more unsavory patrons such as Cash Burridge or Link Cawthorne, that he is not avoiding them or afraid to see them. He tries to analyze his own motivations here, but concludes that his actions may eventually lead to conflict. Later he rationalizes that it is the others who just cannot leave him alone.

Young Cawthorne, for one, has called him yellow and a liar and wants him to step outside (to shoot it out with him). But Nevada remains calm. He has been sitting at the barroom's fire, not drinking or gambling, and still seeing Hettie's face in the glowing embers. He feels put to the test and pleased that he has done what she would have expected of him.

Burridge, however, is in a friendly mood. He talks about his latest deal— "it's cattle, an' it's honest" (43)—getting a ranch in Arizona. He wants Jim to be his foreman because rustlers are taking their toll. Cash feels that the Lacy reputation alone will help to curtail the losses. Nevada, on the other hand, is not too eager to accept the proposition. He tells Cash directly, not meaning any offense, that he doubts the new rancher's chances of going straight—any prosperity will do him in. And, more importantly, another thing about the job: "What I hate aboot it is livin' up to my name" (58).

Grey tells us how Nevada grew to have his reputation. As a boy he had lived among brutal men. He struggled not to be influenced by them, but "by accident, by chivalry to redress a wrong done some one, by passion to survive," he became what fate had meant him to be, what he "seemed unfortunately and wonderfully fitted" for—a Wild West gunman (61). When Cawthorne finally kills a barmaid, beating her to death with a revolver, Nevada/Jim realizes his complete self, and calls *him* out. The chapter ends there, but we know Jim outdraws Link and shoots him, Western style. Then he leaves for Arizona, alone, not with Burridge. "I'll always know, even if I'm forced to be Jim Lacy again, that I'm true to her [to Hettie]," he says (61).

Four years pass. We join Hettie Ide in northern California, also her brother Ben (their father has died). They each miss Nevada very much in secret, not having heard from him all this while. It is only when looking at, and admiring, California Red, the wild horse that Nevada had helped Ben to catch (in *Forlorn River*), that they can open their hearts to each other. The great stallion shines silken, his long mane aflame, a broken horse now but never gentle. Hettie calls him a "beautiful stand-off wild thing" (72).

He needs yet to be tamed, and Nevada's name comes up as the only person who can do the job. Ben had hoped that Hettie had forgotten him (she was only sixteen when he left), but she now says, "Never" (67), and further points out the cause of Ben's malaise—the loss of his "pard" (68). He admits that he has spent a lot of money searching for the easy-going cowpoke with his Texas drawl, but just cannot find him. They both suspect he must have a past to hide.

Then circumstances change. Ben and Hettie's mother becomes ill; a doctor recommends a warmer climate, say, in Arizona. Well, why not move there? Such a change would be good for Ben's soul, and his wife, Ina, wants whatever is best for him. Ben is ever a pioneer and would be energized by moving to new country, still a territory (it would become a state, the forty-eighth, only in 1912). Ina's younger brother, Marvie, always seeking adventure, can come along too. As for Hettie, she knows that Nevada will never return to Forlorn River, but she might see him again in wild Arizona.

So most of the ranchland is sold, as are the cattle, and the group, with a few riders to herd the horses, is off—in covered wagons, four of them, just as in the "olden" days. The family could have taken a train but choose to make the journey an outdoor venture. The ill mother likes the idea. "Work an' livin' outdoors is what I need," she says (98) (a frequent Grey theme).

Hettie feels almost like a girl again, "playing at keeping house" (101). Mealtimes take on a picnic atmosphere: "the smoking fire, the smell of burnt wood, the steaming pots, the new white tarpaulin spread under an oak, the hot biscuits, and sizzling bacon with its savoury fragrance" (105). What we have here is really a joyous, quiet interlude between the heavy drama involving Nevada before and the even more spectacular web of events to follow.

The route takes them through Lineville. A conversation with Mrs. Wood there informs them that gunman Jim Lacy has gone to Arizona. They do not realize she is talking about their "Nevada," and Ben remarks that the territory may not have the healthiest climate if it is filled with Jim Lacys. She replies that Arizona would only be the better for men like him. (Grey likes to put in incidents like this, a chance meeting, or here a missed chance, that changes the course of people's lives — the strange workings of fate ... a divine providence.)

The journey continues, southward to the Grand Canyon, crossed at Lee's Ferry, and into territorial country — "a glory of gold and purple cloud over[hanging] a region of red rock, distant, broken, carved" (119). Hettie has been thinking of Nevada all along: "Might not ... [the] freedom, the hard fare and toil, the kinship with nature — might not these develop character to noble ends?" (116).

Ben is in a hurry to buy a ranch and settle down. He does so quickly, too quickly, a thousand acres of grazing land along the Mogollon Rim — a fabulous panorama, and ten thousand head of cattle, all for forty thousand dollars, just sixty miles from the large town of Winthrop (Grey's fictitious name for Winslow). What a bargain! he thinks. Well, the view is great. Hettie gazes at the outlines and the winding gullies and sublime distances, "that ethereal blending of hues and forms" and cries out: "I can only look — and learn to worship.... Oh, lonely wild land — oh, Arizona!" (136).

The trouble is that Ben has bought the ranch from none other than Cash Burridge, formerly of Lineville, a swindler whom Nevada doubted would ever be honest. So there are not ten thousand cattle, probably only half that number, and those remaining are being rustled away right and left. Tom Day, a neighboring rancher, says nobody knows which of the other ranchers are rustlers and which are not. Even the rustlers do not know who the kingpin is behind the thieves. And it is difficult to catch any of them in the shrubby canyon country, known as the brakes. Furthermore, he and a rough backwoods family, the Hatts, had separately loaned Burridge money, and have a lien on the stock, Day's being worth four thousand dollars. Burridge, in fact, has palmed off his debts on Ben Ide.

Another rancher in the vicinity is Judge Franklidge, a magistrate, who loves his extensive range land for its wild beauty and solitude. One day he and Day are talking about the rotten deal Ben has fallen into. They can sympathize because they also have had a lot of cattle rustled, about ten thousand head, counting Ben and Hettie's loss with theirs.

Lolling on the porch and listening to the discussion is the judge's reliable cowhand Texas Jack, who has also worked for Day. When he hears the Ide names, he "whirl[s] round with a ... suppressed and poignant passion" (155), and says he knows how to deal with the rustlers. He will ride down into the brakes and join them, become a rustler (and a spy). He will have to lie and steal, but if he is successful, all he wants at the end is to have his name cleared, the ranchers' word that they backed him in undertaking this job. Franklidge and Day are skeptical of the venture until Texas Jack divulges his real name. It is Jim Lacy.

Nevada (and Grey) reflects on his sudden decision. What has got into him? He had successfully buried his past in Arizona through his steady, useful service of late. Then, "like a thunderbolt from heaven, an inevitable, irresistible fate had confronted him" (162). Yes, he still loves Ben *and* Hettie and must respond chivalrously (again) to their new predicament, as a modern knight errant. Yet what an irony that the fame he detests, being a gunman, is the only thing that can save them—that is, if he does not stop a bullet first. "How sweet and terrible!" (163).

The Jim Lacy in "Nevada" is a mastermind, an artist really. He rides away, turns his horse loose, catches a freight into New Mexico, emerges from a barbershop as a changed man, buys a set of dandified clothes to match Lacy's reputation, also a horse, and rides leisurely into Winthrop. There he saunters about and meets Rose Hatt, the "only decent one of a bad lot" (143), and learns about her evil half-brother, Cedar—she describes him as "just plain cactus an' side-winder rattlesnake mixed up with hell" (169). (Grey must have smiled when he wrote that.) He also learns that her boyfriend is Marvie, Ben's brother-in-law. What a tangled web the author weaves for him to decipher!

On succeeding days he lounges about bars. His conversation starter is that he is looking for a "pard" (180), a cowboy who broke out of jail in New Mexico. That way he will hear the gossip of the raw life of outlaws, the riffraff that has come into Arizona from the territory to the east. He suspects that the kingpin rustler is a survivor of the bloody Lincoln County war fought there between cattlemen and rustlers.

He hears nothing good about Clan Dillon, whom Ben has hired as his foreman. Then, later at a dance, he overhears the same Dillon speaking "ungentlemanly" to the woman he loves, Hettie Ide. She breaks away, and when she is safely gone, Nevada steps in. The confrontation, the byplay of words before Dillon is knocked flat, is something that Grey does extremely well. He has an ear for dialogue, of course fitting the speech to a Western setting.

Nevada's coup is meeting Cash Burridge and saying, "Just got in, an' am lookin' for trouble" (195). Burridge has gambled away the fortune he made swindling Ide, has joined the rustlers, and is therefore open to Nevada's offer that he, Jim Lacy, wants to partner with him. In this way the gunman inveigles himself into the evil camp, gets to know its territory and who's who. He is back in a world of kill or be killed.

The first death occurs on the streets of Winthrop. We do not see it, just hear it, but Hettie sees the gunman walking away, the famous Jim Lacy, and recognizes—Nevada! She can only think he is one with the rustlers, a vicious murderer. Or has he but killed someone solely evil, as he had done at Forlorn River? "Over and over again," writes Grey, "this stream of consciousness eddied through [her] mind, like conflicting tides" (223).

Meanwhile, Ben has deep concerns, of his own: California Red has been stolen. And although the horse is later returned, Ben seems to be a bit out of things, not seeing the machinations of his foreman and now not understanding young Marvie's interest in Rose. He asks Hettie wistfully, "[A]m I growin' old, thick-headed, absent-minded?" (309). It is these little added touches that make Grey a good writer. Hettie recovers from her sorrow somewhat to aid the star-crossed young lovers, Marvie and Rose Hatt, and let nature revive her senses—"there was no deceit, no blindness, no vacillation" in *it* (224).

Nevada arranges for the horse to be sent back. He argues with the other rustlers that Ben will create more ruckus over losing California Red than losing most of his cattle. For this advice, he is complimented for "the slickest piece of headwork ... seen on this range" (258). However, in his stolen moments from the gang, when getting a pail or two of water, Jim Lacy reverts back to his Nevada character, lover of "the life and color and mystery of nature" (263)—like Hettie. He longs to be able to wander freely about Arizona again.

That time is about to come. The rustlers hole up in the seclusion of the Hatt ranch, where Nevada gets a chance to talk to Rose alone. She reveals that the big boss of the rustlers is Clan Dillon, Ben Ide's foreman. But before he can act on that lead, Nevada has to make one more heist with the rustlers to stay in "good" standing with them, driving a large herd of cattle south over the Mogollon Rim to a waiting buyer (he informs Franklidge and Day beforehand of the theft).

Nevada has two calls more to make. One is to ruffian Cedar Hatt, who is endangering Rose's life. He arrives just in time to see Marvie kill Cedar, in self-defense. Then it is on to Dillon, for the big showdown. So far, we have seen none of the Lacy gunplay in this book, only heard it or heard about it later. Now Grey provides a graphic description, with a full audience of cowboys for the event: "the very air round the Ide ranch seemed congested, heavy, sultry, ominous with menace" (322).

What is most dramatic, though, is the reaction of Hettie and Ben Ide to the incident. With Dillon dead, and positively identified as a Lincoln County rustler, Ben comes upon the gunman known to him only as Jim Lacy, the stealer of his cattle, and California Red, the man he has put out a reward for and vowed to hang, and sees—the man he has been seeking all these last years. Ben's about-face is immediate and passionate: "You're Nevada to me—my friend—my pard. An' so you'll be forever" (348).

Hettie's response is completely different. She now knows Nevada's behavior was wild but great, an act of courage on behalf of her and Ben's own well-being, and she, she had failed in faith. She was the weak one. It is only next day that she can get up her nerve to see him and talk to him, and all is well.

A summing-up of the role of gunmen/vigilantes in the West has already been given by Judge Franklidge (expressing Grey's viewpoint):

> There are bad men and bad men. It is a distinction with a vast difference. I have met or seen many of the noted killers.... These men are not bloody murderers. They are a product of the times. The West could never have been populated without them. They strike a balance between the ruffians, outlaws, strong evil characters like Dillon, and the wild life of a wild era.... [W]e could not be pioneers[;] we could not progress without this violence. [We need] the snuffing out of dissolute and desperate men.... [O]nly hard iron-nerved youths like ... Jim Lacy can meet such men on their own ground [362].

Note: *Nevada* sold more than two million copies.

24
The Shepherd of Guadaloupe:
Love and Malice

Three-quarters through Zane Grey's *The Shepherd of Guadaloupe*, 1930 (serialized in *Collier's*, 1928), Virginia Lundeen, the heroine, sees a motion picture: "It happened to be a western melodrama of ancient vintage, and in spite of ... a plot that had no semblance to any possible life, a villain who was a perfect counterfeit of Malpass, miraculous hairbreadth escapes from flood, fire, avalanche and glass-eyed pursuer, it diverted her mind, amused, disquieted, and thrilled her" (261). Since the time is shortly after World War I, the movie is a silent one, and the author is chuckling a bit at his own Western romances and the opinions voiced by some sophisticated critics of them. Yes, August Malpass in *Shepherd* is the typical stereotyped villain, with not one good feature in his make-up, and the plot is certainly melodramatic. But Grey need not have short-changed himself about the setting. He meticulously researched the areas he wrote about, knew them at firsthand, and captured the spirit of Western life there.

This novel is set at the Forrest Cottonwoods Ranch, a dozen miles west of Las Vegas, New Mexico, where Cliff Forrest, the hero, grew up. His father, Clay, is a tough Westerner, a pioneer of the area, who was proud of the huge cattle herd he ran. But when its market value dropped to next to nothing, he was forced out by Jed Lundeen, a squatter on the ranch who had loaned him money, apparently gained from a silver mine. Now Clay and his wife live in what had been Lundeen's small adobe dwelling, while the Lundeens occupy the former Forrest home, a palatial Spanish residence. (The two men have become sworn enemies.)

This change in fortunes had occurred unbeknown to Cliff, serving overseas in the war. The first chapter describes him aboard ship, badly wounded, coming home, an embittered man. Grey has written about veterans in other books, for he felt strongly that the war "left greed, selfishness, lawlessness, and crookedness paramount in the hearts of almost all men. I fear my patriotism has been dealt a blow" (in Jackson, 75). In *Shepherd*, he speaks of a "futile" sacrifice, "wasted years," and the "inspired fighting fervor" that Cliff had gone to war with, dying "in the ghastly reality of the truth" (11–12). He is twenty-eight.

After stepping off a transcontinental train at Las Vegas, Cliff is driven to Cottonwoods, in a hired car, still thinking it is his home. He cannot "get his fill of gazing" (31) at the surrounding country. In this he is like Grey himself and all Grey's "heroes." He notices the wildlife, from quail to jack rabbits, and the sight gladdens him, as does the open rangeland. "No changes here!" he thinks (32). Nature is an inspiriting constant.

Then he arrives at the white-walled, red-roofed mansion and is stunned to learn it is not his home. A saving grace is that he is greeted by someone who cares—the Lundeen daughter, remembered only as the red-haired girl he used to tease, now a young woman of twenty-one. (They had met aboard ship, and on the train, but had not recognized each other—she herself had been away the past five years.) Cliff faints. It is too much for him, in his weakened condition. We learn that he had been teenaged Virginia's idol, and still is. Cliff, however, sees her now as the daughter of the man who robbed his father.

And all this has been engineered by arch-villain Malpass. At one time only a business acquaintance of Lundeen, he had worked with the former squatter to get Clay Forrest into debt, then gone through the courts to take away his land and stock. From that point on the two schemers have been thick as thieves, running the ranch and mining interests; Malpass, however, knows that he has his associate under his thumb, that he can take away the property as his very own at any time. He is the brains behind the crooked deals, the "lawlessness" Grey saw erupting after the war.

What Malpass is chiefly after is Virginia as his wife for the status that marrying her will give him. He threatens her that if she will not consent, he can expose her father, sending him to jail, while nothing can be proved against him, August Malpass. She is shaken even more when she realizes that because of business dealings, her father has promised her to this horrible man. She hates his complete personage—his dandified air, immaculate garb, his olive-tan face and sleek black hair. His "long cruel Mexican spurs" (62) symbolize the kind of individual he is, a devil incarnate as his very name means—bringing evil to pass. (Virginia's feelings, however justified, are tainted somewhat with what would now be called racial profiling.)

Fortunately, Virginia has as a confidante Ethel Wayne, a friend intuitively wise, a matchmaker (and -breaker), of whom she says, "Ethel, you're a conscienceless, unscrupulous, terrible young woman, but, oh, what would

I do without you?" (120). And Ethel's varied response is—"I'm a punk fair-weather friend, but try me in a storm" (201); she is "piflicated with joy" (198) to be of service. It is she who will help plan "to throw a monkey-wrench into that Malpass threshing machine" (120).

Grey knows he has created a standout secondary character and lets her appear often in the story. We get to know her mainly by what she says and how she says it. Her speech is just the right mix of cliché and unique, flamboyant expression to catch our ear. For instance, in furthering Virginia's romance with Cliff (and so hindering Malpass's advances), she gives this counter advice to her friend: "Fiddlesticks! You talk like a ninny! It needs only one to start a love-affair, especially if it's the girl" (53). Of Cliff, she says much later in the story, that she likes him "as if he were ten brothers of mine all in one" (201). Grey or one of his characters call her "wise little monitor" (53), "a small whirlwind" (99), "this volatile bit of femininity" (116), and "sly little fox!" (124).

In all this turmoil Virginia has at least regained her friendship with Cliff, and they do have something in common—their love of nature. She feels an "allegiance" to it (111); and when she watches a sunset, the "gorgeousness and riot of intense gold, pink, silver, and blue over that far-flung expanse of desert ma[k]e her ache with the glory of the West" (65). (Henry David Thoreau, too, used this sumptuous word "gorgeous" to describe the setting sun [*Journal* 2:296].) Cliff observes "white blinking stars" through the gnarled branches of a cottonwood and feels they "have a secret they [want] to share with him" (80). (Nature can teach us, as Thoreau, again, relates, if only we will be its pupils [*Journal* 1:471].)

Cliff's first job is tending a small rural store. When his strength fails him in walking home one evening—he actually collapses—Virginia is there to rescue him, not only bodily but with words of hope and encouragement that he desperately needs. He thinks he is dying. She convinces him that he is not the only one with troubles. How can she save herself from the machinations of Malpass and her father? With a clever bit of psychology, to make him forget his own worries, she advises that he help *her*. He suggests that for protection she better "marry someone else pronto" (88). And she, like Priscilla Mullens in Longfellow's poem, *The Courtship of Miles Standish*, says in effect, "Why don't you speak for yourself, Cliff?" Her proposal is for a covert marriage that can be revealed in a time of crisis. He, not daring to express his own love for her, thinks that such a marriage, of convenience, would be taking advantage of her and says he would "only be a burden" (89). The matter is dropped, each unaware of the other's real feelings.

Malpass later hits Cliff Forrest across the face with a riding whip, sensing that he is a rival for Virginia's hand, and wreaks further vengeance by setting the store afire. After further run-ins with enraged fathers and Malpass's physical attack on Virginia, Cliff does speak for himself—and he and Virginia marry secretly, as a temporary safeguard for her.

Cliff then secures work as an accountant in a nearby town's general store. There he is espied by Malpass, who has come in with a huge order, which he will cancel if Cliff is not dismissed. Heated words are exchanged, Cliff in his "liberated passion" (162) jeering that Virginia is his *wife*! and whipping out the marriage certificate as proof. Malpass slashes out, again, with his riding crop. It is time for a showdown, not on main street but in a crowded store.

Cliff, backed against a counter littered with teamsters' gear, feels behind him a "blacksnake," and starts cracking it. Malpass, an up-to-date devil, draws out a small automatic pistol. Dodging Cliff's darting, curling whiplashes, he shoots wildly, hitting a bystander and giving Cliff a slight flesh wound. But the old-fashioned whip wins out, and Malpass drops to the floor. Cliff escapes, jobless, feeling he has betrayed Virginia by divulging the marriage.

When the two fathers hear that their children are married, another showdown occurs, though again not in true Western style with six-shooters. Lundeen assails Clay Forrest with "I'm packin' somethin' that'll hit you harder 'n any bullet." What follows is a war of words, more powerful and dramatic than the previous blacksnake-pistol skirmish. Each man is shouting that it is his family that has been disgraced the most. For abject and dispossessed Forrest the marriage is the "end of pride," the "conclusive stab to bleeding vanity." For Lundeen, the new husband is "dirt" under his daughter's feet. If she had *loved* him, he would "have killed her with his own hands." He brags that he has given his daughter a choice: either divorce Cliff or get out. Forrest retorts that this is white-trash talk: he is giving his son no choice at all—he must get out, period (169–72). Cliff has the final say before leaving for good. He tells Lundeen: "You're no father"; he tells his own father: "You're ... a doddering old idiot. Locked in your insane hate." To both he says: "Now, you cowards, go out and kill yourselves!" (173–74).

The next we hear of Cliff, it is November, and he has become a shepherd working for a local Mexican rancher on the desert—the land of sage and sand. He has chosen a desolate life for a war veteran, still ravaged by his wounds, his wage a few cents a day. With him are the rancher's lad as assistant and four dogs. The sheep total three thousand. Each night he sits before a bed of glowing coals, feeding it with bits of stick and sage in order to warm his hands. He has a racking cough but an instinct to survive. To him the desert is serenely beautiful, filled with a "strange somber mystery" (219). In time it will mend his soul and his body.

His specific job is to guide the sheep south three hundred miles to Guadaloupe Springs, their winter range at a lower altitude: "Sunrises of pale rose with fan rays, ice on still pools that soon melt[s], lonesome full hours with the bleating sheep, sunsets of gold and red over purple walls" (231)—so the days speed by, days from which to gain strength and endurance.

One touching (and telling) incident occurs at these winter quarters. One January morning he discovers the loss of fifty sheep. They have been stolen. It is easy to follow moccasin tracks and sheep hoofprints in the sand, and Cliff gives chase—across the Mexican border. He has his rifle and a box of shells along, also a bag with some mutton and salt, parched corn, and hard biscuits. He treks a few dozen miles and comes upon the thieves' camp at night, finding his quarry "dead-to-rights," so to speak—they have no weapons.

What he sees is no band of Malpassian bandits but some Mexicans, "a poor, ragged, starved lot," about their fire, cooking a sheep, "which task was manifestly of profound importance." They are jabbering amongst themselves, one of them a woman with a baby at her breast. Lying about is the meagerest of camp equipment, also a few dogs, catching the scent of the roasting sheep (237). (To me there is a faintest suggestion of the Christmas scene.)

For Cliff, it is an epiphanic moment. Quietly he crawls away, leaving them to their roasted mutton, with the thought, "Poor peons" (237). His employer can afford to lose a few sheep; if not, he will pay for them. Bedding down elsewhere that same night, he knows that he does not want to be anywhere else but on the desert. "Bitterness had gone from his heart.... What a man needed was silence, loneliness, ... to be in contact with the earth and the elements.... Here the stars ... now spoke to him" (238–39). Next spring when he herds the sheep and their new lambs back, just five miles from his parents' dwelling, he knows that his own home will be "the desert henceforth" (318).

Meanwhile, when Virginia fled from her parents, the same day as Cliff's departure, she took refuge with Ethel Wayne at Colorado Springs. Good old Ethel! She goes into "ecstasies" on learning of the secret marriage and becomes a "clenching-fisted, blazing-eyed little fury" on hearing of Lundeen's casting out his daughter (202). Virginia, for her part, calls her friend an "indefatigable and relentless romancer" and a "crazy, lovesick schoolgirl"; Ethel's reply is—"You bet your life I am. That's why I know things.... I'm sure death on these affairs of the heart." Her reaction to Virginia's assessment of the marriage as strictly a matter of Cliff's goodwill and helpfulness is one terse word: "Bunk!" (204–5).

Virginia stays with Ethel for three weeks, giving them time to tour the city, bent on a lark—and Grey opportunity to show his talent as a humorist.

The women hire a horse and hack with an old driver to explain the sites. First he tells them about himself, in a Mark Twain (or Huck Finn) manner: "I hail from Indianer. Fust come West in 'sixty-eight. Was a lad then an' the redskins made me an orphan. Reckon that everythin' the West could give I got—'cept six feet of ground, an' I near got thet a hundred times" (206).

Ethel, with a mischievous wink, is just the person to lead him on and asks whether he was ever married. His reply of "Lot of times, on an' off" draws her comment: "Well, that's fine. Then you didn't find marriage a failure, like so many people of today?" And his response: "No, indeedee. Marriage is all right, if you kin change often enough" (207). The whole conversation, of four pages, is a riot. Zane Grey was obviously enjoying himself writing this book. Earlier in the story he had Virginia ask a question, seemingly aping the critics who most often accused him of overwriting: "Why this extravagant mess of words?" (116).

Virginia's stay in Colorado is not only for amusement and consolation. She had previously suspected something crooked about Malpass's silver mine at Cottonwoods and had visited the site with her two faithful cowboys (personally hired to look after her fine horses—she loves to ride). They had ridden up to it, seen the rusting machinery, sheds, rail tracks, and trestles; one of the men had checked out the tunnels but found no evidence of any real miners' work carried on. (The investigation permits Grey to comment on how man despoils nature, changing a place of picturesque charm to one of "sordid ugliness" [179].) Now Virginia consults a mining engineer, Jarvis by name, in Denver, who believes the mine was "planted" (211), to deceive her father. He will come out for a thorough investigation.

When he does so, what follows, in human terms, has as much "ugliness" as the original despoliation. While Jarvis is in the mine, Virginia awaits him in the old mine office. Instead, Malpass appears and grapples with her. Moments later, the engineer comes in, with damning evidence. Malpass shoots Jarvis with his automatic, badly injuring him, and the tussle with Virginia resumes. A table collapses, a stove is kicked down, and Virginia, this good-hearted girl, bites, pulls out Malpass's hair, and hits him with the stove's poker.

All this is just a preliminary round, for Lundeen appears. He hears Malpass's account of things, with Jarvis gasping out, "He lies!" as does Virginia. The father, already having second thoughts about being led into crookedness by Malpass's cheating ways, realizes he himself has been cheated. He bellows out that his associate *planted* the mine, *manhandled* his daughter (notice which he mentions first), and Malpass shoots him too. But Lundeen comes on like a bull, "lowering and blood-lustful." Now the real battle occurs, continues outside—Virginia faints—and ends on a broken, tottering trestle bridge over a ravine, both men dying in "awful retribution" (283–86). This is stark pictorial drama, for a movie, say, but perhaps too dark, too graphic in its description, for the general tone of the book.

Circumstances greatly alter for Virginia, for the huge Lundeen estate is now hers. Her first reaction is to exchange homes with Clay Forrest and his wife. She is more comfortable in the old adobe house of her childhood. It is now spring again, but she has not been reconciled to her legal husband. He thinks she must have divorced him—in fact, had been so informed earlier by Malpass (the evil that men do continues to live after them, as Shakespeare has said [*Julius Caesar*, 3.2.80]).

It is at her "new" quarters that Virginia receives Ethel Wayne for a visit. That "galvanizing scion of modern feminism" wants to hear the latest news, her friend's story "backward," from present to past. Ethel's asides, observations, and advice are delightful as usual. She calls her host Bertha, the Sewing-Machine Girl (the title character of a stage melodrama of the time); also, fittingly, Desdemona, Melancholy Mag, and Pollyanna, as each incident is told. Her exclamations include "Served him right" and "You darned fool!" When Virginia says that she bought the sheep Cliff shepherded so that he would not lose his job (thwarting another Malpass machination), the "scion" wants to know if she raised his wages. But it is in actually getting the two together again that she is most forthright: "We're no longer vassals of men. We don't have to wait"; and "After all, it's a matter of love. We're not trying to put over any crooked stuff" (306–12).

So, a little bit of stratagem, and Virginia and Cliff are reunited, in a shepherd's tent, explaining away any misunderstandings, confessing their love for each other. She can buy all the sheep on the range, and he will drive them for her. He need not give up the desert; she can ride out to be with him. For her, he is "My shepherd!" (335).

25

Rogue River Feud:
Low Ebb and Recovery

It may be true that not many of us would include *Rogue River Feud* among Zane Grey's best novels or list it as a personal favorite. Certainly its publishing history bears out this estimate. First published serially in *The Country Gentleman* magazine in 1929 (entitled there as *Rustlers of Silver River*), it did not attain book status for almost two decades, until 1948, nine years after Grey's death. Yet the book deals with themes, often very well, that were central to his more popular novels; for example, man and nature in *The Vanishing American* and *The Call of the Canyon*, and the fate of World War I veterans in *The Shepherd of the Guadaloupe* and, again, *The Call of the Canyon*.

This chapter will consider these themes in the Rogue River setting, a salmon spawning waterway in Oregon, one of Grey's favorite fishing spots, sometimes fished with his entire family. Chapter 1 is wholly about the river, not people. Like Walter Scott (*The Fair Maid of Perth*, 1828), James Fenimore Cooper (*The Prairie*, 1827), and Thomas Hardy (*The Return of the Native*, 1878), Grey emphasizes the natural background. His inspiration comes from nature, and his characters (and their actions) grow out of, are conditioned by, that setting. So here we follow the river's course from an icy cold spring at its mountain source, through cascades and canyoned wildernesses, the fir-encroached beauty of an early-day mining camp called Solitude, and eventually on to Gold Beach at the ocean.

At the river's mouth swarm salmon ready to travel back upstream to their natal gravel beds. En route they face shallow bars, rapids, and other perils, so that only those with strength and endurance reach their goal; none escape "without the wounds of battle" (3).

We meet Keven Bell, the book's hero, in chapter 2. He, like the salmon, is returning to his home, at Grants Pass on the upper reaches of the Rogue, after four years in the military. But he never got to serve overseas, for a cannon, which exploded during training exercises, broke away part of his lower jaw. It was crudely patched up with an iron fitting, but he was left with some memory loss and the sight of one eye also impaired. Despite two years in an army hospital, he remains a "wreck" (7), so he tells his father (his mother has died while he was away). Will he have the strength and endurance to succeed in civilian life?

In the first half of the book, it appears not. Keven is a disheartened man. The army, he feels, taught him "not to care—to revert to savagery" (7). He has lost faith, and his father can only sympathize with his situation: "The damned sordid, rotten part of the world that seems in power. The destructive forces!" (7). Such was particularly Keven's outlook because one of his commanding officers, Gus Atwell, had spread malicious rumors about him in order to cover up his own misdeeds.

His mother's dying wish was that Keven return home to the Rogue, where its waters would cure him. This is his wish too, for he remembers his boyhood enjoyment of the river, drifting on its current, listening to its murmur, fishing for steelhead trout in its shaded pools. The only thing he can think of doing to stay in touch with the river is to net-fish for salmon at its mouth. But there are obstacles along the way. He has become addicted to alcohol, having started to drink whisky to alleviate his physical pains; also, he has partnered with an old boyhood friend, Garry Lord. Garry, although a fine hard-working man when sober, is something of an alcoholic himself, so both a good and bad influence.

Still, there is the river, which they will have to travel down some one hundred miles to their fishing grounds. Keven has already experienced his first sense of peace on coming to it. A sporting goods storekeeper tells him something about the Rogue: "Every bend ... beckons—every pool may bring better luck. Life should be like that" (19). Yes, fishing is like life, and the splendid Rogue symbolizes the very stream of life.

Keven begins his new venture on a bad note. Some Saturday-night drinking has brought out a hidden devil in him, and coming upon his tormenting commander from army days, he breaks a vase over Atwell's head, knocking him unconscious. Then he rushes to join his partner at the river. They were going to leave next day, but now, fleeing arrest, they ship out at night, in a boat made by Keven's father. Keven accentuates his farewell to things by flinging his army uniform into a campfire along the shore with "violence and finality" (23), hoping to be done with the corruption he had experienced in the military.

The downstream journey allows Grey to describe in detail what Congress has since designated as one of America's nineteen "Wild and Scenic

Rivers." That the traverse is also a flight from the law adds color to the account: "Swifter current caught them; the banks blurred; the stern of the skiff rocked and dipped"; then "they bounced high ... and went over straight as a die into a long buffeting incline" (25). Meanwhile, Keven recognizes an affinity with the river, "if only the freedom and loneliness it embodied" (27). He will glory in poverty, privation, whatever. He has the river.

The flight goes through Hellgate Canyon, past Galice, and the Almeda Falls, where police are waiting (the spelling of some of the place-names has changed since Grey's time). But the fugitives are not stopping and choose to shoot the falls, successfully, as the policemen open fire. It is this scene that is displayed on the dustjacket of the Grosset & Dunlap edition. With the river going through two mountain ranges, the Cascade and Coast, there is much wild and scenic landscape to view—at Grave Creek Falls, Rainie Falls, Tyee Rapids, Winkle Bar (where Grey will own a small cabin), Mule Creek Canyon, Solitude, Clay Hill Rapids, and the communities of Illahe and Agness. Eventually the river slows and widens on its final push to the sea.

The two men have escaped the law for now (although Keven will later serve a month's sentence), but their job of net-fishing is formidable because of the opposition of hooligan gangs of fisherman already there. They simply hate upriver rivals—hence, the Rogue River "feud"—and will stop at nothing to thwart their efforts, even pouring sulphuric acid over Keven's drying fish-nets. In this they are supported by a big canning corporation, which has encouraged these same gangs to use illegally sized nets to gut the bay of as many fish as possible. Keven sees that corruption is not just restricted to wartime activities.

Here it is really Grey who is angered by the rape of his beloved outdoors. He assembles various complaints besides fish depletion in a half-page tirade by Keven's partner (82)—the mowing down like hay of forests in Washington, white cedars cut simililarly in Oregon, and redwoods in California "goin' like hotcakes." The latter should stand forever, he claims, because "they're so few, an' so grand, an' somehow part of America." Thus practical concerns are not the only issue. And there is another issue as well in this statement about the loss of trees: "It'll dry up our rivers"—an ecological assessment, surely, from the author back in 1929! Worst of all, the governments of the time, those "short-term guys," stand with their "greased" hands behind their backs. Grey, in fact, is furious.

When Keven and Garry try to take up the game violators' undersize nets at night in order to have evidence against them, the two men are caught unawares, Garry clubbed senseless with an oar while Keven springs at the assailant with a fish knife, killing him in self-defense. Then he makes his escape, alone, walking up the river, fleeing "into the fastnesses of the Rogue wilderness" (95). Nature comments on this wild, dark night, with its oppressive atmosphere and lightning flashes and finally a mountain cloudburst.

So ends the rather bleak first half of the book: Keven, a disabled, mistreated, embittered war veteran, unsuccessful at his first job, is now a "killer." The events to follow are in sharp contrast as he must quell a different feud, one within himself, and begin his slow recovery. He walks as far as Solitude and comes upon Beryl Aard, a girl he had known before the war and a child of nature (the woods were her school), now a spirited young woman of twenty. She had fallen in love with him four years earlier. She still loves him, unconditionally, but before that love can reach fruition in marriage, she and Keven will need to work out some things together. She knows what she wants in a husband, and what she does not want.

Keven, because of his cloudy memory, does not recall her, but once she talks of fly fishing, his mind grows clear. She tells him: "The river was your god. I was jealous of the river. You loved it best, and then the water ouzels and the steelhead" (103). Keven will work for her father, and the Rogue will truly be his salvation now, along with the back-to-nature life it engenders. It will make up for everything he has lost, she assures him. With a woman's instinctive wisdom and patience, she feels—as do we readers—that what she is going to do in guiding his recovery will be for his own good as well.

First, he has to overcome his alcoholism, no mean feat, and Grey, a complete teetotaler himself, refers to Keven's struggle ten or more times over the next few chapters: "that serpent of fire within coiled and gnawed" (123). But with temptation finally under control, he begins to sleep better and regains his appetite, welcome signs in overcoming his rundown condition. Beryl is ever encouraging and understanding.

What Keven has yet to do is to forget past ills and, in Grey's words, lose himself in that "vague sensorial perception" (134) of the world about him; that is, to become a man again "who reveled in his senses, ... to smell and see and hear and feel his way back to realization of his [primal] state" (147). For doing so, he has a model in Beryl, a "one-eighth" Native (122) who loves the wild. He watches her as they stroll together, she unconsciously holding an oak leaf and pine needles, smelling them, then unthinkingly caressing the firs, listening to falling water, and seeing every living creature before he does. We sense her animality, something that a lot of us have mostly forfeited in our urban, fast-paced, high-tech life.

Grey has a Thoreauvian sensuousness, nowhere better illustrated than in his earlier novel of the 1920s, *The Vanishing American*, but well exemplified in *Rogue River Feud* too. He has a gift for describing nature with an appeal to the senses, but instead of doing so in the first person, in a personal reflection, he does so fictionally through his characters. A fine example comes at the end of chapter 16.

When I finished reading the chapter, I simply stopped, went back and re-read, aloud, the last page and a half, just to grasp more fully the marvelous flow of words, the rich sensuous imagery of this prose-poetry. Here Keven is looking down on Beryl's favorite view of the Rogue, able to see it now as she does and so show us his return to full health, mental and physical. I will quote from the last paragraphs:

> he was gazing ... over wooded basins and black canyons, over labyrinthine mazes of gold and red and magenta, ... to the ragged iron cliffs, and to the tiny blue-and-silver thread between.... The gulf in the green earth yawned beneath; the mighty slopes flowed down; the river wound its way to be lost; the lilac haze spread across the valley. The white clouds sailed to cast their shadows. And the soaring golden eagle black-barred the sky. Low and far away roared the river. Up the cool heights wafted the woody smells.... And the past of man merged in the present, strange and vague to peering eyes, yet strong and attainable in the scents of the earth [151].

For me, this page and a half is the climax, not of the plot but of the book itself, the high point—as contrasted with the nadir, the skirmish and killing over fishnets earlier at Gold Beach. Things happen quickly from here on. Keven comes to love Beryl as she him—much of their togetherness occurs on the shores of the Rogue, fly-fishing for steelhead (she's the better fisherman, incidentally). They journey by horseback to the nearest train, travel to Portland, and get married, Keven also getting his jaw permanently mended and his bad eye tended to. Then it's back, this time to Grants Pass, Keven's hometown, for shopping. There they meet Keven's father, still in good spirits, learn that the rumors against Keven have been squelched (and his army commander's activities exposed), that his name was cleared in the fishnet affair (even the violators apprehended), and that Garry, his fishing partner, was not killed or drowned but is alive, married, and running a little fish shop nearby.

All these happy endings and the slaphappy frontier humor in Keven's revealing of his own good fortune to old acquaintances may be a little much for some readers, but things fittingly quiet down: the couple are back at their old Solitude fishing grounds on the Rogue, which, we know, has meant so much to Keven's recovery. Beryl refers to her husband as "My fisherman, whom I've promised to love, honor, and obey all my life. Oh, dear!" The "Oh, dear!" tells us that she will still be her own strong self—as well as a faithful companion too. Their marriage will be a happy one: "And the river glide[s] on..., its eternal song, low and musical, near at hand, droning sweet melody from the rapid at the bend, and filling the distant drowsy air with its soft thunder" (218).

26
Robbers' Roost: Road to Regeneration

We never know Jim Wall's real name, yet he is the main character of Zane Grey's *Robbers' Roost*, 1932 (serialized in *Collier's*, 1930). He hardly shows heroic qualities—has once helped to hold up a bank and a train, then later shoots a man and only escapes hanging by breaking out of jail, after killing the jailer to do so. "Been shooting my way out of one jam after another" (18) describes his life thereafter. Grey writes, already on the first page, that he was someone "who had left events behind him" (1). But an unfeeling thug? hardly that either. He takes special care of his horse, Bay, addressing him affectionately as "old boy" (10). Sunsets are a particular attraction to him, and he seeks out vantage points the better to enjoy the scenic vistas before him. Of course, as a sometime gunman, he needs to be alert to everything around him and "misse[s] nothing" (12): "So many damn fools wantin' to try you out!" (13), his new acquaintance, Hank Hays, tells him.

When they meet, Hays is out recruiting men for his boss, an English rancher, Bernie Herrick, who is trying to make a go of things in the Henry Mountains of southern Utah. Having bought ten thousand head of cattle, Herrick hit upon the idea of hiring gunmen as part of his crew to protect his herd from the many rustlers in the area. The problem is that some of these hired "gun-toters, and plain out-an'-out bad men" (16) are themselves rustlers out to steal Herrick's herd. Really, there are two distinct bands of thieves working "for" the rancher, each trying to engineer the big heist before the other one can. Hays heads one such outfit, Bill Heeseman the other.

Now, in his "rolling-stone career" (19), Jim throws in his lot with Hays, even though he feels a dislike for and disgust with the man. The whole situation, however, interests him and appeals to his "thirst for adventure" (19). "He had been a lone wolf for so long that the society of any class of men would have been a relief" (29). Still, he cannot help "meditat[ing]" over his position—he is that kind of man—and in an hour "hung suspended between dusk and night," with the soothing sounds of nature about him (running stream and coyotes' far-off cry), he ponders his position. Every man, he thinks, has some "caverns of memory" of a better life, maybe an earlier life with parents and siblings (40–41). What has changed and why? Why doesn't he just ride off, away from this skullduggery? It seems as though nature is intimating a better world for him elsewhere, yet he lingers.

Before he and Hays arrive at Herrick's ranch, they must pass through the brakes country about the Dirty Devil River, a hellish area that shows nature at its "most awful, grim and ghastly" (47). This speaks to the moral level Jim must descend to in order to work for a rustler. At the ranch Jim notes, with his usual keen eye, that not one of Hays's associates is a cowman. He is indeed in a den of thieves, but is there any honor among them? It is a question Grey poses several times as the story proceeds.

Grey individualizes each of these men with some unique trait. The eldest is constantly squeezing his clammy hands; another is bluff and hearty; a third, gimlet-eyed. The fourth, a wiry fellow, Smoky Slocum by name, suspicious of Jim immediately, sniffs about him, weasel-like. Then there are the two additional men hired along with him, a brooding malcontent and a happy-go-lucky cook. Jim himself remains quiet, soft-spoken, not one to seek quarrels—altogether the attitude of a gunman who is his own man. He well knows that his security lies "solely in being able to instill doubt and fear" (53). There is already some antagonism among the group.

Jim is warmly welcomed by Herrick, who recognizes the new hand as someone really knowing something about cowboying. Further, Jim's manner shows him to be better educated than the other employees (he had been a country-school teacher in his late teens, we learn). He is now given the job of foreman/bookkeeper. Hays, Herrick's superintendent, is still Jim's boss—in two ways, on the ranch and in the rustlers' camp. That Jim has so quickly gained Herrick's confidence will help in secretly stealing the cattle.

Then a complication arises with the upcoming arrival of Herrick's sister, Helen, age twenty-two, determined to live with her bachelor brother. Both Jim and Hays are affected personally. Jim has already considered how good it would be to remain on the ranch, "to have a home" (62), but he does not like the idea of a handsome young woman being around, not with all the ruffians working there—eleven in Heeseman's outfit, eight in Hays's. He may be the only robber adhering to one article of the unwritten code of the West—respect for women. Yet he cannot be squeamish without being treacherous to fellow gang members. Though uneasy about things, it seems at least for now, he can shrug his shoulders and let whatever will be, be.

Meanwhile, Hays continues scheming. He has changed his mind about going slowly regarding the cattle heist—"Never mind why" (66)—and wants to get at it right away. What his men do not know, except Jim, is that Helen Herrick is the reason. "Nature had endowed Jim with sensitiveness and life had dealt him iron" (72). He is ever "trying to pierce through the back of Hays'[s] head" (86). He senses that greed has overcome Hays, and power. The man could have stolen the whole herd at any time from under the Englishman's nose, as planned; now he can abduct Helen as well, for a huge ransom.

The members of his gang come to an agreement about the grand cattle theft. Five of them will pretend to quit Herrick's employ, being touchy about gunman Jim. What they will do is hide out in the Dirty Devil brakes and drive Herrick's herd, a few thousand at a time, fifty miles to Grand Junction to sell them there, at forty dollars a head. There is some need to hurry with the process, for Heeseman and his men will soon notice the sudden decline in stock.

Heeseman, in fact, calls on Jim, when he feels something is astir, for he knows that Herrick's new foreman is a cut above the others. He tells Jim just one fact, then leaves—that Hays had been his partner once, and doublecrossed him. Jim can ponder that! What sticks in his craw is the duplicity of Hays. Having so acted once, he can have something up his sleeve again. Jim feels confirmed in his earlier suspicions regarding Hays. By giving Jim such acumen here and elsewhere, Grey is able to analyze the character of the rustlers, both camps of them, at first hand as it were. His psychological probes make *Robbers' Roost* one of his better novels. New facets of some trait, revealed as the plot enfolds, make for interesting reading, especially those displayed in the "thronging thoughts" of Jim himself, who grows throughout the story. Men of his type, says Grey, make a "complexity of self-preservation" (78).

It is April now, and Herrick asks Jim to get Helen by buckboard from the stage at Grand Junction. In the crude, wild West of Jim's world of late, she is a vision—"dancing, laughing violet eyes," a "pulsing vitality." His blood is "heated." Then he discovers she has keen senses for nature, like his: "I want to see, to smell, to feel, to gloat," she says (98). When he stops to let her enjoy a vista, her awed silence is "amply eloquent" (104). They set off again, at breakneck speed, so that she can indulge what she calls her "wild strain" (101). But as fast as he drives, he cannot go "fast enough to escape from himself" (105). He is smitten.

In his position as foreman, Jim is later asked by Herrick to accompany his sister on her rides across the ranch, to acquaint her with the country (and she can ride like a Tartar). Jim thinks it is a good time to tell her that she cannot continue such rides alone—he warns her of a possible kidnapping.

She thinks his caution is absurd, and the two get into a real spat, nasty and nastier (Grey, again, as in other books, shows his mastery in writing dialogue). Still, when in adjusting her saddle, their faces almost meet, he, "without a thought, in a flash," kisses her (125). Here is the stuff, surely, of typical, predictable, Western *romance*; one can picture the accompanying illustration that would appear in a pulp Western magazine.

And there is more. He roughly and menacingly continues his arduous advances before, like a "maddened giant" (126), throwing her aside. He has *two* motives for his action, he tells her: his love and his wish to frighten her, to protect her from men worse than himself. This is the Wild West, and she and her brother better go back to England before they are both ruined. Who knows which motive is foremost; likely one fostered the other. He says he will leave.

She, in horror, recognizes his double motive, yet with further thought is "fascinated by something looming" (127), and after a mostly silent ride home, she, ahead of Jim, advises him not to go. "Who could make anything of a woman?" (128), Jim is left to ponder.

Things are fast coming to a head. Back at the ranch quarters, there is a showdown in Hays's gang. Smoky and his fellow drivers in their cattle thefts have, without consultation with Hays, disposed of all the rest of the herd in one huge drive instead of continuing with several smaller ones. Now the rustlers have to leave, immediately, before Herrick, or Heeseman, find out. They plan their escape for that night, but Hays is upset. Jim has revealed to the others their leader's wish to hold Helen hostage. That now seems balked, which surmise Hays affirms, but who knows? Hays will join his men later, along with one associate.

Jim has to ride out with the group. Despite some misgivings he assumes that his fears for Helen are far-fetched under the circumstances. Honor among thieves!—it seems that Hays will be as loyal to his men as they are to him. And they do not want their situation complicated by having to harbor a woman for ransom.

When Hays and his companion catch up to the rustlers next day, a third individual is with them. He *has* kidnapped Helen. There is near mutiny; Smoky roars out that Hays has double-crossed them, calls him a cheat and a liar. They will take Helen back at once, but, as Hays explains, they cannot; Heeseman and his outfit are on their trail. What's more, Hays's associate is badly wounded. They need to get away, and fast.

Which they do. Hays leads them through the hellish brakes country of the Dirty Devil River, an appropriate refuge for evil perpetrators. There is a brief skirmish with Heeseman's crew along the way, evil fighting evil. Then Hays's gang eludes its rivals in a maze of canyons, tracking ever downward (fittingly) and through a dark night (naturally enough), until it finally descends "into a black, round hole" (157), to a hideout, a robbers' roost. The men can live there indefinitely, but they know that Heeseman, with reinforcements, will eventually find them. That will mean a final gunfight, a kind of armageddon—if the Hays outfit can remain a cohesive group.

There is no doubt that Hays has betrayed the rest. *Dishonor among thieves* is the verdict. He not only has doomed himself but also the comradeship within the group. The woman has changed it: "her presence alone mean[s] disintegration, disruption, and death" (165). Jim assures Helen, in secret, that he will get her out of this mess, one way or another. To do so, he enlists the aid of Smoky, the only other member, he intuits, who will respect womanhood. "Wal, you're a sharp cuss, Jim," Smoky declares (170). They will see that Helen gets treated like a lady.

The downfall of once mighty Hank Hays, and consequently of his gang (his little kingdom), has begun. Grey describes, and analyses, the fall step by step. Major incidents are reflected in Hays's gaze as "lightnings of a desperate soul" (192). First, his associate in the kidnapping dies of his gunshot wound; he had revealed to Jim and Smoky that Hays had taken $16,000 from Herrick and jewels from Helen during the capture—spoils not divided among the rustlers. Jim tells the others "and le[aves] the poison to brew" (200). Furthermore, a thwarted Hays shoots one of his men over a gambling dispute. This leader, we see, is something of a Jack Kells figure (in *The Border Legion*).

Another morning dawns balmy and sweet; "mockingbirds are bursting their throats" (209). Jim thinks such music is indeed a "mockery" of all the trouble they are in. But nature is certainly *not* commenting on the hell that is forthcoming. (Maybe it is forecasting what will eventually follow.) Hays begins the day by doling out his double-cross loot, but maintains that he will keep Helen for himself. She, however, unnoticed and sneaking up behind him, steals his gun out of its holster. The others quickly bind him hand and foot. At that instant Jim returns from his cliff lookout post, saying the Heeseman bunch is approaching. They will need every man for the upcoming fray, including Hays, who is now unbound.

The battle is detailed over nineteen pages (chapter 14). With five men left, Hays risks his life in sneaking around the enemy—"there was something gloomy and splendid about him then" (229). With two more men killed, Smoky tries the same tactic. Hays, "grand in his disregard of life" (236), is able to kill Heeseman; Smoky "plug[s] [who] know[s] how many" before he "cashe[s] in" (238). Finally, all that are left to fight the rival rustlers are Jim, a wounded Hays, and Helen, who had been hidden in a cave.

Jim, ever astute, realizes that Hays had been fighting not for his lost leadership nor any honor among fellow robbers, but for *Helen*. That accounts for his "infernal blaze of unquenchable hate" (243), and he draws on his only real rival left—Jim. But Jim can draw faster. The last shot is fired.

There is really no time to waste now for Jim and Helen. They must get away quickly before others come. And a storm advances. Lightning rips and thunder crashes, and they ride off in the heavily falling rain. The difficulty is that they must head out a new way to avoid remnants of the Heeseman gang. Jim does not know the brakes country. Two days' travel should get them out of this Dirty Devil land, which has now turned to gumbo mud.

The end of the second day finds them on a ledge in a gorge with an impassable waterfall before them, caused by the continuing downpour, and no trail behind, for it has slid away. They spend the night huddled together, fearing death by drowning in a torrent or smothering in an avalanche. Whatever time is left them will be a "nameless terror" (268). She, completely played out, falls asleep in his arms, while he ponders: "What had he ever done with his life that he should long to prolong it? ... A ne'er-do-well, a failure, a rolling stone, a robber, a killer! Could he pray to save it now, to go on being the same kind of hard, wicked, useless man? No, by the God she whispered of—he could not. He would not..." (270).

The ledge holds, and the storm ends. They can go on and do—with some help along the way—to her brother's ranch. Jim feels he has done his duty and must leave. He cannot imagine Helen ever loving him, a onetime denizen of a robbers' roost. This man—who "missed nothing" (12), whom nature endowed with "sensitiveness" (72), and whose astute intuition "pierce[d] through" people's minds (86)—still cannot "make anything of a woman" (128). It is only when Helen takes him back to the place "where it happened" (294), his first kissing her, that he comes to his senses and knows that she will return his love. It's what he *is* that has made her love him.

Jim Wall encapsulates what Owen Wister saw as the typical Westerners in *The Virginian* (the first Western ever written, 1902): "In their flesh our natural passions ran tumultuous; but often in their spirit sat hidden a true nobility, and often beneath its unsuspected shining their figures took a heroic stature" (24).

27

The Trail Driver:
An Arduous Trek

Texas was rapidly becoming a cattle empire following the Civil War, but with no railhead for shipping its Longhorn cattle (first brought out by early Spanish explorers). It was Jesse Chisholm of Scottish-Cherokee descent who first drove a herd north across Indian Territory (later Oklahoma) in the mid–1860s, forging ahead on a trail named for him, more or less where Highway 81 is today. In Kansas it steered for Abilene on the Kansas Pacific Railroad. Later, a branch swung westerly as the railway, ever pushing onward, created a nearer railhead at Ellsworth. Trail driving on the Chisholm lasted only a relatively short time, roughly 1867–1875.

Other trails were used too. The Western Trail, 1876–1885, connected with Dodge City on a more southerly line—the Atchison, Topeka, and the Santa Fe Railroad. It crossed the Red River, Texas's northern boundary, not at Red River Station as did the Chisholm, but 125 miles farther west at Doan's Store. Zane Grey in writing *The Trail Driver*, 1936 (serialized in *McCall's*, 1931), confused the routes of these two trails, the Chisholm and the Western, but otherwise the incidents he described are true to what typically happened on this kind of arduous trek.

Grey chooses the year 1871 for his drive. The previous three years had seen one-and-a-half million cattle move up the Chisholm. Then in 1871, the cattle traffic was so much that thirty outfits were waiting to cross the flood-swollen Red River, with herds "backed up for 40 miles" (McDowell, 83). Grey speaks of the year appearing "destined to be the greatest for cattle-drives north" since Chisholm started the first one (1).

Adam Brite of San Antonio, the middle-aged boss of the trail drive in Grey's novel, has already made one drive in spring. Now buying as many cattle as possible, he essays to drive a herd of four thousand five hundred, really two herds in one—the usual number is two thousand head. He will need at least ten drivers, "the hardest-driving and hardest-shooting on the ranges" (2).

The job is not an easy one, with storms, floods, sleet, and drought some of the natural hazards. A lightning strike may set a whole herd to stampeding, as may the annual northward migration of buffalo. Then there are possible attacks by Native bands, and Grey does not blame them—their way of life is being threatened by the white man's slaughter of these same buffalo. He concludes chapter 1: "Many a driver ha[s] failed to reach the end of the long Trail" (12). (The Chisholm was six hundred miles long.)

The assembling of Brite's drivers reminds me of the marshaling of Captain Ahab's crew in Melville's *Moby-Dick*, 1851. Brite's cowboys reveal a similar broad cast of characters, each of whom is individualized with some unique trait or mannerism. The foreman, Joe Shipman, also known as Texas Joe or just plain Tex, is only twenty-four but has already done three drives. He has eyes "singularly direct, and a lazy, cool little smile" (3)—a handsome fellow. His wage is thirty dollars a month. The others, we assume, receive less.

One of them, hired on the spot, is a gunman, just escaped from a shootout over a card game. Brite has some second thoughts about "harboring an outlaw on the dodge" (11), but then considers that he is fortunate to have Pan Handle Smith along—chapter 2 ends with this statement: "The Old Trail was a rough and bloody proposition; ... anything might be met upon it" (28). Smith, it seems, is the same character who goes by the name of "Panhandle" (one word) as the hero in *Valley of Wild Horses*, written four years previously. We see him now in his early, wilder young manhood.

The rest of the cast are Texas Joe's young pard, Less Holden; the tenderfoot Bender (no first name); the black cook, Alabama Moze (no last name); a Californian, Whittaker (no first name either); and a quintet of riders who come along with half the herd that Brite bought, each a Texan under twenty—the boss loves Texans and is a father figure over them, indeed over his entire crew. These five are Deuce Ackerman, San Sabe (with Mexican blood), Rolly Little, Ben Chandler, and Roy Hallet. (Note the strong "Western" names of all the hired men.) By the drive's end (and its aftermath) only one of them, excluding the foreman and the cook, will survive—Pan Handle. The outfit will have been "tried," as Brite says, or, as Texas Joe adds, tried by "what happens along" (16).

The first evening "along," some dozen miles out of San Antonio, nothing has gone awry: "The sun set in a cloudless, golden sky. An occasional bawl of a cow from the stream bottom broke the silence. A cooling zephyr of wind came through the grove, rustling the leaves, wafting the camp-fire smoke away. Brite had the satisfaction of being on the Trail again" (17).

That same evening, Reddie Bayne, a sixteen-year-old, rides into camp and is given the job of wrangler, guiding the two-hundred-horse remuda that accompanies the cattle. Reddie is really a girl and so informs Brite. He is the first to suspect a developing romance between her and his foreman, not because of a display of any kind feelings between them but because of the caustic jibes they exchange. The boss is a wise father figure.

In one instance Texas Joe yells at Reddie not to swim her horse back across a river because of the adverse current. (He is concerned for her safety.) Back she comes anyway "with suppressed excitement, her eyes large and dark and daring." "Sorry I scared you" is her comment (128). The banter continues: "I ordered yu back. Did yu heah *thet*?"—"Course I did. Laws! Yu'd woke the daid" (128).

Meanwhile, the drive continues, with its varied sense impressions, including "the incessant stir of cattle, ... the never failing smell of dust, manure, and heated bodies" (44). Grey is not squeamish about mentioning unpleasant sensations, just as earlier he had tempered the morning's "magnificent spectacle" of cattle moving on with the sound of gunshots ("attesting to the fact that the drivers were shooting new-born calves that could not keep up with their mothers" [33]). And along the way Brite is ever wondering, as in chapter 3, "how many head of stock, and how many drivers, [will] never get to Dodge" (35).

Troubles start happening. Rustlers nab some of the outlying cattle, also make off with a few horses. "[T]wo-bit stampeders," Brite calls them (63), who collect a few head here and there from legitimate herds to finally get enough to drive as their own cattle. Two such rustlers are Wallen and Ross Hite. They and their men draw up in a semicircle about Brite's camp and claim that Reddie is their truant hireling. When it becomes apparent that their intention is to abuse her, Texas Joe's gun flashes red before Wallen can even reach for his, and the latter pitches from his saddle. Such deadly response presages what will happen later to one of Brite's men, Roy Hallet, when he proves traitor to his outfit and agrees to secretly aid Hite. At a court martial to get at the facts, Hallet draws but Pan Handle fires. (Hite will receive a similar comeuppance, again from Pan, before the story ends.)

Other troubles relate to the logistics of the cattle drive itself, cattle bogging down in quicksand, for instance, or wind and rain rousing the herd overnight and starting it to drift off course. The men survive the extra exertion of working in total darkness, braced by their "profanity [left unstated] and grim humor" (60) appropriate to the situation, but their mounts are completely spent, useless for the rest of the drive. Likewise, a hailstorm causes considerable grief, covering the ground half a foot deep with walnut-sized pellets. The cattle are stunned, lying on the ground or staggering along, while the drivers, bruised and bloody, resemble men in a fistfight.

River crossings tend to be the most perilous of all trail activities in actual loss of human life, let alone cattle being swept away and not rounded up—or melded, accidentally or on purpose, into other herds. At the Colorado River, still in Texas, Brite loses Ben Chandler, who had felt called upon for extra derring-do to offset his original siding with Hallet's treachery (despite fatherly Brite's forgiveness, or maybe because of it). He is swept four miles downstream with half the herd that he is trying to save, does successfully beach them, but drowns in the process. And these cattle, unprotected, are easily stolen by Hite.

Even the little Wichita River presents problems because a freshet is roaring along. In the interval of waiting for the water to recede, the drivers rescue what is left of a pioneer wagon train after a Comanche raid, by attacking the Natives. While this is taking place, Hite and his men steal the remaining half of their herd. Nature, Grey notes, is unaffected by this double slaughter—of the pioneers by the Comanches and of the Comanches by the trail drivers. Brite observes: "how peaceful, even pastoral that [Witchita River] valley scene! The river glided on yellow as corn; the summer breeze waved the grass and willows; flowers bloomed along the banks and birds sang; the sky spread a blue canopy overhead, accentuated by white cloud-sails" (192).

Brite and crew seem fairly relaxed about the two thefts. Let Hite drive the huge herd for a while; foreman Joe and Pan Handle will get it back when an opportune time comes along. That occurs during a nighttime storm and deluge of rain. The two men enter the milling herd from opposite sides and take potshots at Hite's cowboys during lightning flashes. It is another night to remember: "thunder burst[s] like disrupted mountains.... But before that reverberation roll[s] away another zigzag rope of lightning divide[s] the dense cloud" (216). The plan works, even better than the marksmen intended. Next morning they come back with their cattle, totaling six thousand! (Hite had annexed fifteen hundred elsewhere.)

Now on to Red River. It is this watercourse that usually gives the most trouble—more drivers are lost at its various crossings than at all the other rivers combined (McDowell, 84). However, Grey devotes only one short paragraph to Brite's herd swimming it, at Doan's Store. True, four hours are needed, and a hundred Longhorns lost.

Brite and company are now in Indian Territory. Here direct actions of the Kiowa and Comanche tribes interfere with the drive. The Kiowas one night stampede the tail end of the herd, the cowboys needing three days to round up the cattle. The delay means that two other herds pass them by, getting first jump at better areas of grazing. Comanches can be a bigger threat, but when they appear, Brite is very generous in handing out beef, tobacco, flour, and beans—doing so he calls "this missionary business" (248)—and averts bloodshed.

A swollen, unnamed creek then claims another driver. The downhill course to the water would ordinarily have killed hundreds of the herd too, with the onrushing animals knocking down and trampling dead the ones ahead, but the high and strong water flow immediately sweeps away those first entering it out of harm's way downstream. Not so for San Sabe, the Mexican vaquero fronting the maddened herd. Ironically, he usually had quieted the herd each evening with his haunting Spanish folksongs, a "magic," says Grey, that soothed the Longhorns' restlessness (53).

After crossing the south branch of the Canadian River, yet another memorable night befalls the drivers (364–69). Brite gives a warning: "Boys, we're in for a galvanizin'." The atmosphere is charged with electricity, a phenomenon caused by a storm whose charge floats about like a visible fire around horses' manes and ears and about people's heads. This seems like magic too, supernatural, and Grey uses terms such as "singular," "mysterious," and "fiendish" to describe it. We call the phenomenon St. Elmo's fire.

It can also be seen about the masts of ships. Ahab in Melville, again, points to the ghostly phosphorescence acting as a white flame to guide his sailors to the great white whale, Moby Dick. Grey sees the "fire" as a psychological oppression to be endured by the drivers and the driven. The cattle are frozen in their tracks; the horses hide their heads against each other; the men are mesmerized, caught in a brimstone nightmare and freed from it by only "the reality of the sunrise, ... the solid earth under their feet[,] the grazing stock." Texas Joe sums up the experience: "All the hell I ever deserved I got last night."

The drive has now lasted three months. There is one more noteworthy experience, an obviously physical one, before trail's end—the buffalo stampede. Grey uses nine pages to describe it (274–83). What is most interesting is its onset, gradually recognized for what it is, and the follow-up reaction of cattle and cowboys. At first the drivers hear something—"like the wind in the pines," then "like low thunder." Then the event becomes visual—"a peculiar yellow, billowing smoke ... rising. Dust clouds!" A cowboy yells, *"Stampede!"* and the realization dawns that both people *and* cattle are "trapped in a circle," and that they all could be "pounded by millions of hoofs into a bloody pulp." The yellow cloud "blot[s] out the sky halfway to the zenith." The gap lessens between cattle and rampaging buffalo. The stampede mania at once claims the world, the ground shakes, and sound vanishes, lost in a *deafening* roar, in an encompassing "flood of fur covering the whole prairie."

For once a river's appearance is a blessing. The Cimarron saves the drivers and their herd, or most of them, as the thundering buffalo split around an island. Bender and Whittaker have gone down, are dead, and one thousand cattle are lost. It takes several days for the surviving drivers to round up five thousand others, five hundred more than Brite started with.

Roaring Dodge City welcomes them all. The sale of the herd brings in more than seventy thousand dollars; Texas Joe and Reddie agree for once—to marry, Joe skipping the usual post-drive drunken orgy; Pan spots Hite in the "city," outdraws and kills him, right on the busy street. The lawlessness of Dodge is nowhere better illustrated than in the crowd's reaction: "A rush of feet, excited cries, a loud laugh, then Pan Handle ... wrench[ed] his gaze from his fallen adversary.... He sheathed his gun and strode on to join Brite. They split the gathering crowd and hurried down the street. Dodge roared on..." (301).

Grey had just described the town's activity: "Laughter without mirth ran down the walk. The stores were full. Cowboys in twos and threes and sixes trooped by, young, lithe, keen of eye, bold of aspect, gay and reckless." He then added: "It might have been the march of empire," but then qualified that statement with this addendum: "the tragedy of progress" (300).

The "progress" is seen in the fate of three of Brite's teenaged drivers. Much earlier in the book, in chapter 3, Grey had characterized trail drivers as having "no thought of the morrow," just an "unalterable obligation" to stick to the job and finish it (34). So here we have Less Holden, Rolly Little, and Deuce Ackerman on a hotel's porch steps, sober, but up to some horseplay to pass the time. The play becomes a little rough, then turns to blows and finally deadly gunfire—all die. Grey, with superb writing, has built this seemingly harmless episode into an ironic twist of all the good fellowship engendered by the hard trail drive and the boss's constant fatherly concern for his faithful boys.

Brite's brief, elegiac comment also reveals the author's grasp of the complexity of human nature: "Poor, wild, fire-hearted boys! ... All in less than a minute! My God! ... Oh, the pity of it, Pan! To think thet the grand game spirit of these cowboys—the soul thet made them deathless on the trail—was the cause of such a tragedy!" (299).

28

Thunder Mountain: Gold-Rush Cowboy

The setting of *Thunder Mountain* is the Sawtooth Mountains of Idaho. The novel was first serialized in *Collier's*, 1932, and published as a book in 1935. It is a marked contrast to such works as *Desert Gold*, 1913, and *Tappan's Burro*, 1923, where lone miners wander the desert looking for the precious yellow metal. In *Thunder Mountain*, we have a mad stampede for it, and a tent town springing up with its plethora of dance halls and gambling dens. Here Zane Grey has an opportunity to explore the gold-rush mentality over a whole book.

First he tells us why all this mineral is present in the sandbars of a meandering steam feeding into the Salmon River. A looming mountain's southern face slid downward in the long-ago past, leaving gold bearing silt and gravel in the valley below, shorn from rich veins higher up. The mountain remained unstable—a low rumble "seemed to growl" (2) from its interior every so often. When a beaver heard the thunder and saw tremors across her pond, she and her cub immediately left, fearing for their safety. Years later, a group of fugitive Native Americans sought shelter in this valley with its abandoned beaver dam. But the chief heard a moan, as from "a subterranean monster ... in the bowels of the earth" (5), and they left, believing the Great Spirit had warned them, disregarding the fact that one of the Natives had grasped a handful of wet sand there flecked with golden flakes.

That Native in his old age informs two prospecting brothers, Sam and Jake Emerson, of his find. They, with a younger third brother, Kalispel, head out for the valley. Sam is fascinated by the layout, Jake sees it to be a gloomy hole, and Kalispel loves it, not because of any mining possibilities but because it is a beautiful wilderness stocked with game. He will hunt food for the camp, a sport he enjoys, while the others hunt gold, a more arduous task. This is not a fair trade-off, but it shows his happy-go-lucky manner, also his immaturity in not accepting his full responsibilities for the trio. He has been a cowboy in Montana, getting into a few scrapes, now glad to be rescued from that hard life. What he wants is a little ranch somewhere "and a wife to keep him straight" (10).

The brothers hear the thunder too, Jake and Kal thinking landslide, with Sam the wisest, speculating on an earthquake. The mountain, with its thunder, is like a character in the book, a chorus in a Greek play, commenting on the action. At one point Kal sees it as a clock recording time, nature "audit[ing]" its books and noting the brevity of man's life (105). In another instance it is downright menacing, waiting. Kal speaks to it as if it were more than a clock, as if it were indeed a person: "Thunder an' grumble, old man.... You'll never bury me an' my gold" (153). Later, it seems to reply with "warning whispers of catastrophe" (186), "waiting there for the great hour of its existence" (199).

But everything starts out all right for the three brothers when the story begins. Kal likes the intimacy of the place, walled in as it is, and gives himself over to daydreaming—"a still sweet, drowsy languor pervaded the place" (15). Jake, meanwhile, pans the sandbars and finds gold everywhere, in prodigious amounts, and informs Kal that his dream of a cattle ranch will come true. Kal lets out a whoop, and is answered by Sam from upstream. He has found the mother lode and brings back a huge slab of quartz, all he can lift, veined with gold. Then they hear another sound, the mountain rumbling a "faint deep thunder of warning" (23).

After some discussion, the brothers decide what to do. Sam will stay and guard the site, Jake will take the quartz to mining men in Boise and sell a half-interest in their holding for no less than a hundred thousand dollars, and Kal will go to Salmon for supplies. (Mum's the word so far as the whereabouts of the strike.) They should be back in a month. It is Kal's adventures en route that we follow—he now becomes the central character of the novel.

There is some problem with Grey's choice of "hero." Often the main protagonist in one of his Westerns is a determined, focused, hard-working individual. Literary critics may throw up their hands at such portrayal, but the imaginative reader can ascribe whatever interior attributes and motivations are necessary to fill out his character as the action proceeds. When the hero is simply an easy-going, loquacious, "pretty wild" young cowboy (42), there is not much inner man to figure out. In this regard *Thunder Mountain* appears to be one of Grey's lighter works, with less philosophical depth and psychological probing than found elsewhere—what some critics call his overwriting. Here the author's plan, for the most part, is to show Kal's life on the surface and get on with it. Kal, after all, has "a Westerner's point of view," as he himself says, and glibly considers his job as but a string of "gamblin'-hells an' dance-hall girls—red liquor an' gun-play—all in the day's work!" (42).

Even Kal's speech, spattered with more *damn*'s and *hell*'s than is usual in Grey's writing, becomes part of the book's style: just let 'er rip. Thus we have such expressions as "Why, you damn fools!" and "Accident, hell!" and "My Gawd!" But the author stops short of anything more expletory in having Kal say of an adversary: "I never learned rotten cuss-words enough on the range to fit you. So I won't try" (48, 50). He can speak with his gun, instead— in true Western fashion. The expletives, incidentally, do not help to give Kal a more forceful character (if that indeed was the intention in using them), for they remain very much just a clichéd form of speech.

On arriving in Salmon, Kal rescues a young woman, Sydney Blair, saves her father from being swindled, and when he is about to be arrested for "interference," calls the just-deputized lawman's bluff with his hand ready at his hip where his gun is holstered. Bewildered by the girl, he is no longer buoyed up merely by being in the great outdoors, watching its sunsets, listening to its rivers flow: "All [is] certainly not well with him, for these things [stir] a new and pervading melancholy" (51). Grey describes the scenery here in matter-of-fact terms to match Kal's mood. (Grey is usually more florid, and fluid, when describing nature.)

The upshot is that Kal asks Sydney and Blair to accompany him back to the valley to take part in the rich gold strike. They accept, the daughter knowing that Kal, as she tells him, is impudent, conceited, and domineering, but she trusts him. Their little flirtation while mixing biscuit dough is well dialogued by Grey (80). He repays her faith in him by saving her from drowning when they need to plunge across a river. To him she is a girl "of an infinite variety of moods," including shyness (84). Happiness is within his grasp, he feels, and he has his "continual reversion to nature, to the lonely silence of the hills" (85), to thank for smoothing some of the rough edges of his personality.

But when they can finally look down into the valley, they see it swarming with people, a tent city rising, and Kal is inconsolable. The mountain growls "ominously" (89). He rushes down and finds that one Rand Leavitt has staked the quartz claim and there is no brother Sam anywhere. When the guard swings his rifle at the questioning Kal, the cowboy draws and fires, killing the man. Leavitt appears, assuring Kal and all the miners thronging about that he overtook only an abandoned site. Kal has no choice but to flee, not even going back to the waiting Blairs. He does not want to face Sydney with blood on his hands. Hiding in a clump of firs across the valley, he drinks a whole flask of whisky to blot out his misery and falls asleep.

He wakes up a few days later, confronted by Blair, who tells him his much-disillusioned daughter had seen him lying there "like a sodden beast" (100), this after professing his love for her, then killing and drinking. Kal resolves to make a new start, give up liquor, prove Leavitt to be a robber and murderer of Sam (confirmed later), and show himself a resourceful and dependable suitor. Doing so will take time—methodical investigation and upright behavior. (His ensuing to-ing and fro-ing some readers may find tedious.) In the interim, the community booms, an outgrowth of the biggest gold rush ever in Idaho: "A tent town, a saw-log, clapboard town full of miners, gamblers, adventurers, women, merchants, pack-drivers, freighters. All bent on gold. An awful mess..." (103).

Grey comments on the "stark, ghastly, hideous, defacement of nature" (108) made by the many miners. Kal's job is to become acquainted with most of them and gain their confidence to help with his "detective" work. He also has to keep up some pretence of mining so that Leavitt will not become suspicious of his real goal. As it happens, he finds a good store of nuggets at his hideout—a fact he keeps hidden. What he does openly is hunt game to supply meat to the miners, as he had done for his two brothers when they first made their strike. Then Jake returns and tells his tale of being robbed of the quartz lode before he ever got to Boise. The robbers started the stampede to Thunder Mountain.

By now there are more than a thousand miners in the camp, with the owners of saloons and gambling and dance halls reaping the biggest harvest. One of them is a man named Cliff Borden, with whom Kal already had a run-in back at Salmon where he got supplies. Working for Borden now, as then, is a "dance-hall-girl" called "Nugget" (Ruth), also a previous acquaintance. She is a respectable girl, really a great-souled young woman, who allies herself with Kal in his private investigation work. She knows that Borden and Rand Leavitt are in "cahoots" in trying to run the mining community (123–24). Meanwhile, Sydney Blair is hardly civil to Kal. She is being courted by Leavitt, whom she considers a splendid, generous man. What she does not know is that he is also trying to see Ruth on the sly—a two-timer. The plot thickens.

Kal has not yet given up on Sydney, though their conversations have become argumentative, even sarcastic. She is convinced of his "utter shamelessness" (155) when, spying on him, she sees him with the dance-hall girl in her quarters. She feels betrayed. When Kal asks whether all decent thoughts about him are dead and gone, she replies, "Yes, thank God. You are a strange mixture of chivalry and baseness. You don't know what honor means" (157). She thinks *he* is the two-timer, making up to Ruth, whereas he was only helping to settle differences between the girl and his young friend Dick Sloan (he is killed in a mining dispute later).

Kal's sense of heartbreak and defeat is softened by his exercises outdoors—climbing heights, smelling fir and pine, sensing the utter wildness of the mountains about him. Still, he has to see Sydney again: "her eyes [are] all the more wonderful for their tragic pride and scorn" (196). He must convince her of the dire consequences that will be hers if she does not stay away from Leavitt. She, on the other hand, wants to hurt Kal, and lets Rand kiss her, in Kal's (hidden) presence. At the same time she asks him where he hides his gold so that her former love can overhear. The poor, lonesome cowboy can only ponder—"what [does] he know about the many sides of a woman?" (200). One thing is certain: the old romance is over.

Now Kal makes use of the revealed information to "steal" Leavitt's gold, knowing that much of it was stolen from Sydney's father (it is returned to him) and the rest really belonged to his still-missing brother, Sam. And it is Ruth who tells Sydney about Leavitt's double dealings and his vilifying Kal. Sydney's womanly intuition makes her realize that Ruth loves Kal, secretly, more than she could and would make the better wife for him. Yet when Syd and Kal meet again and he asks her what she will do, she cannot help faltering: "Is there nothing—for you—and me?" (218).

It is a last, and unsuccessful, attempt at reconciliation, although for a moment Kal has one wild hope of taking her, and his gold, and heading out to where *she* belongs—he feels she is a lady "far above [him], too fine for the bloody West" (219). But he knows *he* belongs in the West, where there is work for him to do: wipe out Leavitt and Borden "an' scare the rest of them stiffer 'n a crowbar" (233). Ruth, his confidante, is aghast at this notion when he tells her about it, but then says that he knows best. Kal strides away to complete his task, thinking that *here* is a gal who understands a man like him, a man of action.

What happens is that Kal shoots two of the men who killed Dick and gets a confession implicating Borden. Then it's an imminent shoot-out between the two, what Sydney has called "the man-to-man thing" (202). A mob gathers, and Grey understands mob psychology. When Borden hesitates in coming out onto the street, the throng is all on Kal's side: his "status [rises] to that of a chivalrous and honorable man" (242). It offers to bring out Borden. Then someone cries, *"Burn him out!"* followed by "Lynch him!" in a wave of shouts (244). Only the quick work of the sheriff allows for a regular code-of-the-West confrontation, and it is a drawn-out affair, Borden emptying his six-shooter from a fair distance before Kal takes one deliberate, deadly shot.

Borden's last word is *"Nugget?"* (249)—a revelation of love? Who knows? Kal says he will look after her. "The hour [is] past sunset, crimson and gold, tranquil and sad. The relentlessness of man, with his love, his hate, his avarice, [does] not intrude" in nature (249). It remains calm but will have more to "say" shortly.

Fall equinoctial rains come. Many miners plan to leave, including the Blairs and the Emerson brothers, with Ruth. Apparently, she has always loved Kal, telling him: "Don't ask *any* woman ... how she comes to love. It can't be explained" (256).

But the Leavitt matter has not been settled, and Rand, who has had his cronies appoint him judge of the community, has arranged for vigilantes to arrest Kal for banditry. Leavitt has witnesses ready to convict him in an outdoor court, and a gallows waiting. Sydney steps up with poignant words to prove Kal innocent—we wonder if Grey's characterization of her may not be one of the best things in the book. But her testimony is not needed. For Thunder Mountain THUNDERS—Avalanche!

A melee of people run for their lives, all except Leavitt, who rushes back to save his ill-gotten gold (that Kal had previously removed) and is himself buried. The mountain's mile-high face has slipped down—"like a billowy sea on end" (282). What is worse is the slower, three-feet-a-minute horizontal movement of all the rock debris, inexorably destroying the whole town and leaving a hundred-foot dam—with eventually a hundred-foot-deep lake backed up for two miles, and broken, tilted houses floating on it. Grey's description of the landslide and its aftermath, covering a dozen pages, is excellent.

The miners who had planned to leave, leave, and others too. Kal buys a ranch and marries Ruth, who was a cowgirl once and will be a fine pioneer wife. The minister's commendation is interesting: "It is a hard country, this glorious West of ours. It takes big women to stand it.... They are making the West. Who shall remember in threescore years, when this broad land will be prosperous with cities and ranchers, that the grandmothers of that generation, ever were, let us say, dance-hall girls? And if it were remembered, who could bring calumny against the strong-souled mothers of the West?" (298–99). Who indeed!

29
Knights of the Range: Western Chivalry

"Knight" is a suitable term to describe the Western cowboy. Medieval warriors in armor were the hirelings in the feudal system, engaged by manor barons to defend their castles and other property. Horsemen were they, hence chevaliers (cf. French *cheval*, a horse) or caballeros (Spanish horsemen). They acted chivalrously, protecting the ladies and/or courting them with due grace, following a code of honor. It is helpful to keep such a background in mind when reading Zane Grey's *Knights of the Range*, 1939 (first serialized in the *Chicago Tribune*, 1935), a yarn about cowboys, armed with six-shooters, fighting off rustlers on behalf of their employer, a young woman in this case.

The time, place, and plot are outlined in the first chapter, in a discussion between ranch owner Lee Ripple and his foreman Cap Britt, a former Texas Ranger. The aged Ripple is soon to die of heart problems and wants Britt to know what is in store for him. Ripple's daughter, Holly, age seventeen, has just returned to the Don Carlos Rancho after a nine-year absence at school and will take over the sixty square miles of ranch with its stock of fifty thousand cattle and five hundred horses (the range is still dotted with buffalo too). She had a rich Spanish-Mexican mother (the large ranch came from *her* father) and has inherited her looks and temperament as well, but Ripple hopes that her years at school have Americanized her. The year is 1872; the place, northeastern New Mexico, still a lawless Territory.

Both men anticipate problems. The price of cattle is rising as the railroad moves west, now as near as Las Animas, Colorado. This fact means a "heyday" for rustlers flooding in (7), and an end to the "drowsy langorous atmosphere of the Spaniards" (11), with their hospitality to all. Britt envisages the "bloodiest" times to come (6), with horse thieves, desperadoes, and Eastern riff-raff joining the movement. The only solution, he feels, is to hire cowhands that are wilder and tougher than any rustler gang and make the job so attractive that they will feel a loyalty to their boss and stay. Ripple is dumbfounded but gives in to the plan: he sees his daughter, innocent "like an unfoldin' rose, ... mistress of the hardest outfit of cowboys ever thrown together in the West" (12). Holly thinks: "How perfectly wonderful! ... I shall fall in love with every single one of them.... Bring on your wild cowboys!" (20).

Chapter 2 begins two years later. Ripple has died, and Britt, alone, is riding the range, only to confront eight horse thieves, including one of the last riders he had hired, trying to run off fifty unbranded horses. When Holly happens to ride up, the leader tries to "rustle" her too, that is, kidnap her, but is stopped by one of his own men, Renn Frayne, for wanting to make himself and the others "accomplices in a crime Westerners never forgive" (34). In this graphic account that Grey does so well, the leader urges his men to "bore" Frayne ("bore" is a more powerful verb than "shoot")—so much for honor among thieves. Frayne outdraws them and kills both the leader and the second in command. The others skedaddle, what with Britt's drawing as well.

Frayne has a "terrible presence" (34), a "stern image of bronze" (37). When Holly wants to thank him, he says curtly not to mention it. She proffers him cash, a ring, even a horse, but he will accept nothing, then asks if she has not more sense than to ride the wild range alone. The question is abrupt, but maybe it shows he is concerned about her welfare. When she retorts that she does as she pleases, he rejoins that she is a "headstrong little fool," further a "spoiled young woman," and a "child, too" (39–40).

Her various responses have brought on this calling down. It seems that she wants someone to stand up *to* her, not just *for* her. She may be testy but is not really offended, and she wants control: she asks whether he will work for her—"fight for my rancho, my cattle, my horses, for *me*!" (43). She does not care what he has been before. Frayne lowers his head, and, gunman and loner that he admits he is, accepts the offer.

Thus he joins a troop of seventeen other cowboys on the Don Carlos Rancho. Brazos Keene is the youngest of the lot, of Holly's age, "the wildest, the most untamable," his fresh face and clustering blond hair proclaiming his joyous youth and concealing his "magnificent lawlessness" (65). He loves Holly, but she wants him only as a brother. His closest friend is Laigs Mason, who will later give up his life to save Brazos. Ride-'Em Jackson is a black cowboy, and through him Grey can make some indirect comments on racial discrimination. Others have nicknames telling where they are from—Bluegrass, for example, from Kentucky; still others, names telling something of their character—Stinger, Skylark, and Rebel Ben Sloan. Then there are three

Mexicans; Cherokee, a Native American; and Jim, a stoop-shouldered cowboy of "uncertain years" (70).

Cap Britt has assembled here a crew as varied as Captain Ahab's seamen in *Moby-Dick*, 1851. While Melville sees his characters' whaling venture as a metaphysical search for the meaning of things, Grey sees his "Rowdies of the Saddle" (79) riding out as solid empire builders, "more than trappers, traders, gold-seekers, freighters, soldiers, and pioneers" (77). Grey is not dealing with philosophical abstract concepts, but with the very real idea of the West. He has Holly expand on this notion in her banquet speech to her men (there are touches in it similar to Ahab's "Quarter-Deck" exhortation to his crew that they join him in his quest).

Holly begins: "What a splendid part you are unconsciously playing in the opening of the West" (139). She wants to make them conscious of this, conscious of the area's greatness, and their own greatness too. She provides some historical background: they are following in the footsteps of the Spaniards in Mexico who came north for gold, leaving behind horses that were ancestors of today's wild mustangs; of padres who established Santa Fe and the beginnings of the Old Trail (the famous Santa Fe Trail) that her cowboys all have ridden. The railroad is being built—they are responsible for that because of the cattle they raise. She dubs them Knights of the Range. She will double their wages; make them proud riders—loyal to her, to other good rancheros, and to the West. The Knights jump up and shout their support. They have a common cause.

When the tumult subsides, Frayne responds at length, convincing his fellow cowboys of the "inevitable law of right itself" and the value in "chivalrous friendship among themselves" (157). They cannot go back on a game girl who supports her men. Holly knows now that she loves Frayne, and flees to her room, where, composed, she exults over him: "You [just] won yourself a friend—a sweetheart—a wife!" (158).

At the dance to follow, Holly is proposed to by a big-time rancher, her nearest neighbor, heavy-jowled Sewall McCoy. He says that if they join outfits, his would give hers a respectable name; together they would be strong enough to withstand any rustlers. If not, he is thinking of "throwing in" with a Russ Slaughter. The repartee between the two, Holly constantly correcting him (166–68), is highly amusing—once again Grey excels at this—and revealing too. Britt had previously asked her to talk to McCoy and draw him out, and she does that. Now the foreman as well as Frayne, are convinced that it is McCoy and Slaughter who are behind all the rustling.

The next day we have some Western highjinks for further amusement. The Slaughter outfit has a bucking bronco and challenges the Ripple cowboys to ride him. Of course, their honor is at stake, and bets will be placed. What the Slaughter men do not know is that Ride-'Em Jackson can stick on any horse. Three other Ripple riders will try before him and fall off, if not bucked off first. Then, with the mustang's owners raising the wagers and with jeering at its height, Jackson will ride. Even Holly bets—a staggering five hundred dollars (her rider to get half if he wins). Brazos announces the terms of the final attempt—"two to one odds..., whole haug or none" (185). And the Ripple boys win, big, laying more grounds for animosity later.

Not many days thereafter, eight of the Ripple riders leave on a cattle drive—of thirty-five hundred steers down the trail to the railhead, Las Animas. Frayne is in charge and gets some last minute instructions from Holly. He is to take payment *in cash*, an amount of perhaps one hundred forty thousand dollars. Frayne is aghast at the responsibility placed on him. What if the money is lost or stolen? Holly again shows her trust in her men, particularly Frayne. He calls her "you child" in appealing to her—if something bad happened, she would never believe in him again. But she has a womanly reason for her action: "She had at least driven this man into a betrayal of feeling. It was so sweet, so beautiful..." (193).

Now she has only to flap her red scarf to get the troop moving. She does so, and gives it a final whirl in replacing it around her neck. Frayne says, "*Adios*" (194), and mounting his horse, rides off. Holly watches the moving line of red and white cattle and then notices Frayne on his black horse, catching up. Trailing from him is a streamer of red—her scarf. She had not noticed his taking it. Grey does not further elucidate, nor has to. Renn is her knight, her champion, riding to "battle," wearing her token. When the trail drivers return, successfully, Holly waves the money aside, as if it were nothing at all, and kisses Frayne for being back, and safe. Now it is his turn to break—and run. As a reticent man, a gunslinger, having a "sweet, beautiful, innocent girl ... fall in love with [him]" (216), he does not know what to say.

Cattle rustling at the Don Carlos Rancho continues, increases in fact. Two of its riders have double-crossed the others, the true Knights, and now, sided with the McCoy-Slaughter group, have stolen as many as three thousand head—so Rebel Sloan reports after spying on the outlaw camp. Foreman Britt at once organizes a night raiding party: "An hour later eight horsemen, on bays and blacks, darkly-garbed and heavily armed, r[i]de silently away" (230). There will be no mercy shown. They surprise a bedded-down company of seven. Four are shot, two strung up, and the last forced to talk, incriminating the ring leaders; he is told to leave the country. Two Ripple men have been somewhat injured in the gunfire; Laigs Mason has taken a bullet meant for Brazos. He asks for a smoke but cannot inhale, wants to play a final round of cards but cannot see, although the morning sun has risen. "Pard—sing—Lone Prairee," he says (243), then dies in his friend's arms.

This is gruesome, heart-wrenching stuff, and Grey pauses in his narrative (starting chapter 11) to say that the last six years of the 1870s were the bloodiest ever in New Mexico (and in all the West) because of the influx of conscienceless adventurers into the Territory, corroborating what Britt had prophesied at the start of the book. Just the Lincoln County war alone spelled the death of three hundred men. In the spring of 1875, Holly Ripple has to end the open hospitality of her home to all newcomers, a tradition previously maintained by her father and grandfather.

Two more bloody incidents occur at the ranch that year. Reading Grey's descriptions of them is like seeing a great Western movie unfolding. In the first Britt rides off on a May morning up Gray Hill to a lookout once used by Apaches in waylaying caravans moving along the Old Trail. There he meets Ride-'Em Jackson, who has been spying on the movements of ten rustlers for the last three days. His fellow Knights, seven of them, are bunched at a convenient location elsewhere, waiting for the right moment to make their attack. We not only get a Cinemascopic view of the running battle as seen through the eyes of Jackson and Britt in eight pages of gripping prose, but half of that is written in a kind of sportscaster's monologue. Later, when two of the rustlers trying to escape approach the lookout, Jackson himself rushes out with his rifle and dispatches them, shouting "*Slow down—white trash*" (266).

The whole incident is a response to what Grey calls "the opening gun of the season" (253), the shooting of a defenseless rancher, named Doane, by the McCoy-Slaughter faction—he had but questioned McCoy's honesty. McCoy then bragged that Britt might get the same (also Renn Frayne).

A quiet interlude precedes the final showdown, and we learn more about Holly's personal situation. She now shares her home with Doane's daughter, Ann, left destitute by the rustlers' actions. Born in a prairie schooner, she has all the traits of a pioneer girl, being strong, able, willing, unphased by hardship. In addition, she is "frank, droll, simple, big hearted, and wise." Grey sums up her character in one word—"Western" (268). She is going to marry one of Holly's ranchhands, Skylark, and Holly needs her presence, her discourse on things, to complete her own education—remember, Frayne had called her a child (and note Grey's flair for writing natural-sounding girl-talk). Holly comes to this self-appraisal: she has been too girlish, too aristocratic as well. She realizes her respect for Frayne has increased "in proportion to his restraint" (272)—something she would not have admitted earlier.

Then one morning Holly awakes with a boding premonition. Something is up. She makes her way outside, finally through the corrals, and sees on the slanted runway up to one of the barns a great circle of men—cowboys and ranch owners. A cattlemen's organization, led by McCoy and another rancher, Clements, confronts the Ripple band, accusing it of being the area's rustlers. Their proof is that some of the Knights have been caught rustling, true enough, and that Frayne has an outlaw past. Slaughter is soon to arrive with more evidence.

The drama, the action, cannot be captured in a few words of summary. Holly runs out to Frayne, crying out her love for him, the man she will marry; Frayne outdraws McCoy's gunman, Rankin; Brazos and five of the Knights ride in from a separate skirmish with a dead Slaughter draped over a pack horse; and Brazos, "terrible in his cold-blooded fury," takes control. He has proofs, jotted down in Slaughter's own notebook of nefarious dealings with McCoy. Brazos—that "frivolous, care-free" youth, now "hard as flint" (212)—shoots McCoy, twice, once for having insulted Holly, the second time for his grudge against Frayne. Then he turns on Clements, who bought Ripple stock from Slaughter, and "bores" him too. Half an hour later, he rides away, forever. The other Knights bow "to the fate and the greatness of their comrade" (300).

Holly and Frayne marry on her twenty-first birthday that summer, and recall something of Brazos's previous "fun-loving, devilish glee" (348). Before he left, he had arranged with her cowboys (Frayne excluded) to tell the bride on the wedding morning that more rustlers were raiding the cattle; Frayne would have to ride with them at once—he could not get married that day. Holly would have to wave them on with her red scarf again. Of course she is beside herself, wrings her hands while running to and fro—before she sees it is all a joke. She is furious, at first, but soon comes round to say of her faithful merry-making Knights of the Range, "Bless their hearts!" (306).

30
Woman of the Frontier: The Best Years

Shortly into *Woman of the Frontier*, author Zane Grey has one of the characters say, "[T]he woman settler does the bigger share of the work, an' never gets the credit due her" (37). What Grey accomplishes in this novel is to give Lucinda Huett, representative of all such real-life women, the plaudits she deserves. Actually, the praise is doubled in a way, for the book was first released as *30,000 on the Hoof*, 1940, a year after Grey's death, then again in 1998, with son Loren Grey restoring about eight pages of the original manuscript to chapter 6 (and some additional material elsewhere) in the retitled version. In them Lucinda is raped in an act of personal vengeance against her husband, Logan, by a Native adversary, Matazel. The incident, although not described, was considered offensive by the original publisher and excised. Allusions to it in the 1998 version show the great anguish endured by the heroine, and her even greater strength in recovering from it—she keeps the violation of herself secret from Logan. (Page references are to this 1998 Leisure Books edition by Dorchester Publishing.)

The straightforward prose carries the story forward right from chapter 1. There are no frills, embellishments, only the facts. It is 1895. Logan, then a bachelor, has just been released from service as an army scout in Arizona, where he gained the enmity of Matazel. He remembers a unique canyon in the Mogollon forest, south of Flagg (Flagstaff), an ideal location to start a ranch, and rides there. Miles long, it provides grazing for thirty thousand cattle, Logan's estimate of an ultimate dream herd—without the need for extra cowhands since the animals cannot climb out. Grey's description is matter-of-fact: "The brook made several turns between the gradually leveling slopes. Scattered pines trooped down to the deep blue pools. The bench on the east side had waited for ages for the homesteader" (18). This reads like a true unvarnished account more than a fictional one.

Even Logan's feelings are somewhat bland, showing "neither passion nor romance" (19), as he plans his future. He will need a wife—she will certainly improve the chances of success for his venture—and decides on a girl, Lucinda, he had known in Missouri, who was "sensible" (19). It does not occur to him that he "would be dooming her to a lonely existence" (20). So he wires her to come West and marry him. He figures that would eliminate time wasted in courtship so that they could get the ranch, and their home on it, started before winter.

Surprisingly, she agrees to come to Flagg, by rail, and he begins rigging up a covered wagon for their "honeymoon" journey of four nights on the road to what he has named his Sycamore Canyon. He spends all the money he has in loading the conveyance with practical goods, and "last" (25) a box of candy for her. When we first meet her, we see she is not without practicalities either, saving her money from teaching school, which she started at sixteen, all the time "training herself to become a pioneer's wife," Logan's bride. She is described as "steady, plodding, dutiful, unsentimental," but she knows that deep within her she is "half savage" too (27)—happy to be away from her former stylish, comfortable surroundings.

Lucinda is not prepared for the Wild West, however. She has an uneasy fear about the wilderness and is overcome by the strangeness of everything. The wind is foreboding, "whispering death to her girlish hopes and dreams," and she is aghast at being shut in on all sides by canyon walls. The combination of wind and walls drives her frantic at times; yet she senses about her "an atmosphere of pioneer enterprise, of adventure, of struggle" (35). She will not back down. She realizes that her role is to give heartfelt support to her husband's vision and, in fact, amazes him by doing so when he feels down because of cattle losses to cougars. "Why ... bless your heart!" is his exclamation (80). It is his first real expression of love for her.

They are a team, man and woman of the frontier, working together to establish a home and ranch in the wilderness, with Lucinda becoming the stronger of the two. It is now Logan who often is the discouraged one, for setbacks continue to occur, and each time she, his partner, "encourage[s] him." To his repeated question, "What would you do, Luce?" her answer is praise of his industry and strength that can overcome the difficulties. Always he "brighten[s] and cast[s] off his pondering dark moods" (91). (It may be that had she also affirmed that times were unjustifiably tough, he would not have been downcast so often. Sometimes the male ego merely needs someone else to acknowledge that, yes, the situation *is* trying, to be assuaged.)

With the birth and naming of their first child, George Washington Huett, we see something of the parents' (perhaps unconscious) sense that their stumbling pioneer efforts are worthwhile, are helping to build a nation. Certainly, with motherhood, Lucinda herself gains added strength for her own duties—"she [is] as happy as she had been miserable" (92) at the start of their venture. Also, she has a new way to comfort Logan after the winter's toll on the cattle herd and the summer's shriveling of their first season's planting: "But, husband dear, look at our baby" (93). She sets him right about priorities, and he knows that his tribulations are only a lesson to be learned—his wife and child are what really matter.

Unfortunately, a different trouble awaits them, real horror in the personage of Matazel (in chapter 6). It seems as if Lucinda's earlier premonition of a "fearful wilderness" (27) now is realized in spades, embodied in that human denizen of this wild land. He appears when Logan is away, "an incredible and terrible blow from this raw and savage wilderness"—how Grey describes the rape (112). Critic Stephen Tanner, in an article in *Zane Grey Review*, says that the language creates the impression "that the rape of the individual is incidental to a more significant ravishment by the wilderness itself" (42). The act is symbolical, producing from the union a second child, Abraham Lincoln Huett: another reference to frontier nation-building and here also a metaphorical "blending" (Tanner again) of two opposing worlds, the wild and the civilized, to create a new West. Of the three sons born to Lucinda—Grant is the third—only Abe survives at the end to carry on the work begun by the parents to give their efforts a nation-building permanence.

Grey has carefully developed his story to lead up to the high drama of chapter 6. Lucinda first hears about Matazel three chapters earlier when Logan tells her how, as an army agent, he had captured the Native and that the captured man had threatened to get even some day. He mentions that Matazel's appearance is of a "noble red man" (47), someone to have caught Lucinda's fancy. There is a further ironic statement in chapter 5 after Logan returns from Flagg with supplies the first spring. Left home by herself, Lucinda tells her husband that she was so lonely she "would have welcomed an Indian ... or even a grizzly bear" (86) (a Native is paired with wild nature). Logan also says that though Matazel has escaped from his reservation she need not worry about him—he is far away.

Fall arrives, and Logan leaves again for supplies. This time, Lucinda, alone once more, walks out to gather wild grapes. Her happiness over little George helps her to see the loveliness of Sycamore Canyon, with all its trees aflame in autumn colors. She had never seen beauty there before although she had lived in the canyon for a year. Now everything is "invested with a glamor" (99). But the sunny weather does not hold; neither does her joy. A strong wind, her arch-enemy, begins to blow, and an equinoctial storm ensues.

The wilderness seems blighted, and she lies "stiffly" in her bed at night, about her the "black sky" and "the frenzy of the wind." She remains starkly awake "until she [is] deaf and numb, insensible to pain and terror" (104). This preludes the appearance a few days later of—Matazel, who "get[s] even!" (108).

One of Logan's greetings on coming home is—"You're the smartest little wife in Arizona." Lucinda can only think—"What [does] he know about the travail of a frontier wife" (112); she does not explain what *she* knows. (Her travail will be even greater with Abe's birth in a cowshed next year.) But life has to go on, she thinks—difficult for her because "she always [has] thought and felt too acutely" (98). Yet she cannot fail Logan, and that is that. She *must* forget, if possible; keep on, if (seemingly) impossible. And she does, stoically, day by day, month by month. (A few years later, Logan kills Matazel in a forest shoot-out, not described by Grey, not mentioned to Lucinda.)

When fall comes round again, Lucinda, now with two babies, accompanies Logan to Flagg on the annual stocking of goods for winter. The several days' adventure is good for her morale, a rejuvenation of her soul, and Grey captures well this new, gayer woman of the frontier in just two lines when they return: "'I'm glad to get back,' Lucinda announced as if telling herself something new and exciting. 'After all, it's home'" (135).

Another year passes, Grant is born, and more years go by. Logan in his less obsessive moments of building up his ranch, realizes what a wonderful helpmate he has, to the point of describing his ambition as "lousy" because of the toll it costs her to live in such isolation (132). He can never forget her "uncomplaining steadfast loyalty" (125), although he does not lose sight of his own goal of thirty thousand on the hoof. Lucinda for her part finds the habit of work growing so strong in her that it is not only satisfying but necessary for her well-being (a Zane Grey tenet). Going to town is wonderful, a chance to store up memories for the coming winter, but while there the only "luxury" she treats herself to is the buying of a box of jars so she can put up preserves for her family back at the ranch.

Logan and the three boys are Lucinda's world now, Abe being her favorite son because of the suffering she had in bearing and birthing him. He, in turn, is the most obliging of the children, the most reliable. Sometimes she affectionately (and unconsciously) refers to him as "the little savage" (142), while proudly (and ironically), Logan speaks of his "Indian yell" (173). Brother George calls him a "handsome Indian" outright (215); Grant listens to all this banter good-humoredly. There is a family togetherness here, and when the boys chance upon a deserted child, named Barbara, she becomes a sister to them. The family is complete.

Meanwhile, hot summers come, followed by still autumns and the white months of winter. And these pass "as if time were not" (141). Then another spring, summer, autumn, winter. Grey is writing a saga of many years, and there are repeated references to the intervals of time: "winter fled apace, and the seasons rolled on" (162); "the toil early and late in the fields, and the other manifold tasks of the growing ranch made days and seasons fly by on wings" (217). Logan kills a cougar attacking his cattle, single-handed with a spade, before it almost kills him; the family fends off a pack of wolves, Lucinda using a pitchfork; the children have their share of wild pets that need tending—bear cubs, a fawn, chipmunks, and an owl—along with their usual chores. Slowly the ranch grows, and Logan says, "Lucinda, you're a pioneer wife" (161). It is the greatest compliment he can give her.

The children become adults—George a born stockman, Abe a superb woodsman, Grant a hard-riding cowboy, Barbara no longer a "sister" but a competent, courtable woman for the three sons. Her true background is revealed to them only when they are young adults. Grey excels in describing this revelation by Lucinda, the controlling family figure. We see how each of the four react individually and to each other—also the parents' response. All this is part of chapter 12, two-thirds through the book. It is Abe who will win Barbara.

With grown-up children to help build the ranch, the Huett herd doubles, triples, quadruples "while the seasons [speed] by" (218). Success is imminent, and with it the plot momentarily loses some of its drive. Yes, there still are difficulties—with rustlers, for example—but the physical struggle of wife and husband is no longer primary, no longer a desperate attempt to gain basic necessities. Grey strikes a responsive chord in the reader, the bit of caveman mentality still lurking in each of us. The fittest *have* survived; the remaining struggle is more sophisticated, artificial—not the elemental securing of a home and livelihood in the wilderness, but a maintaining and improving of them.

As this happens, the roles of Lucinda and Logan are exchanged for a time—Lucinda even faints when her husband suffers a slight wound in a shoot-out with the rustlers, while Logan's fortitude intensifies to achieve his dreamed-of herd. He "so inspire[s] them all with his great idea, his driving passion, that long habit of work, of sacrifice[,] ha[s] left them unable to slow down, to begin to see the prosperity that has really come" (218).

World War I intrudes, however, and something "deep, primitive, mystic—a something inherited from the mother of the race" (243)—whispers in Lucinda's ear. Her sons will go to war, and she will lose them. Again, Grey is at his best in building up, over fifteen pages (243–58), to the climax of her emotions, that "blinding shock to her consciousness" (245). She realizes that men have always loved to fight, "from ... remote aboriginal days," but it was "the women who bore sons, and therefore, the brunt of war" (252). She relives in her mind the birth and growth of each of her sons, particularly of Abe, who will marry Barbara before going overseas. She recalls her too—as a little girl rescued on a lonely road "so long ago and far away!" (254). At the wedding supper she will be happy with her family members—"if to be happy [is] to rise above" her (and their) agony (255). Lucinda is the dominant person in the family once more.

Logan decides to sell his thirty thousand cattle (a number finally reached!) at high wartime prices and leave the ranch to live in Flagg during the war. He is happy and proud, smoking a cigar, his thumbs stuck behind his vest. Grey's comment is cryptic: "The business of the world [does] not halt for heartbroken mothers" (256). With the departure of the troop train, while Lucinda and Barbara bear up despite their sorrow, he runs alongside with some frivolous remark for Abe, as excited as his waving sons.

After thirty-three years of ranching, Logan completes the deal for his cattle—only to be swindled of the whole payment, $865,000, by a government supply agent. The logistics of the robbery are dramatically told. Attempts are made to recover the money, without success, so that Logan finally goes to Washington, DC, to get justice there. He sees himself in time of war as a "miserable outsider among [a] swarm of grabbing humanity" (289). Moreover, he is bamboozled of an extra $2,500 by some shyster lawyers, who claim they can help him. Then comes the fateful news—George and Grant killed in action, Abe missing—and his soul cries out, "*Would God I had died for you! Oh, my sons, my sons!*" (295) (echoing David's lament for Absalom, 2 Samuel 18:33).

He is beaten, crushed, punished by his own greed—he "should have lived for his family and not his cattle" (295). His assessment of the war is now grim: "leaders ... played politics as Westerners played poker.... [M]en who furnished ... young men for gun-fodder were patriotic fools.... War in modern times held no glory" (294). All of chapter 16, from which these excerpts are taken, places Grey among authors that editors of *The American Tradition in Literature*, volume 2, 1967, would call masters of "Critical Realism" or of "Realism and Naturalism" at the turn of the nineteenth century, men such as William Dean Howells, Theodore Dreiser, and, one could add, Frank Norris (*The Octopus*, 1901). He is not writing romance here.

Logan, back in Arizona, is, as he says, "done" (295). But Lucinda, with amazing strength, knows what may cure him—returning to Sycamore Canyon and starting again. At first he sits pathetically at the unfinished stone corral that he and his sons were building when they first heard of the war (cf. Wordsworth's shepherd, Michael, in a poem of the same name, who, hearing of *his* son's wayward course in life and permanent departure from home, returned "many a day" to the sheepfold they had begun working on together and "never lifted up a single stone" [156]). But Logan's missing son returns— and discovers a remnant of the great herd hidden away in one of the many draws of the canyon.

Lucinda's hope that they can begin to pioneer once more is fulfilled. The old struggle is renewed. Zane Grey is again saying, as he did in *Wanderer of the Wasteland*, that life's greatest achievement is not in a goal reached, but in the striving for one. Willa Cather, a premier American author, puts it another way in one of her short stories in *The Old Beauty and Others*, 1948. "Our best years," she has a character say, "are when we're working hardest and going right ahead when we can hardly see our way out"; and "people are happiest where they've had their children and struggled along and been real folks and not tourists" (135–36).

Lucinda and Logan in their ongoing travail have shown themselves as such real folks, not romantic figures, in which Lucinda is the dominant one, a true *Woman of the Frontier*. The novel is one of Grey's finest works.

31
Western Union:
A Great Achievement

Sometimes admirers of Zane Grey may just like to dip into a novel with a straightforward plot, more or less predictable characters, and enough solid outdoor action in a Western setting to hold their interest—in other words, a pleasant read. If the book is based also on a specific historical event of their country's growth, readers can experience, vicariously, the thrill of nation building from the comfort of their easy chairs. Significant information can be garnered along the way, along with the surge of pride at the achievement. Such a book is *Western Union*, 1939, Grey's last published work during his lifetime. It details the building of the last stage of the continental telegraph line, about 800 miles, from Goldenburg in central Nebraska to Fort Bridger in the southwest corner of Wyoming. (Grey had access to the Western Union Company's records for his research.)

The year is 1861. The Civil War had begun that spring, and young Wayne Cameron of Boston, age twenty-four, finds himself between "the devil and the deep sea" (2), as he puts it: the entire story is written in the first person. His mother supports the North and his father the South. So he heads West, to be out of the turmoil, and boards a stagecoach to Omaha, Nebraska, for the telegraph company's construction camp on the North Platte River farther on in the state (the telegraph is following the Oregon Trail). Having been inspired by a newspaper clipping about the great project, still in his pocket, he hopes to get a job there.

The story thus starts with a fast stage ride, and it keeps this pace over the next chapters as the plot and characters develop. The stage driver alerts Cameron that one hazard during the construction will be Native attacks— and for good reason. The "redskins hev a grievance against the whites" for taking over the West and starting to kill off their mainstay, the buffalo. He predicts that in ten years or more his people will be killing the animals for their hides (mainly to provide pulley belts for machines in burgeoning factories): "White men are mostly wasters, as well as bein' greedy and unscrupulous" (17).

When Cameron speaks for "the tide of empire" (America's need to expand), the driver counters that this was the Native's country, that he was robbed and depraved by liquor, and that he will be forced to inhabit but the country's waste places—"it shore ain't a purty picture" (7–8). This, we can have no doubt, is Grey speaking once more of his Vanishing American.

Before the first chapter closes, the stagecoach passes a wagon train of settlers, another feature boding ill for the Native Americans. And aboard one of the prairie schooners a pretty girl, with a "luster of ... rippling hair" (9), returns Cameron's wave, an event, we may be sure, boding ill and/or well for the future young worker on the telegraph line. Much has already been revealed to the reader.

In the next chapter, tenderfoot Cameron arrives at the construction camp. A drunken rowdy shoots at his feet to make him dance, but he is saved from further embarrassment by a young cowboy from Texas, who has an "almost girlish ... charm." When Cameron shakes his hand, he finds that the man, Vance Shaw, also has a soft hand, "almost like a girl's," but a grip of iron (19–20). Grey may have had some idea of developing these unexpected traits in his tall, slim gunman, for that is what he is, but these feminine attributes are never referred to again. Instead, we note his dark clothes, his smell "of leather and horseflesh and smoke" (21). (We learn later that he had once been a Texas Ranger whose preference had not been only *arresting* low-down hombres.) His shorter, roughhanded buddy is Jack Lowden.

Both men, dusty and shabby outwardly, have an intent look, as having just survived tough times successfully, but appear friendly and approachable. Cameron warms to them at once and forms a trio with them. Then a third cowboy, Tom Darnell, really down-and-out, comes by, and the other two stake him to a meal. All four seem to "get along tip-top" (27), despite varying backgrounds. The Civil War is not being fought out West, and the Texan cowboys, knowing that Cameron's father is a Southerner, think of their companion as "half a rebel anyhow" (27).

What binds them all is their wish to "throw in" together and "help this grand gazebo Creighton to beat the hell he's up against" (29). Edward Creighton, chief engineer of the telegraph project, seems to them "as big as all outdoors," a true leader, and they agree that the "laying of the telegraph line will beat any deal ever made in the West" (28). They are caught up in the adventure. All like outdoor work, the cowboys are trail-wise, and Cameron, though a tenderfoot Bostonian, has a year's study in medicine at Harvard that might be useful.

Here are *Four* Musketeers, "all for one, one for all," the motto of the three adventurers in Alexandre Dumas's famous book (119). Cameron, the one most different in the group, vows "to win and hold these three cowboys, no matter what it cost" (37). There is even an echo, in their enthusiasms over fitting out a prairie schooner as their home, of the three teenage chums from R. M. Ballantyne's *The Coral Island*, 1858. In fact, Grey has Cameron say that "both Shaw and I felt like boys at a game as we fixed the wagon" (75).

Cameron is chosen "boss" of the housekeeping arrangements by drawing cards, he feeling both frightened and thrilled in holding the position, the others assuring him that he will be conscientious if nothing else. And one more person joins the foursome when it rescues dance-hall Ruby, Shaw's girlfriend, who has been mistreated by *her* boss, Red Pierce. So that she can escape detection, she dresses in boys' clothes, with Shaw painting her face to look Mexican (shades, here, of Tom Sawyer and Huck Finn). Incidentally, she takes the side of many women regarding the Civil War—"not wanting war at all" (118).

Construction work begins, a digging of holes and raising telegraph poles, twenty-five to a mile. It is interrupted when the wagon train catches up, and Cameron saves the life of Kit Sunderlund, the girl with the "rippling" chestnut hair. He calls her to jump from her buckboard, with its runaway team of horses, right into his arms. Both are knocked over. He has already fallen, however, "head over heels in love with her" (108). But Kit is a spoiled, rich belle of the ball from Texas, a former acquaintance of Shaw, who describes her as a "natural born flirt," leading men on (112).

If a romance is to flourish between idealistic Wayne Cameron and Kit, he would be wise to ignore her: she will only want the more what she cannot have, and in time she may learn something of forbearance and being faithful. This is exactly what happens: Cameron is never free from duty, however much he may wish to court Kit. When he is done with his manual chores, he still has to tend to cuts, bruises, burns, broken limbs, gunshot wounds, fever, and dysentery of his fellow employees. He is the only one there with some medical training. Indeed, he is thankful he can help the others—it is as if he had already taken the Hippocratic oath. He marvels how much the work and endurance are making a man of him and how his comrades at their tasks are becoming increasingly dear. He concludes with Grey, that they all work the harder because of Creighton's faith in them.

Six noteworthy events occur during the building of the telegraph line that try the resources of everyone. (Grey has described such happenings before but never all in one book.) The first is a prairie fire. Shaw scents a faint whiff of smoke in the air before any of the others. Night falls, with the sky a "strange red" (128), and all the stars blotted out. The blaze is headed their way, blown along by a fierce "norther" (124). The whole camp at once is a beehive of activity, seeking refuge on sandbars in the nearby river. Soon even the red sky is changed—by "rolling, mushrooming, billowing clouds ... in colors of yellow and black and white" (133). What follows, in Grey's description, are phrases such as "monstrous wall of flame," "hear that roar," then three terse adjectives: "magnificent, hellish, appalling" (134, 135, 136). The heat wave strikes; fiery embers land on the schooners' canvases, the oxen's backs, and workers' clothing. Cameron is up all night tending to people's burns.

Sunderlund's wagon-train has also suffered, and Cameron rides out to aid the people there, particularly Kit, who has burned her foot. She is still in a pet, apparently for his not keeping an engagement with her after the runaway. To her squeals of pain (from a superficial burn) and her calling him a "brute," he responds with terms of "baby" and "girl." She then sarcastically replies, "Very noble of you, Mr. Cameron," and he, nettled, says, "Oh, shut up" (146–47). Her real source of anger is having seen Ruby in his wagon and believing the worst. Before he leaves, he informs her that "that little dance-hall girl is bigger and finer than you and far more worthy" (150). A lovers' quarrel, surely.

After the construction camp reaches Julesburg, Colorado, a second overall disruption occurs—attack by Natives. This is typical Wild West fare, with "yelling and shooting and whirling of dust and smoke" (172). Fifteen accompanying soldiers are killed, and five of Creighton's men; he himself has a gunshot shoulder wound—and Cameron an arrow in his thigh. This the young medic calls a mere scratch and again tends to the injured. The real loss is Ruby, who, in the turmoil, has been kidnapped by her former employer.

Leaving Colorado to re-enter Nebraska and proceed northwest along the North Platte River once more, the telegraph crew meets with severe drought, a third disruption of its work. The men are exhausted from the heat, their lips blistered, their eyes seared: "it was difficult to breathe or move" (190). Then comes a fierce prairie storm, a cloudburst. Cameron's senses, as he says, are "strained to their limit," what with the "splitting crack of ropes of lightning," the "pungent odor of brimstone," the "thudding impact of water," and the "weird unreality" of the cataclysm (196). The downpour, we are told, is Creighton's salvation, and work proceeds, ever onward, now within sight of Chimney Rock.

It is at this point that Grey, composing his last book (much of it dictated rather than written, due to failing health), seems to grow somewhat weary. His use of conversation has always been a highlight of his work—its naturalness, rightness, sharpness. Now we find within half a page (200–201), a character saying "What the hell?" and "Hell, no!" and another's comment, "Shore as hell." This may well be how cowboys talk, but "hell," if not used sparingly in literature, loses all impact as an expletive, and makes for weak rather than strong writing. And within the same half page Vance Shaw once more uses his favorite expression—"shore as God made little green apples." Since he says this perhaps a dozen times, we can only tire of it. (His "it's dollars to doughnuts" [195] also appears too frequently.)

The action in the book, however, continues strong. Shortly after the deluge, more trouble comes a-galloping—a buffalo stampede. Again, Shaw is the first to detect a possible disaster, hearing the low rumble of hoofs before the animals appear. Luckily for the camp, he knows what to do. The wagons are lined up in a wedge facing the oncoming herd, with two of the oldest wagons placed farther ahead to be set afire. Two men from each wagon remain in front to shoot and kill the leading buffaloes forming a barricade of dead animals. The other men stay behind to keep their own stock from stampeding. The thundering herd will not be stopped, but it can be split and partially redirected. Grey's description of hearing the yet unseeable herd is a good one: Cameron puts his ear to the ground and thinks he has pressed it on a gigantic seashell, its sound being the rumble of rampaging life. The ground shakes under him.

Buffalo, even not stampeding, still cause problems because their rubbing themselves on the telegraph poles push them over. Creighton thinks that spikes nailed partway into the poles at an appropriate height is the answer. Twenty-five poles go down before he discovers that the animals, with their thick hides, *prefer* the spiked poles for scratching their backs and relieving themselves of vermin or dried mud from wallowing. There is some roughhouse humor here, which Grey enjoys relating, when Creighton orders Shaw to kick him for such gross stupidity.

Chimney Rock is reached, a relief for Cameron, who becomes loquacious at his first sight of it at a five-mile distance "in the transparent atmosphere of dawn" (219). During early morning hours, he is not so physically tired from his routine work, or so tied up in it mentally, that he cannot stop to give a full description. Such extended relation of natural phenomena is less common in this book than usual, appropriately so because it is a first-person account. (His previous observations of nature were typically short, coming, too, when he felt more at ease—at bedtime in noticing the "sough of the wind" in nearby trees and the "blinking of ... great white stars" while "thrilling" to coyotes' yelping [78]—or next morning in seeing the "ruddy sky grow suddenly resplendent with the rising sun" [81] [see Blake, 36].)

Now, before Chimney Rock, Cameron speaks these apt words about what it represents: "After so many weeks ... of flat barren prairie, there was something soul-freeing in the sight of this landmark.... I saw it look like a great white sentinel beckoning the travelers to its shelter and to the pure water that it marked. That day we ran the five miles of telegraph poles in a state of mind that was in the nature of a celebration, with one day, at least, given over to the forgetfulness of bitter toil" (219). Finally, the crew is in Wyoming to complete its work, stringing a line across to Fort Bridger. (There they will meet another crew working up from the West Coast.)

Wyoming Territory soon presents a fifth major concern for the telegraph construction workers. The Laramie River is in flood and has to be crossed. All this is graphically described over a dozen pages, the like of which we have witnessed in several Western movies. First the crew helps Sunderlund's wagon train and its cattle over to the other side, difficulties arising because floating trees get tangled up with the wagons and harnessed oxen. When Cameron and Darnell bring their own schooner across, the crest of the flood is just coming through, creating more anxious moments. In the course of the various critical situations, Cameron again proves himself a hero, saving Kit Sunderlund's life; quarrels are forgotten, and the two become engaged then and there—he having to be reminded that a girl has to be asked first, she *happening* to have her mother's engagement ring with her.

Kit heads to the Sweetwater Valley ranch her father is starting, Cameron back to his job with the telegraph line forging ahead. One clear morning he spies along the western horizon what he thinks is a line of magnified clouds, unlike any he has seen before. Darnell tells him he is having his first look at the Rockies, specifically the Wind River Range. Approaching South Pass of the Continental Divide, the "musketeers" learn from a Pony Express man that Ruby is being held there. The four set out to free her, the pair of Cameron and Darnell finding Ruby and shooting their way out of the gambling den to effect her escape. Darnell sacrifices his life in protecting them.

In a rented buckboard, Cameron flees with the girl to leave her at Kit's ranch. Kit, who before had been jealous of their association, now takes pride in his action and calls him a "regular knight of the West": the tenderfoot from Boston has earned his spurs. If we detect just a little note of sarcasm in her remark, it is softened by her lovely warm smile as she adds, "You know me—how—how funny I am..." (286). (It is a nice little touch by the author.)

The story is drawing to its close. One final disruptive event occurs, a blinding snowstorm after the crew gets through South Pass. But this is dismissed in a few sentences. A wagonload of telegraph poles is at hand to provide fuel for a huge bonfire while the storm rages, and work then proceeds quickly to Fort Bridger.

It is a time for tributes and best wishes all round. Cameron, with Grey, has already praised his close companions on the telegraph crew: "These wild, fiery-spirited cowboys had never been understood by Easterners.... [S]omething in their lonely life ... made for greatness" (291). Now, the first transcontinental message on the new line, from California to President Abraham Lincoln, congratulates him upon "the completion of a great work" that will bind "both the East and West to the Union" (295), comforting words during the Civil War. And readers in their easy chairs, with their freshly gained knowledge of the event, will indeed take pride in the achievement, and in Zane Grey's writing of it.

Bibliography

Austen, Jane. *Jane Austen's Letters*. Collected and edited by R. W. Chapman. 2d ed. London: Oxford University Press, 1952.
———. *Pride and Prejudice*. New York: E. P. Dutton, 1976 (first published 1813).
———. *Sense and Sensibility*. Edited by Mary Lascelles. Everyman's Library. New York: Dutton, 1906 (first published 1811).
Ballantyne, R. M. *The Coral Island*. London: Collins, 1947 (first published 1858).
Billard, Jules B., ed. *The World of the American Indian*. Washington, DC: National Geographic Society, 1974.
Blake, Kevin. "The Geography of Zane Grey's *Western Union*." *Zane Grey Review* 28, no. 1 (May 2013): 22–23, 36–37.
Bradley, Sculley, Richmond Croom Beatty, and E. Hudson Long, eds. *The American Tradition in Literature*. Vol. 2. New York: W. W. Norton, 1967.
Cather, Willa. *The Old Beauty and Others*. New York: Alfred A. Knopf, 1948.
Cooper, James Fenimore. *The Prairie*. Chicago: Thompson & Thomas, n.d. (first published 1827).
Defoe, Daniel. *The Life and Adventures of Robinson Crusoe*. Akron, OH: Saalfield Publishing, n.d. (first published 1719).
Dickens, Charles. *A Christmas Carol*. Afterword by Clifton Fadiman. New York: Macmillan, 1963 (first published 1843).
———. *David Copperfield*. London: Macmillan, 1988 (first published 1849–50).
Dumas, Alexandre (the Elder). *The Three Musketeers*. Washington, DC: Regenery Publishing, 1998 (first published 1858).
Emerson, Ralph Waldo. "Self-Reliance." In *The Selected Writings of Ralph Waldo Emerson*. Edited by Brooks Atkinson. Modern Library College Editions. New York: Random House, 1950.
Fox, John, Jr. *The Trail of the Lonesome Pine*. New York: Charles Scribner's Sons, 1908.
Friesen, Victor Carl. "The Cowboy Life." In *Forever Home: Good Old Days on the Farm*. Calgary: Fifth House/Fitzhenry & Whiteside, 2004.
———. *The Spirit of the Huckleberry: Sensuousness in Henry Thoreau*. Edmonton: University of Alberta Press, 1984.
Goethe, Johann Wolfgang von. *Faust Part One & Part Two*. Translated by Charles E. Passage. Indianapolis, IN: Bobbs-Merrill, 1965.
Grey, Zane. *The Heritage of the Desert*. New York: Harper & Brothers, 1910.
———. *The Last of the Plainsmen*. New York: Outing Publishing, 1908.
———. *The Last Trail*. New York: Outing Publishing, 1906.
———. *Roping Lions in the Grand Canyon*. New York: Grosset & Dunlap, 1924.
———. *The Spirit of the Border*. New York: A. L. Burt, 1906.
———. *Stairs of Sand*. New York: Harper & Brothers, 1943.
———. *Zane Grey on Fishing*. Edited by Terry Mort. Guilford, CT: Lyons Press, 2003.
Gruber, Frank. *Zane Grey*. New York: World Publishing, 1970.
Harding, Walter. *The Days of Henry Thoreau*. New York: Alfred A. Knopf, 1965.
Hardy, Thomas. *The Return of the Native*. New York: Harper & Row, 1966 (first published 1878).

Henley, William Ernest. *Poems*. London: Macmillan, 1921.
The Holy Bible [King James Version]. New York: Thomas Nelson, n.d. (first published 1611).
Irving, Washington. "Rip Van Winkle." In *The Sketch Book*. Toronto: Copp, Clark, 1892 (first published 1819).
Jackson, Carlton. *Zane Grey*. Twayne's United States Author Series. New York: Twayne Publishers, 1973.
James, Henry. "The Art of Fiction." In *Partial Portraits*. London: Macmillan, 1894 (first published 1888).
_____. *The Wings of the Dove*. New York: Modern Library, 1937 (first published 1902).
James, Will. *Smoky, the Cowhorse*. New York: Charles Scribner's Sons, 1926.
Jones, Landon Y. *Great Expectations: America and the Baby Boom Generation*. New York: Coward, McCann & Geoghegan, 1980.
Karr, Jean. *Zane Grey: Man of the West*. New York: Grosset & Dunlap, 1949.
Keats, John. *Complete Poems*. Edited by Jack Stillinger. Cambridge: Belknap Press of Harvard University Press, 1982.
Kipling, Rudyard. *Rudyard Kipling's Verse*. Definitive Edition. Garden City, NY: Doubleday, 1946.
Longfellow, Henry Wadsworth. *Favorite Poems of Henry Wadsworth Longfellow*. Introduction by Henry Seidel Canby. Garden City, NY: Doubleday, 1947.
Mathew, David. *Acton: The Formative Years*. London: Eyre & Spottiswoode, 1946.
McDowell, Bart. *The American Cowboy in Life and Legend*. Washington, DC: National Geographic Society, 1972.
Melville, Herman. *Moby-Dick*. Edited by Alfred Kazin. Riverside Editions. Boston: Houghton Mifflin, 1956 (first published 1851).
Norris, Frank. *The Octopus: A Story of California*. Garden City, NY: Doubleday, 1901.
O'Hara, Mary. *My Friend Flicka*. Philadelphia: J. B. Lippincott, 1941.
_____. *Thunderhead*. Philadelphia: J. B. Lippincott, 1943.
Pauly, Thomas H. *Zane Grey: His Life, His Adventures, His Women*. Urbana: University of Illinois Press, 2005.
Pfeiffer, Charles G. *So You Want to Read Zane Grey and Don't Know Where to Start*. 4th rev. Columbia, SC: Author, 2006. [24 pages].
_____. *Zane Grey: A Study in Values—Above and Beyond the West*. Aurora, CO: Zane Grey's West Society, 2005.
Porter, Eleanor H. *Polyanna*. Laurel, NY: Lightyear Press, 1977 (first published 1913).
Rawlings, Marjorie Kinnan. *The Yearling*. New York: Scribners, 1938.
La Rochefoucauld, Francois, Duc de. *La Rochefoucauld: Maxims*. Edited by F. C. Green. Cambridge, UK: University Press, 1945 (first published 1665).
Schaefer, Jack. *Shane*. Boston: Houghton Mifflin, 1949.
_____, ed. *Out West: A Western Omnibus*. London: Andre Deutsch, 1959.
Scott, Walter. *The Fair Maid of Perth*. London: J. M. Dent, n.d. (first published 1828).
_____. *Marmion*. In *The Poetical Works of Sir Walter Scott*. Edited by J. Logie Robertson. London: Oxford University Press, 1921.
Shakespeare, William. *Twenty-Three Plays and the Sonnets*. Edited by Thomas Marc Parrott. Rev. ed. New York: Charles Scribner's Sons, 1953.
Smith, Henry Nash. *Virgin Land: The American West as Symbol and Myth*. Cambridge: Harvard University Press, 1950.
Steinbeck, John. *The Grapes of Wrath*. New York: Viking Press, 1939.
Stevenson, Robert Louis. *Across the Plains*. Cambridge: Belknap Press of Harvard University Press, 1996 (first published 1892).
Tanner, Stephen. "Founding a New Society in the West: Male and Female as Coordinate Forces." *Zane Grey Review* 24, no. 2 (June 2009): 13–14, 41–42.
Tennyson, Alfred, Lord. *The Poems of Tennyson*. Edited by Christopher Ricks. London: Longmans, Green, 1969.
Thoreau, Henry David. *The Journal of Henry D. Thoreau*. Edited by Bradford Torrey and Francis H. Allen. 14 vols. as 2. Boston: Houghton Mifflin, 1906; New York: Dover Publications, 1962.
_____. *The Maine Woods*. Edited by Joseph J. Moldenhauer. Princeton: Princeton University Press, 1972.
_____. *Walden*. Edited by J. Lyndon Shanley. Princeton: Princeton University Press, 1971.
_____. "A Winter Walk" and "Walking." In

Excursions. Edited by Joseph J. Moldenhauer. Princeton: Princeton University Press, 2007.

Tolstoy, Leo. "How Much Land Does a Man Need?" In *Walk in the Light & Twenty-Three Tales*. Maryknoll, NY: Orbis Books, 2003.

Turner, Frederick Jackson. *The Frontier in American History*. New York: Henry Holt, 1920.

Twain, Mark. *The Adventures of Huckleberry Finn*. Edited by Henry Nash Smith. Riverside Editions. Boston: Houghton Mifflin, 1958 (first published 1884).

Wheeler, Joseph Lawrence. "Solitude and Work—Observations by Zane Grey." *Zane Grey Review* 24, no. 4 (December 2009): 8–9, 34.

———. "Two Roads Merged in White Mountains." *Zane Grey Review* 24, no. 3 (September 2009): 7–9, 26–31.

———. "Zane Grey's Impact on American Life and Letters: A Study in The Popular Novel." Ph.D. diss., George Peabody College for Teachers, 1975.

Wister, Owen. *The Virginian: A Horseman of the Plains*. Afterword by Max Evans. New York: New American Library, 2002 (first published 1902).

Wordsworth, William. *The Excursion*. Edited by Sally Bushell, James A. Butler, and Michael C. Jaye. Ithaca, NY: Cornell University Press, 2007.

———. *Selected Poems and Prefaces*. Edited by Jack Stillinger. Riverside Editions. Boston: Houghton Mifflin, 1965.

Wrigley, Robert E. *Mammals in North America: Wildlife Adventure Stories and Technical Guide*. Wildlife Paintings by Dwayne Harty. Winnipeg: Hyperion Press, 1986.

Index

Aard, Beryl 174–175
Aard, Mr. 174
Abel (Bible) 85
Abilene, TX 182
Ackerman, Deuce 183, 187
Acton, Lord 144
Adam (Bible) 21, 87
The Adventures of Huckleberry Finn (Twain) 93
Agness, OR 173
Agua Prieta, Mexico 45
Ahab, Captain 56, 183, 186, 196
Alabama Moze 183
Alaska 127
Alberta 131
alcohol(ism) 16, 40, 42, 44, 68, 70, 103, 140, 172, 175, 190–91, 208
Alder Creek, MT 52, 56–58
All-Story Weekly 52
Alloway, Chess 35
Almeda Falls, OR 173
The American Tradition in Literature (eds. Bradley, Beatty, Lang) 205
Anderson, Jim 82
Anderson, Lenore 79, 81–84
Anderson, Mr. 78–82, 84
Anderson, Sherwood 3
Apaches 198
Arden 20
Argosy (magazine) 33
Arizona 1, 6, 16, 26, 42, 60, 72, 92, 93, 99–100, 105, 114–15, 119, 125, 138, 154–56, 158–62, 200, 203, 205
"The Art of Fiction" 59
As You Like It (Shakespeare) 20
Asia 61
Atchison, Topeka, and the Santa Fe Railroad 182
Atwell, Gus 172, 175
Auchinloss, Al 72–73
Austen, Jane 13, 73–75
Autry, Gene 154

backwoodsmen 1, 119, 124, 138–143, 160–62
Balancing Rock 19, 23–24
Ballantyne, R.M. 209
bandits 9, 26, 29–30, 38, 40, 43–44, 52–58, 66, 90, 114–15
Baxter, Penny 138
Bayne, Reddie 183–184, 187
"Be Honest with Me" (song) 154
Beam, Jake 115–17
Beam, Madge 115–17
Beasely 72, 76–77
Beeman, Roy 72, 74, 76
Belding, Nell (née Warren; m. Berton; m. Belding) 25–27, 31
Belding, Tom 27–29, 31
Bell, Keven 171–75; river's influence on 171–75
Bell, Mr. 172, 175
Bell, Mrs. 172
Belmont Stakes 62
Bender 183, 187
Bennett, Elizabeth 13
Benton, WY 68–69
Bering Land Bridge 127
Bertha 170
Betty Zane 1, 3, 5, 11–17, 125
Biblical allusions/references 23, 38, 76, 85–87, 102, 107, 139, 205
Billard, Jules B. 129
Bison antiquus 127
Bison bison see buffalo
Bison latifrons 127
Black Star (horse) 22, 59
Blade, Jess 117–18
Blaine, Dall 145, 147
Blaine, Hart 144–45, 147–49
Blaine, Ina (later Ina Ide) 145–50, 159
Blaine, Marvie 145, 148, 159, 161–62
Blaine, Mrs. 144, 148
Blair, Gene 91
Blair, Mr. 190–93

219

Blair, Mrs. 91
Blair, Sydney 190–93
Blake, Jim 152–55
Blake, Kevin 211
Blake, Lucy 152–55
Blake, Mrs. 152–53
Blanco Sol (horse) 27–28
Bland 34–35
Bland, Kate 34–35
Blucher 107, 111–112
Blue Book 65
Bluegrass (cowhand) 195
Boise, ID 189
The Book of Knowledge 12
Borden, Cliff 191–92
Border Legion (gang) 54–58
The Border Legion 3, 52–58
Bostil, John 60, 62–63
Bostil, Lucy 59–60, 62–64
Bostil's Ford, AZ 60, 63
Boston, MA 207–8, 212
Boy's Magazine 125
Brazos River 130
Britain *see* Great Britain
Brite, Adam 182–85, 187; as father figure 184–87
Britt, Cap 194–98
Bruce, Simm 95
Brutus (horse) 133, 135, 137
buffalo 3, 65, 125–31; history 125–29, 131; hunt 126–30; stampede 41, 126, 130–31, 186–87, 211
Burch, Carley 99–104; self-centeredness 100–3
Burridge, Cash 158–59, 161–62
Burton, Nell (daughter) 25–29, 31–32
Burton, Nell (mother) *see* Belding, Nell
Burton, Robert (*aka* Cameron) 25–26, 31

Cabin Gulch, ID 54, 57
Cain (Bible) 38, 85
California 1, 47, 52, 80, 87, 113–14, 127, 144–45, 157, 159, 173, 213
California Red (horse) 146, 149, 159, 162–63
"The Call of the Canyon" (song) 99, 154
The Call of the Canyon 2, 99–104, 171
Cameron *see* Burton, Robert
Cameron, Wayne 207–13; medical services by 208–10
Canadian River 186
canyon country *see* landscapes
Carlisle Indian School, PA 105, 111
Carlos, Don 40, 42–44
Carmichael, Tom 74, 76–77
Cascade Range 173
Casey 3, 68, 70
Casita, AZ/Mexico 26, 28
Cass, Widow 72

Casteñeda, Mercedes 26–27, 29–30
Cather, Willa 42, 206
Catholicism 106
Catlee 129
Catlin, George 128
Catskill Mountains 72
Cawthorne, Link 158–59
Chandler, Ben 183, 185
Chase, Ben 31
Chase, Radford 31
Cherokee (cowhand) 196
Cherokees 182
Chesaldine 37–38
Cheyenne, WY 68
Chicago, IL 26
Chicago Tribune 194
Chimney Rock, NE 210–11
Chiricahua, AZ 42
Chisholm, Jess 182
Chisholm Trail 182
Chocolate Mountains 114
Christ 21, 87, 103
Christianity 106
Christmas 168
A Christmas Carol (Dickens) 94
Cimarron River 153, 186
Civil War 2, 92, 182, 207–9, 213
Clarke, Alfred 12–14, 16
Clay Hill Rapids, OR 173
Clear Lake, CA 145–48
Clear Lake National Wildlife Refuge, CA 145
Clements 199
Cleve, Jim 52–58
Coast Range 173
code (of the West) 4, 69, 76, 122–24, 177, 192
Code of the West 2, 4, 119–24
Cody, William Frederick ("Buffalo Bill") 128–29
Collier's (magazine) 164, 176, 188
Colorado 132, 169, 210
Colorado River 51, 60, 63, 86–87, 114, 185
Colorado Springs, CO 169
Colt (revolver) 33
Colter 97–98
Comanches 185–86
"Composed Upon Westminster Bridge" 49
Concord, MA 5, 6
The Concord Saunterer 6
conservation, nature 4, 71, 100, 125, 131–32, 173, 191, 208
Cooper, James Fenimore 4, 171
The Coral Island (Ballantyne) 209
Cordilleran ice sheet 127
Cordts 60, 62–63
Coronado, Francisco Vasquez de 126, 131
Cottonwoods, UT 18–19, 21

Index

The Country Gentleman (magazine) 59, 72, 78, 92, 119, 132, 171
The Courtship of Miles Standish (Longfellow) 166
cowmen 1–4, 18–20, 39–43, 93, 120, 122, 144, 148, 151–53, 160–61, 164, 169, 182–87, 189, 194–197, 200, 203–6
Cratchit (family) 94
"The Crater of Hell" 30
Creech (father) 60, 62
Creech, Joel 60, 62–63
Creighton, Edward 208–11
"Critical Realism" 205
Crosby, Bing 154
Crusoe, Robinson 36
Cumberland Mountains 138

Dale, Milt 72–77; as "teacher" 73–75
dance-hall girls 68–71, 156, 190–93, 209–10, 212
Darnell, Tom 208–9, 212
Dashwood, Elinor 73–74
Dashwood, Marianne 73–74
David Copperfield (Dickens) 115, 151
Day, Tom 160–62
Death Valley, CA 89–90, 113–15, 118
"Death Wind" *see* Wetzel, Lew
Deception Pass, UT 18, 23–24
Delilah (Bible) 22
Dempsey, Jack 120
Denmeade, Allie 140
Denmeade, Edd 140–42
Denmeade, Joe 140–42
Denmeade, Lee 139–40
Denmeade, Mertie 140
Denmeade, Mrs. 139
Denmeade, Uncle Bill 140
Denver, CO 169
Desdemona 170
desert *see* landscapes
Desert Gold 3, 25–32, 113, 188
The Desert of Wheat 2, 78–84
deus ex machina 87
Díaz, Porfirio 39
Dickens, Charles 4, 94, 151
Dillon, Clan 161–63
Dirty Devil River (and brakes) 177–81
Dismukes 88–91
Distinguished Service Medal 111
Doan, Tom 129–31
Doane, Ann 198
Doane, Mr. 198
Doan's Store, TX 182, 185
Dodge City, KS 129, 182, 184, 187
Don Carlos Ranch 194–95
Dorchester Publishing 33, 200
Dorn, Chris 78–80
Dorn, Kurt 79–84; love of farming 79–80, 84

Dreiser, Theodore 3, 205
Duane, Buck 33–38; self-doubts 33–36, 38
Dumas, Alexandre (the Elder) 209
Durade 65–71
Durango, Mexico 27
Dyer, Bishop 20, 22–23

Eden (Bible) 20
Egyptians 86
El Cajon 39, 43
Elizabeth, Queen, I 20
Ellsworth, KS 182
Emerson, Jake 188–89, 91, 93
Emerson, Kal(ispel) 188–193; as man of action 249–51, 253
Emerson, Ralph Waldo 142
Emerson, Sam 188–89, 191–92
"Empty Saddles" (song) 99
England 179
Erne, Milly 18, 20–21, 23
Euchre 34
Eve (Bible) 21, 87
The Excursion (Wordworth) 108
Exodus (Bible) 76, 86

The Fair Maid of Perth (Scott) 171
farmers 1, 78–81, 84, 151
farmland *see* landscapes
Fayre, Milly 129–31
Federal Indian Agent 105
Field and Stream 18
Finn, Huckleberry (Huck) 3, 93, 140, 169, 209
fires 61–64, 156, 209–10
fishermen 1; commercial 3, 172–73; sport 3, 12, 67, 145, 171–72, 174–75
Flagg (fictitious name for Flagstaff, AZ) 200–3, 205
Flagstaff, AZ 46, 200
Florida 138
Follonsbee, Hank 129
Folsom, NM 127
forest *see* woods/forest
foresters 1, 72, 76–77
Forlorn River 2, 144–50
Forlorn River, AZ 28, 31
Forlorn River (Lost River), CA/OR 145, 147, 157, 159, 162
Forrest, Clay 164–65, 167, 170
Forrest, Cliff 164–68, 170; assessments by 166–68
Forrest, Mrs. 164, 170
Forrest Cottonwoods Ranch 164–65, 169
Fort Bridger, WY 207, 212
Fort Henry, WV 11–14, 16
Fort Worth, TX 129
Four Musketeers 209, 212
Fox, John, Jr. 138

222 Index

France 194
Franklidge, Judge 160–61, 163
Frayne, Renn 195–99
Frisco, CA 155
The Frontier in American History (Turner) 5
frontiersmen 1, 11, 13, 15–16

Gale, Dick 26–32; as joyful adventurer 26–28
Galice, OR 173
Galloway (cattle) 125
gamblers 58, 65–69, 189–91
Gary, Jim 11
Gentiles (non-Mormons) 18, 20
Germany 78–79, 81, 83
Girty, Simon 15
Glidden 80–81
Globe, AZ 115, 117
god 46, 111, 174
God 5, 23, 47, 49, 71, 75, 85, 87, 89, 107, 111–12, 181, 205
Goethe, Johann Wolfgang von 21
Gold Beach, OR 171, 175
gold rush 3, 52, 56, 188, 190–91
Gothenburg, NE 207
Graham (family) 92
Grand Canyon 51, 60–61, 132, 160
Grand Junction, CO 178
Grants Pass, OR 171, 175
The Grapes of Wrath (Steinbeck) 80
Grass Valley, AZ 95
grassy plains *see* landscapes
Grave Creek Falls, OR 173
Great Britain 11, 15
Great Depression 6, 80
Great Expectations (Jones) 120
Great Falls, MT 128
Great Plains 128
Greaves 95–96
Greece 85, 189
Grey, Loren 200
Grey, Zane: beliefs 18–19, 21, 30, 46, 78, 91, 111, 129, 138, 154–55, 163, 164–65, 169, 187; Biblical allusions/references in 23, 38, 76, 85–87, 102, 107, 139, 205; compared to Austen, Jane 13, 73–75; compared to Cooper, James Fenimore 4, 171; compared to Dickens, Charles 4, 94, 151; compared to Melville, Herman 56, 61, 183, 186, 196; compared to other authors 3–4, 21, 36, 42, 50, 53, 59, 65, 72, 75, 80, 120, 138, 141, 143, 166, 171, 181, 205–6, 209; compared to Scott, Walter 4, 19, 171; compared to Shakespeare, William 13, 14, 20, 35, 70, 75, 93, 170; compared to Thoreau, Henry David 2, 4–6, 31, 64, 107–11, 139–40, 146, 166, 174–75; compared to Twain, Mark 3, 93, 140, 169, 209; compared to Wordsworth, William 4, 6, 12, 47, 49, 105, 108, 205–6; dialogue in 2, 22–23, 37, 48–50, 82, 94, 101, 122–24, 137, 147, 156, 157, 161–62, 166–67, 170, 179, 184, 190, 198, 204, 210–11; graphic style 14, 21, 38, 88, 97, 126, 130, 136, 149, 163, 170, 187, 195, 212; on gunmen 2, 23, 76, 157–59, 163, 176–78, 208; humor in 4, 13, 40–42, 68, 119–23, 135, 147, 161, 164, 168–69, 175, 196–97, 211; introspection in 21, 35–36, 73, 83, 91, 95, 124, 133, 135, 158, 181, 196, 198; irony in 160–61, 187, 202–3; love of horses 2, 30, 59–62, 133, 135–37, 145–47, 149, 152, 155; love of nature 12, 108, 121, 165; minor expletives in 190, 211; on Native Americans 4, 15–16, 46, 49, 71, 105–112, 126, 129, 131, 133, 183, 207–8; overwriting 3, 44, 54–55, 88, 97, 102, 137, 169, 189; pathos in 4, 69–70, 88, 124, 149, 187, 192, 197, 205–6; and profanities in 22, 55, 93, 102, 184, 211; psychological probes 21, 36, 54, 69–70, 92, 122, 124, 136, 177–80, 204–5; respect for women 69, 96, 101, 153, 177, 180, 193, 195; on violence 22–23, 31, 54, 163, 198; on war 82–83, 103, 204–5, 209; Western ideals 4, 31, 44, 49, 51, 65, 70, 76–77, 80, 84, 86, 87, 90–91, 94, 111, 122, 124, 181, 193; on work 67–68, 71, 76, 84, 90, 95, 99, 124, 159–60, 203; writing traits 37, 43, 60, 62, 92, 116, 122, 160, 162, 177, 198, 200–1, 212
Grosset & Dunlap 6, 11, 102, 173
Gruber, Frank 58, 108
Guadaloupe Springs, TX 168
Gulden, Sam 52–58
gunmen 1–2, 18–19, 21–23, 33, 35–38, 76, 129, 149, 153, 155–56, 157–63, 176–78, 180–81, 183, 187, 190, 192, 195, 197–99, 208

Hall, Bill 148–49
Hallet, Roy 183–85
Hamlet (Shakespeare) 70, 75
Hammond, Madeline (Majesty) 39–45; becoming free 39–40, 42–44
Hans, Gus 153
Hardin 36
Harding, Walter 5
Hardman, Dick 151–56
Hardman, Jard 153–55
Hardy, Thomas 171
Harper & Brothers 6, 31–32, 105
Hatfield, Bid 120–21, 123–24
Hatt, Cedar 161–62
Hatt, Rose 161–62
Harvard University 208
Hawthorne, Nathaniel 4
Hays, Hank 176–81
Hebrew 86

Heeseman, Bill 176–81
Hellgate Canyon, OR 173
Henley, William Ernest 4
Henry Mountains 176
Heritage of the Desert 31
Herrick, Bernie 176–81
Herrick, Helen 177–81
Hill, Billy 99
Hippocratic oath 209
Hit Parade 99
Hite, Ross 184–85, 187
Holden, Less 183, 187
The Holy Bible 87, 107
horse wranglers 1, 60–62, 132–37, 145–47, 149, 153, 155
horses: broken 2–3, 22–24, 27–30, 59–64, 133, 135–37; wild 132–37, 145–49
Howells, William Dean 205
"Huckleberry Finn" Western 3
Hudnall, Clark 129
Huerta, Victoriano 39, 43–44
Huett, Abraham Lincoln 202–6
Huett, Barbara 203–5
Huett, George Washington 201–5
Huett, Grant 202–5
Huett, Logan 200–6; as family leader 201, 204–5
Huett, Lucinda 200–6; as family leader 202–6
Hugo, Victor 4
hunters 1, 16, 126–31
Hurons 12
Hutter, Flo 101, 103

Ice Age 127
Idaho 53, 246, 191
Ide, Amos 144–45, 147–50
Ide, Ben 144–50, 157–63; love of wild horses 144–49
Ide, Hettie 145–47, 150, 157–63
Ide, Ina *see* Blaine, Ina
Ide, Mrs. 145–46, 159
ideals, Western 4, 31, 44, 49, 51, 65, 70, 76–77, 80, 84, 86–87, 90–91, 94, 111, 122, 124, 181, 193
Illahe, OR 173
Illinois 46, 51
In Memoriam (Tennyson) 75
Indian Territory (later, Oklahoma) 182, 185
Indiana 169
Indians *see* Native Americans
Industrial Workers of the World (I.W.W.) 78–84
"Invictus" 4
Ireland 68
Irving, Washington 72
Isbel, Ann 94
Isbel, Bill 94, 96–97

Isbel, Gaston 92–94, 97
Isbel, Guy 94, 96
Isbel, Jean 93–98; in love 93–96, 98
Ishmael 61
I.W.W. *see* Industrial Workers of the World

Jackson, Carlton 15, 59, 86, 96, 105, 108, 125, 164–65
Jackson, Ride-'Em 195, 197–98
Jacobs 96
Jake (cowhand) 81
James, Henry 50, 59
Jane Austen's Letters (Lascelles, ed.) 75
Jarvis 169
Jenet (burro) 113–15, 117–18
Jett, Randal 129
Jim (cowhand) 196
John (Bible) 118
Jones, Charles Jesse "Buffalo" 16–17, 61
Jones, Landon Y. 120
Jorth, Ellen 93–98; elemental nature 94–98
Jorth, Lee 92–93, 95–97
The Journal of Henry D. Thoreau (Torrey and Allen, eds.) 2, 107–11, 166
Julesburg, CO 210
Juliet 95
Julius Caesar (Shakespeare) 170

Kaidab (fictitious name for Kayenta, AZ) 106
Kane, Paul 128
Kansas 144–45, 182
Kansas Pacific Railroad 182
Karr, Jean 108, 113
Kayenta, AZ 47, 49, 106–7
Kearney, NE 68
Keats, John 141
Keene, Brazos 195, 197, 199
Kells, Jack 52–58, 180
Kentucky 138, 195
Kilbourne, Glenn 99–104
King, Larry Red 67, 70
"King of the Royal Mounted" 11
Kingsley, Florence 40, 43
Kiowas 185
Kipling, Rudyard 4
Klamath Falls, OR 147
Knell 38
Knights (of the Range) 196–99
Knights of the Range 2, 194–99

Lacy, Jim *see* Nevada (cowboy/gunman)
Ladd, Charlie 27–30
Ladies' Home Journal 99, 105, 113, 125, 138, 144, 157
Lake, Joe 47–48, 50–51
landscapes: canyon country 19–20, 23–24, 34, 46–47, 49–51, 59–62, 97, 99–100, 102, 104, 106, 109, 111–12, 132, 137, 160, 171,

173, 175, 179, 181, 200–3, 206; desert 20, 25–32, 42, 45, 47, 49, 59–62, 69–70, 85–91, 106, 109, 111, 113–15, 133–34, 166–68, 170; farmland 78–80, 83–84; grassy plains 126–30, 183–86, 194, 209–12; mountains 29–31, 34, 43–44, 49, 53, 65, 67, 72, 85, 87–89, 104, 109, 114–15, 145–46, 171, 173–75, 176, 188–93; woods/forest 16, 62–63, 72–77, 96–97, 100, 110, 115–17, 124, 134, 138–39, 141–43, 160, 171, 173–75, 200, 202–4
Laramie River 212
Laramie Trail 65
Larey, Adam (Wansfell) 85–91; education in womanhood 87–91
Larey, Guerd 85–87, 91
Larkin, Fay ("Mary") 20, 22–24, 47–51
La Rochefoucauld, Francois, Duc de 53
Las Animas, CO 194, 197
Las Vegas, NM 164–65
Lash, Jim 27–30
Lassiter, Jim 2, 10, 19–20, 22–24, 47, 51, 133; gunman activities 23–24
Last of the Duanes 2–3, 33–38
The Last of the Plainsmen 125
"The Last Roundup" 99
The Last Trail 125
Laurentide ice sheet 127
Leavitt, Rand 190–93
Lee, Allie 65–84
Lee, Allison 66–68, 71
Lee, Jennie 34–38
Lee's Ferry 160
Leisure Books 33, 200
The Light of Western Stars 2, 39–45
Lincoln, Abraham 213
Lincoln County 161, 163
Lineville, CA/NV 158, 160
Linwood, Genie 91
Little, Rolly 183, 187
"Lizzie" *see* Model T Ford
Llano Estacado *see* Staked Plain
Lodge, General 66, 68, 70–71
"Lone Prairee" ["Bury Me Not on the Lone Prairie"] 197
Longfellow, Henry Wadsworth 143, 166
Longhorn (cattle) 182, 185–86
Lord, Garry 172–73, 175
Lost Dutchman Mine 115
Loughbridge, Jim 133, 135–37
Loughbridge, Ora 134–35
Lowden, Jack 208–9, 212
Lundeen, Jed 164–70
Lundeen, Mrs. 164
Lundeen, Virginia 164–70

MacNelly, Captain 36–38
Madero, Francisco 39, 42, 44

The Maine Woods 31
Majesty (horse) 40, 42–43
Malpass, August 164–70
The Man of the Forest 1, 72–77
Manerube, Bent 133–37
"Many Waters" 78, 81
Marco, NM 153–55
Margarita 86–88
Marmion (Scott) 19
Mary, Aunt 94
Masked Rider *see* Oldring, Bess
Mason, Laigs 195, 197
Matazel 200, 202–3
Mathew, David 144
Matthew (Bible) 102
Matthews, Sheriff 153–56
Maxims (La Rochefoucauld) 53
Maysfield, KY 13
McAdam, Sewall 147
McCall's 182
McClure's 86
McCoy, Sewall 196–99
McDowell, Bart 182, 185
Melancholy Mag 170
Melberne, "Mel" 133, 135–137
Melberne, Sue 134–37; maturation 134–37
Melliss, Louise 20, 156
Melville, Herman 56, 61, 183, 186, 196
Mennonite 106
Merry, Tuck 120–21, 124
Mesa (fictitious name for Tuba City) 107
Métis 128
Mexico 26–29, 39–40, 42–43, 45, 117, 127, 136, 152, 165, 167–68, 183, 186, 194, 209
Mezquital, Mexico 45
"Michael" 205–6
Middleton, Jim 140, 142
A Midsummer Night's Dream (Shakespeare) 13
Miller, Alfred Jacob 128
Miller, Ralphe, 14
missionaries 46, 105, 107, 111–12
Missouri 201
mob mentality 36, 57, 112, 192
Moby-Dick (Melville) 56, 183, 196
Moby Dick (whale) 61, 186
Model T Ford ("Lizzie") 120
Modoc 147–49
Mogollon Forest 200
Mogollon Rim 93–94, 115, 160, 162
Montana 52, 153
Monument Valley 60–61
Moran, Blinky (Somers, Frank) 153, 156
Morgan 107, 110–12
Mormons 18–20, 22, 47–51, 113
Moses (Bible) 86
Mount Shasta 146
mountains *see* landscapes
Mule Creek Canyon 173

Index

Mullens, Priscilla 166
Munsey's Magazine 39
Musson Book Company 6
Myeerah 11–12

Naomi (Bible) 23
Nas Ta Bega 47–49, 51
nation-building 13, 15, 27, 42, 66, 68, 71, 76, 124, 128, 193, 196, 201–2, 207–8, 213
Native Americans (Natives, Indians) 5–6, 11–12, 15–16, 28–31, 46–49, 51, 71, 76, 88, 105–12, 126–28, 131, 132–34, 136–37, 147–49, 182–83, 185–86, 188, 200–3, 207–8, 210; as Noble Savage 16, 47, 202; as part Native 13, 93, 174; religion 4, 47, 51, 106–7, 111–12, 188; rights 46, 111; as seen by Grey 4, 15–16, 46, 49, 71, 105–6, 110–11, 126, 129, 133, 183, 207–8; tribes: Apache 198; Cherokee 182, 196; Comanche 185–86; Kiowa 185; Navajo 46–49, 51; Piute 132–33, 137; Sioux 65–68, 70–71; Wyandotte/Huron 12; Yaqui 28–31; white man's treatment 16, 30, 46, 106–7, 111–12, 133, 183, 207
nature: affinity with 89, 105, 107–9, 143, 173; as aid to narrative 1, 29–30, 33–34, 60, 76, 87, 116, 192–93, 202–3; as canyon country *see* landscapes; characters' love 12, 35, 44, 47, 72, 88, 100–1, 107, 114, 117, 121, 133, 145, 160, 162, 166, 174, 176; as commentator on narrative 44, 53, 56, 64, 88, 91, 96, 130–31, 155, 174–75, 180, 189, 190; conservation 4, 71, 100, 125, 131, 173, 191, 208; as desert *see* landscapes; ecology in 4, 75, 79, 88, 122, 173; as grassy plains *see* landscapes; as image 25–26, 36, 42, 74, 89, 99–100, 137, 142, 172, 177, 179–80, 186; influence 27, 30–31, 47, 61, 104, 133, 142–43, 162, 165–66, 168, 171, 175, 177, 190, 211–12; as mountains *see* landscapes; sensuous appeal 6, 59, 76, 96, 102–3, 107, 110, 115, 124, 134, 146, 174–75, 178, 192; survival of the fittest in 75, 85, 88; sustained description 27–28, 39, 51, 76, 87, 109, 110, 116, 175, 193; wildness 1, 39, 59, 64, 75–76, 85–86, 106, 110, 192, 201–2; as woods/forest *see* landscapes
Navajo Reservation 105
Navajos 46–49, 51, 105
Naza *see* Rainbow Bridge
Neale, Warren 65–71; as a romantic dreamer 65–69, 71
Nebraska 65, 67, 207, 210
Neuman 81
Nevada (book) 2, 157–63
Nevada (cowboy/gunman, aka Jim Lacy or Texas Jack) 146–49, 157–63; and gunman activities 149, 157, 159, 162–63

Nevada (state) 146, 157–58
New England 5–6, 20, 72
New Mexico 39, 92, 153, 161, 164, 194, 198
New Year's Eve 99
New York (city) 16, 39, 43, 99, 102, 125, 127
Nielsen, Sievert 113
Night (horse) 22, 59
Nokin, Susie 133–34, 136–37
Nokin, Toddy 133, 136
Nonnezoske *see* Rainbow Bridge
Nophaie 6, 105–12; relationship to nature 105–10; religion 107, 111–12
Norris, Frank 205
North Platte, NE 68
North Platte River 207, 210
Northwest Territories, Canada 127
"Nugget" *see* Ruth

Oak Creek, AZ 99
Oak Creek Canyon 100, 102, 104
The Octopus (Norris) 205
"Ode: Intimations of Immortality from Recollections of Early Childhood" 105, 108
"Ode to a Nightingale" 141
Oella 88
Ohio 13
Ohio River 1, 15
Ohio River Valley 11–12, 15
Oklahoma 182
The Old Beauty and Other Stories (Cather) 206
"Old Book" (Bible) 107
Old Testament 76
Old Trail *see* Santa Fe Trail
Oldring 18–19, 21
Oldring, Bess (Masked Rider) 18–24
Olsen 80
Omaha, NE 67, 207
Oregon 3, 52, 93, 145, 171, 174
Oregon Trail 207
Orlando 20
Othello (Shakespeare) 170

Painted Desert, AZ 60–61
Panamint Mountains 114
Panquitch (horse) 133, 137
"Paradise Park" 77
Pauly, Thomas H. 2
Pearce, Red 55
Pecos River 114
Pennsylvania 105
Pfeiffer, Charles D. 1, 4, 7
Phoenix, AZ 117
Picacho, AZ 86, 91
Pierce, Red 209
Pilchuck, Jude 129–31
Pine, AZ 72
Piutes 132, 137

226 Index

Platte River 153
Pleasant Valley War 92
Pleistocene epoch 127
Plummer, Henry 52
Pocket Books 105
Poggin 38
Poland 127
Pollyanna 170
Pony Express 212
Popular Magazine 25
Portland, OR 175
The Prairie (Cooper) 171
Price, Monty 40–42
Pride and Prejudice (Austen) 13
The Princess (Tennyson) 141
Promontory, UT 71
prospectors 1, 20, 25–26, 87–90, 113–15, 118, 188–89, 191
Pruitt, Andy 129
"A Psalm of Life" 143
Psalms (Bible) 87
Pyramids 71

"The Quarter Deck" 56, 196

railroad workers 1–3, 65–71
Rainbow Bridge (Nonnezoshe or Naza) 47, 57, 111
The Rainbow Trail 1, 24, 46–51
Rainee Falls, OR 173
Randle, Joan 52–58; "missionary zeal" 53–55, 57
Rankin 199
Rawlings, Marjorie Kinnan 138
Rayner, Bo (Bo-Peep) 72–74, 77
Rayner, Helen 72–77
"Realism and Naturalism" 205
Red River 182
Red River Station, TX 182, 185
Remington, Frederic 128
The Return of the Native (Hardy) 171
Revolutionary War 1, 11, 15
Riders of the Purple Sage 1–3, 18–24, 28, 31, 46–47, 59
Riggs, Harve 72–73, 77
Rio Grande 34, 37
Ripple, Holly 194–199; as "lady" to her knights 196–97, 199
Ripple, Lee 194–95
Roaring Twenties 2, 4, 99, 119
Robbers' Roost 2, 176–81
Rocky Mountains 65, 212
Rogue River 171–75
Rogue River Feud 3, 171–75
Rojas 26–27, 29–30
Romance (heroic magnitude) 1, 3–4, 65–66, 71, 75, 131, 142, 164, 181, 205
Rome 85

Romeo 93, 95
Romeo and Juliet (Shakespeare) 93, 95
Roping Lions in the Grand Canyon (Grey) 61
Rosalind 20
Ruby (*The U.P. Trail*) 69–70
Ruby (*Western Union*) 209–10, 212
Ruff, Haze 101
Russell, Charles 128
Russia 127
Rust, Virgil 102
rustlers 18–20, 93, 146, 148–49, 158–63, 176–81, 184, 194–99, 204
Rustlers of Silver River (Grey) 171
Ruth (Bible) 23
Ruth ("Nugget") 191–93

Saalfield (publisher) 11
Sage Hills/Mountains 145
Sage King (horse) 60, 62–63
St. Elmo's fire 186
Salmon, ID 189–91
Salmon River 188
Salt Lake, UT 113
Samaritan (Bible) 139
Samson (Bible) 22
Samuel (Bible) 205
San Antonio, TX 182–83
San Diego, CA 117
San Juan River 132
San Sabe 183, 186
San Ysabel 91
Santa Fe, NM 196
Santa Fe Railroad 129
Santa Fe Trail (Old Trail) 196, 198
Sawtooth Mountains 188
Sawyer, Tom 209
Scotland 182
Scott, Walter 4, 19, 171
Secretariat (horse) 62
Sense and Sensibility (Austen) 73
Setter, Less 147–49
Shadd 49, 51
Shakespeare, William 20, 35; *As You Like It* 20; *Hamlet* 70, 75; *Julius Caesar* 170; *A Midsummer Night's Dream* 13; *Othello* 170; *Romeo and Juliet* 93, 95; *The Taming of the Shrew* 14
Sharps (rifle) 129
Shaw, Vance 208–9, 211–12
Shefford, John 46–51; growing religious beliefs 46–47, 51
The Shepherd of Guadaloupe 2, 164–70, 171
sheriffs 40, 52, 87, 153, 155–56, 190, 192
Shipman, Texas Joe or Tex 183–87
shoot-outs: seen 21, 23, 33, 35, 38, 40, 77, 92, 129, 149, 155, 163, 180–81, 184, 187, 192, 199, 204; unseen 24, 36, 156, 159, 162, 203

Index

Sioux 65–68, 70–71
Skylark 195, 198
Slaughter, Russ 196–99
Slingerland 65–67, 71
Sloan, Dick 191–92
Sloan, Rebel Ben 195, 197
Slocum, Smoky 177, 179–80
Slone, Lin 60–64, 133; determination 60–62
Smith, Bill 151–55
Smith, Henry Nash 5
Smith, Mrs. 151–54
Smith, Pan Handle (*The Trail Driver*) 183–85, 187
Smith, Panhandle or Pan (*Valley of Wild Horses*): childhood 151–52; Western savvy 153–56
So You Want to Read Zane Grey and Don't Know Where to Start (Pfeiffer) 1, 52
soldiers 12, 15, 39, 42, 44–45, 65–66, 82–83, 111, 172, 210
Solitude, OR 171, 174–75
"Solitude and Work—Observations on Zane Grey" 76
Somers, Frank *see* Moran, Blinky
songs, Western: "Be Honest with Me" 154; "The Call of the Canyon" 99, 154; "Empty Saddles" 99; "The Last Roundup" 99; "Lone Prairee" ["Bury Me Not on the Lone Prairie"] 197
Sonora Desert 25, 29
South Pass, WY 212
Spain 26–27, 29–30, 40, 126, 128, 164, 182, 186
The Spirit of the Border (Grey) 125
The Spirit of the Huckleberry (Friesen) 5, 110
Sprague, John 95–96
Springer 97–98
Stairs of Sand (Grey) 91
Staked Plain (Llano Estacado) 127
Stanton, Beauty 69–71
State Agricultural College, WA 79
Steinbeck, John 80
Stevenson, Robert Louis 4, 65
Stewart, Gene 40, 42–44
Stillwell, Bill 39–40, 42–43
Stinger 195
Stockwell, Georgiana (Georgie) 119–24; psyche probed 122–24
Stockwell, Mary 119–20, 122–24
Stonebridge, UT 48–49
Stutz Bearcat (automobile) 43, 45
Sunderlund, Kit 208–10, 212
Sunderlund, Mr. 210, 212
Sunderlund, Mrs. 212
Superstitious Range 115
Surprise Valley, UT 19–21, 23–24, 46–47, 49–51
Sutton, Ellen (Ellen Jorth, the elder) 92–93

Sweetwater Valley, WY 212
Sycamore Canyon, AZ 201–2, 205–6

The Taming of the Shrew (Shakespeare) 14
The Taming of the Wild Heart 14
Tanner, Stephen 202
Tappan 113–18; reliance on Jenet 114–15, 118
Tappan's Burro 3, 113–18, 188
teachers 1–2, 50, 74–76, 107, 119, 138–43, 177, 201
telegraph line 207–13; workers 1, 209–13
Tennyson, Alfred, Lord 75, 141
Tewksbury (family) 92
Texas 3, 67, 76–77, 92–93, 127–31, 151–53, 182–85, 208–9
Texas Jack *see* Nevada (cowboy/gunman)
Texas Panhandle 3, 127–31, 151–53
Texas Rangers 36–38, 77, 194, 208
30,000 on the Hoof (Grey) 200
Thoreau, Henry David 2, 4–6, 31, 64, 107–11, 139–40, 146, 166, 174
The Thoreau Society 6
Thorne, George 26, 28–30
Thorpe, Jim 105
The Three Musketeers (Dumas) 209
Thunder Mountain 188–91, 193
Thunder Mountain 3, 188–93
The Thundering Herd 3, 125–31
Thurman, Cal 120–24
Thurman, Enoch 119–23
To the Last Man 3, 92–98
Tolliver, June 138
Tonto Basin, AZ 92–93, 103, 117, 119, 122
The Trail Driver 3, 182–87
The Trail of the Lonesome Pine (Fox) 138
Tuba City, AZ 107
Tule Lake 144–46
Tule Lake Wildlife Refuge 145
Tull, Elder 18, 20, 22–24
Turner, Frederick Jackson 5
Twain, Mark 3, 169
Twayne Publishers 15
Tyee Rapids, OR 173

Under the Tonto Rim 2, 138–43
Union Pacific Railway (U.P.R.) 66, 69, 71
University of Alberta Press 5
The U.P. Trail 2, 3, 65–71
Utah 20, 22, 46, 60, 65, 71, 132–33, 136, 176

Valley of Wild Horses 3, 151–56
The Vanishing American 4–5, 16, 47, 105–12, 171, 174
Van Winkle, Rip 72
Venters, Bern 18–24, 28, 46–47
veterans (World War I) 2–3, 99–100, 102–4, 111, 164–65, 167, 171–72, 174

Virey, Elliot 89–90
Virey, Magdalene 89–91
Virey, Ruth 90–91
Virgin Land (Smith) 5
Virginia 138
The Virginian (Wister) 181

Waggoner 50–51
Walden (Thoreau) 109, 139–40
Walden Pond 31, 146
Walden Woods 31
"Walking" 64, 110
Wall, Jim 176–181; introspection by 176–78, 181
Wallen 184
Walter J. Black (publisher) 6
Wanderer of the Wasteland 1, 25, 85–91, 113, 206
Wansfell *see* Larey, Adam
Warner, Marian 105–7, 111–12
Warren, Jonas 25–26
Warren, Nell (m. Burton; m. Belding) 25–27, 31
Wasatch Range 65
Washington (state) 78, 173
Washington, George 13
Washington, DC 31, 205
Watson, Clara 140–42
Watson, Lucy 138–43; vanity 139, 141–43
Wayne, Ethel 165–66, 168–70; assessments by 166, 168, 170
Wayne, John 14
Weatherill, John 106
Weatherill, Louisa 106
Wellston, TX 33
West Virginia 1
Western Trail 182
Western Union 3, 207–13
Western Union Company 207
Wetzel, Lew ("Death Wind") 12–16, 43–44
Weymer, Chane 133–37; as loner 133, 137
Weymer, Chess 134–37
Wheeler, Joseph Lawrence 2, 4, 76
Wheeling, WV 11, 13
Wheeling Creek, WV 11
White Mountains 72
"white mule" 140
Whittaker 183, 187
Wichita River 185
"Wild and Scenic Rivers" 172–73
Wild Horse Mesa 133–34, 136–37
Wild Horse Mesa 2, 132–37
"Wild Justice" 50
Wild West 16, 33, 40, 44, 50, 56, 58, 66–68, 76–77, 123, 132, 137, 157, 159, 163, 179, 192, 194–99, 201–2, 208, 210
Wildfire 1, 59–64

Wildfire (horse) 59–64; races with Sage King 62–63
Wilson, Jim 77
Wind River Range 212
The Wings of the Dove (James) 50
Winkle Bar, OR 173
Winslow, AZ 160
"A Winter Walk" 110
Winthrop (fictitious name for Winslow, AZ) 160–62
Wister, Owen 181
Withers, John 47, 106
Withers, Mrs. 106
Withersteen, Jane 18–24, 47, 51, 59; new Mormonism 18–20, 23
Wobblies *see* Industrial Workers of the World
Woman of the Frontier 2, 200–6
Wood, Bate 55
Wood, Mrs. 158, 160
Wood Buffalo National Park, Canada 131
woods/forest *see* landscapes
Wordsworth, William 4, 6, 12, 47, 49, 105, 108, 205–6
"The World Is Too Much with Us" 4, 12
The World of the American Indian (Billard, ed.) 129
World War I 2, 78, 82–83, 106, 111, 119, 164, 171–72, 204–5
World War II 119
Wrangle (horse) 23–24, 28
"Wrangle's Race Won" 3
Wyandotte 12
Wyoming 65, 207, 212
Wyoming Hills 65

Yaqui 28–31; a debt paid 28, 30–31
"The Yaqui" 28
Yashi, Gekin 110–11
The Yearling (Rawlings) 138
Yellowstone National Park 131
Yukon 127
Yuma, AZ 29, 117

Zane, Bess (Bessie) 13
Zane, Betty (Elizabeth) 11–16, 43; moodiness 12–14
Zane, Ebenezer 11–16
Zane, Isaac 11–12
Zane Grey (Jackson) 15
Zane Grey: A Study in Values (Pfeiffer) 4
Zane Grey on Fishing (Mort, ed.) 67
Zane Grey Review 6, 202
"Zane Grey's Impact on American Life and Letters" (Wheeler) 4
Zane Grey's West Society 5–6
Zane's Trace 13

www.ingramcontent.com/pod-product-compliance
Ingram Content Group UK Ltd.
Pitfield, Milton Keynes, MK11 3LW, UK
UKHW041947140426
5217IPUK00014B/693